# The Language of Contention

*Revolutions in Words, 1688–2012*

This book examines the relations between the material and political bases of contentious politics and the construction, diffusion, and endurance of contentious language. Beginning with the language of revolution developed from the seventeenth to the nineteenth centuries, it examines contentious language at work, in gender and race relations and in nationalist and ethnic movements. It closes with an examination of emotions in contentious politics, reflecting on the changes in political language since 9/11 and assessing the impact of religion and recent innovations in electronic communication on the language of politics.

Sidney Tarrow is Maxwell M. Upson Professor Emeritus of Government at Cornell University and a visiting professor at Cornell University Law School. His recent books include a collection of essays, *Strangers at the Gates: States and Social Movements in Contentious Politics* (Cambridge, 2012), and a revised and expanded edition of *Power in Movement* (Cambridge, 2011). He is a Fellow of the American Academy of Arts and Sciences and past president of the Comparative Politics Section of the American Political Science Association. He is currently completing a book on states, wars, and movements.

D1227399

# Cambridge Studies in Contentious Politics

## Editors

MARK BEISSINGER Princeton University
JACK A. GOLDSTONE George Mason University
MICHAEL HANAGAN Vassar College
DOUG MCADAM Stanford University
SARAH SOULE Stanford University
SUZANNE STAGGENBORG University of Pittsburgh
SIDNEY TARROW Cornell University
CHARLES TILLY (d. 2008) Columbia University
ELISABETH J. WOOD Yale University
DEBORAH YASHAR Princeton University

*Continued after the index*

# The Language of Contention

*Revolutions in Words, 1688–2012*

SIDNEY TARROW

*Cornell University*

CAMBRIDGE
UNIVERSITY PRESS

# CAMBRIDGE
## UNIVERSITY PRESS

32 Avenue of the Americas, New York, NY 10013-2473, USA

Cambridge University Press is part of the University of Cambridge.

It furthers the University's mission by disseminating knowledge in the pursuit of
education, learning, and research at the highest international levels of excellence.

www.cambridge.org
Information on this title: www.cambridge.org/9781107693289

© Sidney Tarrow 2013

First published 2013

Printed in the United States of America

A catalog record for this publication is available from the British Library.

Library of Congress Cataloging in Publication Data
Tarrow, Sidney G.
The language of contention : revolutions in words, 1688–2012 / Sidney Tarrow, Cornell
University.
   pages cm. – (Cambridge studies in contentious politics)
Includes bibliographical references and index.
ISBN 978-1-107-03624-6 (hardback) – ISBN 978-1-107-69328-9 (pbk.)
1. Communication in politics.   2. Revolutions.   3. Political participation.
4. Social conflict.   I. Title.
JA85.T37   2013
303.601′4–dc23      2013004055

ISBN 978-1-107-03624-6 Hardback
ISBN 978-1-107-69328-9 Paperback

*For Sue*
*Words can't express . . .*

# Contents

# Figures

# Tables

# Maps

# Acknowledgments

This book has been too long in the making: its beginnings go back to a conference at the University of Michigan in 1990, which marked the first stirrings of attention to meaning among social movement scholars. In Chapter 1, I draw on my chapter from the book that resulted from that conference (Tarrow 1992b), Aldon Morris and Carole Mueller, eds., *Frontiers in Social Movement Research* (1992); and on the work of other participants, especially that of William Gamson. A second effort was a fugitive paper, "Costumes of Revolt" (1992a), inspired by the historical work of Lynn Hunt on the French revolution (1984). It does not appear in this book, but Hunt's work shaped what I have to say about revolutionary symbolism in Chapter 2.

Inspiration also came from a group of Cornell colleagues whom I joined in a project on "Contentious Knowledge" sponsored by Cornell's Institute for the Social Sciences. Rebecca Givan, Kenneth Roberts, and Sarah Soule organized a conference on the diffusion of contentious knowledge (Givan, Roberts, and Soule 2010). The paper I contributed to that conference does not appear in this book either, but I am grateful to those colleagues for the opportunity to develop some of the ideas that will be found here.

If I have learned anything about political communication in writing this book it is largely due to the teachings of W. Lance Bennett, Murray Edelman, and Bill Gamson. Chapter 2 on revolutions is in debt to the work of Dan Rodgers, Jean-Clément Martin, and Chuck Tilly. If the historical sketch of working-class language in Chapter 3 has any worth, it is due to the help of colleagues like Geoffrey Evans, Michael Hanagan, Guy Michelat, and Marc Steinberg. In drafting Chapter 4 on race and rights talk, I was helped by the advice of Kim Lacey, Doug McAdam, Rogers Smith, and Michelle Smith. I want to thank Cynthia Bowman, Mary Katzenstein, Cathérine Le Magueresse, Jane Mansbridge, Conny Roggeband, Abigail Saguy, Lea Sgier, and Verta Taylor for their advice on Chapter 5.

Language is a key component of nation building, and Chapter 6 draws on the work of Aleksander Matovski on Macedonia, Anita Shapira on Israel, and Lynn Hunt on France, as well as on the advice of Eitan Alimi, Shlomo Avineri, and Marc Bernstein. Chapter 7, on love and hate in social movements, is in debt to Ron Aminzade and Doug McAdam's work on emotions, to my own work with Michael Dorf on same-sex marriage, and to that of Jonathan Leader Maynard's work on the language of atrocity (Maynard 2013). The conclusion draws on the original work of Joseph Margulies on American political culture after 9/11 and that of Lance Bennett and Alexandra Segerberg on digital communication. Eitan Alimi, Donatella della Porta, Joe Margulies, Doug McAdam, and David S. Meyer suffered through the whole thing, offering typically kind but trenchant criticisms. None of these scholars bears any responsibility for the inferences I have drawn from their advice.

The empirical core of the study was first developed in talks delivered at Carleton College, the Central European University, the Contentious Politics Workshop at the City University of New York, Cornell's Institute for European Studies, Northwestern University, the University of Florida, Nuffield College Oxford, Stanford University, and the Wissenschaftszentrum Berlin. I am grateful to friends and colleagues at those institutions for the opportunity to expose the ideas and develop the evidence that became this book.

If there is a methodological message in the book, it is that there is no such thing as a master methodology; systematic, archival, and ethnographic approaches are best seen as complements, rather than as competitors. I would like to thank Doug Imig, who first taught me to analyze the words of Reuters press releases about European contention for our book *Contentious Europeans* (2001), and my assistant at Cornell, Chan Suh, who helped me master the intricacies of Google Insight and the Ngram system. Robert Braun tracked down the etymologies of several key terms in both Dutch and German. Marc Steinberg tried to convince me that "thicker" ethnography was both possible and necessary. I hope he will agree that the book has profited enormously from his exemplary work (Steinberg 1995, 1999a).

There is something wrong if a scholar reaches the beginning of his eighth decade and hasn't learned more from his students than they have learned from him. This book profited from the ideas of many former students, especially Jennifer Hadden, Chan Suh, Sarah Soule, Kim Williams, and Bogdan Vasi. I also want to record my debt to my great teacher, the late Charles Tilly, whose intellectual strategy vis-à-vis the "new cultural studies" I have consciously adopted: "Don't ignore the excesses of the cultural turn," he advised. *"Tunnel under them!"*

Susan Tarrow, to whom the book is dedicated, never let a careless word escape her ruthless red pen. If I emerge from this tunnel of words, it will largely be due to her forbearance and her love.

Ithaca, New York
December 2012

# Introduction

On New Year's Day 1994, a previously unknown group startled Mexico by announcing a program of liberation for Mexico's indigenous people. Led by a masked man calling himself Subcomandante Marcos, the group seized the governmental palace in San Cristóbal, Chiapas. From the palace's balcony, they read a vivid declaration to the Mexican people. It declared that a long-suffering people had endured centuries of oppression and deprivation, but finally *HOY DECIMOS ¡BASTA!* (Today, we say, Enough). Soon, people all over the world were paying attention to the Zapatista Army of National Liberation (EZLN in Spanish).

At various points in the declaration, the authors identified themselves in these terms:

- A product of five hundred years of struggle
- Poor people like us
- People used as cannon fodder
- Heirs of our nation's true makers
- Millions of dispossessed
- "The people" as described in Article 39 of the Mexican national constitution
- The Zapatista Army of National Liberation
- Responsible, free men and women
- Patriots

Announcing a revolution on behalf of Mexico's poor, dispossessed, indigenous people, they called for "us" to rise against "them."

That revolution did not take place. But the Zapatistas soon made an impact on Mexican politics. Within Chiapas, they held off threatened

suppression by the army and forced the national government to start nego-
tiations over peasant property rights. On a national scale, they started a
more general campaign for indigenous rights. During the spring of 2001,
they staged a colorful march from Chiapas – Mexico's southernmost
state – to Mexico City itself. The march publicized demands for enforce-
ment of local autonomy laws the legislature had passed in response to
concerted pressure from indigenous people all over the country, backed
by international activists.

In the course of the insurrection, the Zapatistas acquired an impres-
sive national and international reputation and a following across the
world. Electronic websites and mailing lists, operated mainly by foreign
supporters, broadcast their messages across North America and Europe.
Those connections brought activists, funds, and enthusiastic statements
of solidarity to Chiapas from as far away as Italy (Hellman 1999). Many
of these outsiders interpreted the Zapatista mobilization as a form of
resistance to the recently enacted North American Free Trade Agreement
(NAFTA). For that reason, they saw it as a welcome addition to the
worldwide antiglobalization efforts that were beginning to unfold in the
1990s. In 1996, the Zapatistas drew thousands of supporters to a "First
Intercontinental Encounter for Humanity and against Neoliberalism" in
the jungle of Chiapas. One observer argued that "the interest and attrac-
tion generated by the EZLN beyond its national borders is matched by
no other movement in the post–Cold War period" (Olesen 2005: 12).

Indigenous identity was hardly a new idea in a country like Mexico,
which is made up of literally hundreds of indigenous groups. Its 1905 revolution was, in part, the struggle of indigenous peasants to assert their
rights to the land. It was no accident that the leaders of the Chiapas
rebellion named their organization after revolutionary leader Emiliano
Zapata (Womack 1971). What was new in 1994 was the combination
of the very local and the very global and the use of the new instrument
of the Internet to spread their message: claiming to speak on behalf of
an indigenous identity inherited from the past and resisting NAFTA, the
Zapatistas triggered an international movement of solidarity and inspired
many indigenous groups in Latin America and many who were not but
who embraced the transnational "Zapatista" label (Hellman 1999).

The Zapatista rebellion employed many of the contentious performances typical of the region in which it was born. But it was also an
episode in the formation and diffusion of contentious language, about
which we know a lot less. Thanks to the work of Charles Tilly (Tilly
1995a, 1995b, 2008), we have learned a great deal about repertoires of

action; but we know much less about what Tilly's student Marc Steinberg calls "discursive repertoires" (1999b). This book focuses on such repertoires. I argue, with Steinberg, that "discursive repertoires are reciprocally linked to the repertoires of collective actions that groups develop to realize their goals" (1999b: xii). I argue, further, that contentious language that takes hold successfully in one context tends to diffuse to others, but it often changes its meaning and its referents in the process.

## Origins

Some books result from a plan; others emerge accidentally: this one was born from a dismissal. In the spring of 1964, as a mere stripling of a PhD student, I was invited to serve as a rapporteur at a conference in the Italian villa of Frascati (LaPalombara and Wiener, 1966). At that conference, I approached the dean of Italian political science, Giovanni Sartori, hoping to interest him in the interviews I was doing with Italian Communists. "Interviews," he scoffed, his Florentine nose in the air. "If you base your research on interviews with Communists, all you will learn about is *verbal* behavior!"

I was at first crushed, then angry, and, finally, provoked into thinking about a meaning of Sartori's *battuta* that he couldn't have intended: that verbal behavior *matters*; that words can tell you more than speakers intend about their meaning; and that the mobilization of words can actually change how people act collectively. In my interviews with Communist activists, for example, I had noticed that the Leninist term "cadre," which originally referred to groups of militants, had been transformed in Italian Communist parlance to mean an *individual* militant – a *quadro*.

At the time, I didn't know what to make of this transformation in meaning. Perhaps, I speculated, it was the result of the change from a Leninist party to the "party of a new type" that Palmiro Togliatti had built after World War II. If that was true, it might have been a sign of the de-collectivization of the party's mentality decades before its leaders liquidated Leninism. In 1964, I was an unreconstructed structuralist whose interests were far removed from such "cultural" questions as language (Tarrow 1967), so I let it go. But the meaning of political words continued to haunt me as my work shifted from Italian Communists to French mayors. Nurtured by my experiences in Italy, my idea was that a mayor was a militant who had been delegated to lead a commune on behalf of his party. How surprising, then, to find that the first French mayor I interviewed in 1968 insisted he had nothing to do with politics! "*Moi, je ne fais pas de politique!*" ("I have nothing to do with politics!") exclaimed the mayor of Maussane-les-Alpilles, the village my wife and I had moved to in the South of France. Was this only a political cover for conservatism, I wondered, masquerading as *apolitisme*? Maybe it was, but when even mayors associated with the Left repeated the same mantra, I began to think that I had encountered words that mattered.

This was the instinct that led me to carry out a matching set of interviews with French and Italian mayors (1977). That comparison unearthed a fundamental difference in how local elites interacted with the state: in France, through "apolitical" ties with the prefecture and the state administration; and in Italy, through the mayors' ties in the party system. French mayors who used the word *apolitique* to describe themselves might not be pure administrators, but their roles led them to keep their distance from the party system, whereas Italian mayors who continued to see themselves as party militants developed clientele ties through their parties to get what they needed from the state. Words matter!

## Protest Repertoires

Language turned up again in the analysis I did of newspaper articles describing the social movements of the late 1960s and early 1970s in Italy (Tarrow 1989). Under the influence of Charles Tilly, I had become interested in the actions of these movements as they performed on the public stage of Italian politics. "Performance" was no exaggeration: "Politics in Italy," wrote Joseph LaPalombara, "is a form of *spettacolo*" – by which he meant "not entertainment but certainly an ongoing drama, something out of the ordinary, that pervades life and demands attention" (LaPalombara 1987: 88).

Using standard computerized technology and coding, I first tried to fit the multiple public performances I was finding into preformed coding categories – categories like marches, sit-ins, demonstrations, and, later, street fights and clandestine violence. What took me longer to understand was that minor changes in the language of contention could denote major changes in behavior. Take the term "Il popolo di dio" (the people of God), which was first employed by Pope John XXIII at Vatican II. When a dissident priest employed the term in a poor neighborhood of Florence, it came to mean something more threatening to the Catholic hierarchy (Tarrow 1989: Ch. 5). I came to see that by examining such changes in language, I could track and better understand longer-term changes in behavior.

Tilly understood this well, and that was why, in his final book, *Contentious Performances*, he paid microscopic attention to the words used to describe how actors engage in "contentious gatherings" (2008). Words, Tilly taught, are never mere epiphenomena but reflect the contexts of social and political change. That was the influence Tilly had on my work when he suggested I look for the links between action and its framing by those who observe and construct it.

Does the use of a particular locution produce changes in behavior? As I struggled to catalog the action formations, the actors who used them, and the repertoires they formed in the Italy of the late 1960s and 1970s, a new movement was emerging in the social sciences – "culture studies" – for which language was crucial. In place of the names that had guided my earlier work – Marx, Gramsci, Tilly – names like Bakhtin, Bourdieu, Derrida, and Foucault became guideposts for a new generation of scholars. This "cultural turn" brought a new dimension to the study of collective action, social movements, and political contention.

I was at first frustrated by the abstractness of the new terminology and annoyed at the clublike attitudes of some of its adepts. Yet hidden within the rapidly evolving concatenation of theories, countertheories, and semitheories that came under the umbrella of culture studies was an insight that resonated with what I had been finding in my empirical work: that the symbols, mentalities, and narratives that actors employ can track real-world changes in contentious politics. Not only that, as new words for contention diffuse across social and territorial boundaries to new actors, such words can tell us how meanings change as the same words are used by different actors. That was the instinct that inspired me to write this book.

## This Book

Chapter 1 lays out the theoretical framework of the book and places it in the vast cornucopia of approaches to the culture of contention. I do not attempt to survey all of this literature but instead review studies from history, political science, sociology, and anthropology that help us to examine changes in the language of contention. I argue that changes in contentious language can best be seen as they emerge from critical historical junctures (Collier and Collier 1991) – what I have elsewhere called "cycles of contention" (Tarrow 2011). During such episodes, people come together in conflict with others and constitute new collective actors through the forms their actions take, what they call them, and

what they call themselves. Two main sets of variables – symbolic resonance and strategic modularity – link these linguistic changes to actors'
political contexts and are largely responsible for their durability and diffusion. With each step in the process of diffusion, the book shows, the
meanings of contentious language shift in response to the new political
contexts in which actors attempt to apply them.

Chapter 2 begins with the first actors who gave deliberate attention
to the invention of political language: the French revolutionaries. French
Republicans endowed their own and other languages with a bundle of
terms, many of them new – like Jacobinism, Thermidor, and the Terror –
and others inherited from the past or borrowed – terms like "patriots,"
"convention," and "rights." Revolutions, I argue, are not only critical
*political* junctures (Collier and Collier 1991); they are also *linguistic* junctures, because they provide people with stories that they apply to other
episodes, soldering the experiences of forms of collective contention onto
ordinary language. Three revolutions (the English, the American, and the
French) and one revolutionary secession (the American Civil War) provide
the historical linchpins for the analysis of three key terms – "patriots,"
"conventions," and "terrorism" – chosen because their invention spanned
revolutions from 1688 to the present.

Chapter 3 turns to the world of work, starting with the key words
"working class," whose use diffused only in the 1830s and 1840s. Many
other contentious terms emerged from this period as well – beginning
with the diffusion of the verb for the withholding of labor – "to strike" –
and, in France, with *grève*. Along with the timing and the variations in
the Industrial Revolution, political events and political practices provide
a guide to how and where such terms were diffused, and the language
strategies used by authorities show the power and limits of the repression
of popular language.

Chapter 4 examines the relationship of rights and race, using the tangled skein of the ways black Americans have been described and described
themselves in the past century. The remarkable changes in the naming
of this long-subjugated group tell us much about black progress in the
twentieth century but also about the ingenious resources of racist language as the century reached its end and a mixed-race president was
elected in the United States.

In the modern history of gender relations, the "renaming" of actors
was, at times, a deliberate strategy of feminist activists, whereas the use of
traditional gendered language was a less deliberate, but no less effective,
strategy of their opponents. Chapter 5 pays particular attention to early

twentieth-century debates over "birth control" and explains why the term gave way to "family planning." Next, we turn to the appearance and normalization of "male chauvinist" and "male chauvinist pig" and then to the "naming" of sexual harassment and its diffusion from the United States to Western Europe.

Chapter 6 turns to conflicts over naming of citizens, territories, and nations, in the varied cases of the French revolution, the creation of the state of Israel, and the naming of the new state of Macedonia in the former Yugoslavia, an action that triggered the ire of its Greek neighbors. The chapter traces the double face of the construction of naming – internal and external – and underscores the conflict between redemption and the creation of new and more potent identities in the creation of nation-states.

Two words that have always been at the heart of contentious politics are "love" and "hatred." The "beloved community" of American civil rights workers and of those advocating same-sex marriage were inspired by love, whereas anti-Semites and white supremacists are driven by hatred. Although these emotions are obvious to most participants in contentious politics, scholars have only begun to try to understand how "emotion *work*" relates to the emotions of those who are mobilized by social movements. But they have paid less attention to how love and hate intersect in episodes of contention. Those themes are examined in Chapter 7.

The book's conclusion turns to three fundamental problems: first, how should we understand the role of contentious language? Are the words for contention merely expressive of what people want to accomplish through protest, or do they actively structure how they go about making their claims? Second, how have the new and revolutionary forms of communication that came into their own in the first decade of the new century affected the language of contention? And finally, has a more globalized world produced a greater unity of words of contention, or has it devalued political language?

"What's in a word?" the final chapter asks. You can already anticipate the answer I will offer: "In a word, lots!"

I

# Repertoires of Contentious Language

September 17, 2011: a group of young people carrying tents, cooking equipment, and sleeping bags sets up camp in a privately owned but public square in downtown Manhattan, near the New York Stock Exchange. As they describe themselves, "Occupy Wall Street is a people-powered movement that began on September 17, 2011 in Liberty Square in Manhattan's Financial District, and has spread to over 100 cities in the United States and actions in over 1,500 cities globally." The protesters claim to be fighting back against the corrosive power of major banks and multinational corporations over the democratic process and over the role of Wall Street in creating an economic collapse that has caused the greatest recession in generations. The movement, they argue, is inspired by popular uprisings in Egypt and Tunisia and aims to expose how the richest 1 percent of people are writing the rules of an unfair global economy that is foreclosing on our future.[1]

Media savvy and well connected nationally and internationally, the Wall Street protesters are soon joined by sympathizers from around the country and abroad.[2] By late October, there are at least 250-odd

[1] http://occupywallst.org/about/.
[2] A number of websites tracked the diffusion of the movement to various regions of the United States and abroad. Probably the most reliable account comes from the *Guardian*, which published an interactive map of sites (http://www.guardian.co.uk/news/datablog/interactive/2011/oct/18/occupyprotestsmap-world, visited on Nov. 22, 2011, and regularly updated. Particularly interesting is the link between OWS and a Spanish-born network called *Los indignados*, whose occupation of city squares spread across Europe and the Middle East roughly in parallel to those of their American homologue. For a brief account, see http://www.clarin.com/mundo/indignados-Espana-extienden-Europa_0_484151851.html.

TABLE 1.1. *Main Locations of OWS Protests, September 17–November 30, 2011*

| Location | Cities | Location | Cities |
|----------|--------|----------|--------|
| State public buildings | 37 | Parks | 58 |
| Federal buildings | 3 | Plazas, squares, commons | 44 |
| Banks | 12 | Streets | 35 |
| Chambers of commerce | 1 | Downtown/Centers | 18 |
| University campuses | 35 | Bridges | 2 |
| Other | 20 | | |

*Note:* The table contains information on the location of OWS protests in 265 cities from the press and from self-reports by protesters.

occupy sites across the country in which some form of occupation is being mounted. Map 1.1 shows the occupy sites that were recorded over the first ten days of occupations alone.

The New York City occupation goes through a number of phases, punctuated by support from trade unions and sympathetic public figures and the periodic intervention of the New York Police Department, Mayor Bloomberg, and the ever-present media. Reporters are at first puzzled ("What do they *want*?" asks more than one of them), then fascinated (some see it as a homologue to the tea party movement), and, finally, bored. For their part, the occupiers busy themselves keeping order in their rapidly growing tent city, listening to speakers whose words are spread by a distinct human microphone chain, and, as winter creeps up on the toe of Manhattan, keeping warm. In late November, a small group breaks away to march on Washington, but the attention of the media is diverted by the brutal pepper-spraying of another group of protesters by campus police in Davis, California. After this, the movement continues to spread, first across the United States and Canada, as Map 1.1 shows.

As it diffuses across the country, the movement diversifies in the kind of places its activists occupy. In forty-four cities, the activists copy the New York pattern by setting up tents on public squares, but another forty groups pitch their tents outside state or federal public buildings, fifty-eight in parks, and thirty-five on city streets. Increasingly, college campuses become the sites of occupations, as Table 1.1 shows.

When the activists first camped out on a square near Wall Street, many Americans thought they were inventing a new form of demonstration – and indeed, Occupy Wall Street (OWS) was more creative than the set-piece marches that have marked American politics in recent years. But the OWS protesters were using a basic form of protest that has marked

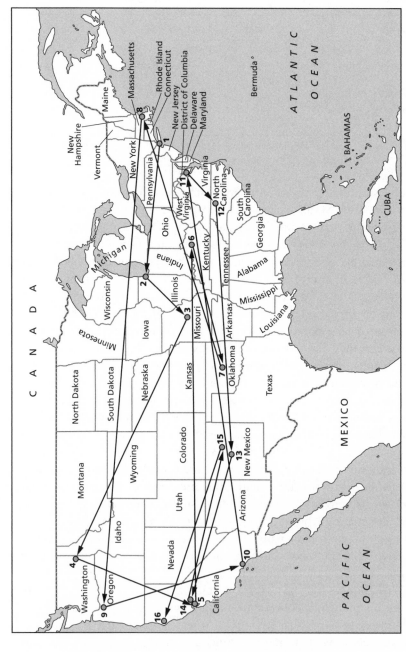

MAP 1.1. Occupy Sites in the United States Through October 1, 2011. *Source:* The Occupy Together Web site (www. occupytogether.org).

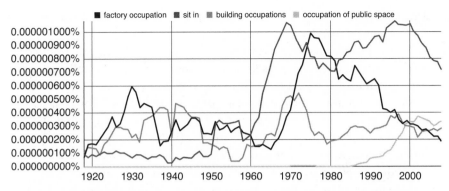

FIGURE 1.1. Various Forms of "Occupy" from an Ngram Analysis of Books in English, 1914–2008. *Source*: http://books.google.com/ngrams.

U.S. and European history for almost a century. We first see it in the occupation of Italian factories after World War I by workers trying to prevent themselves from being locked out of their workplaces (Spriano 1975); it reappeared with the "sit-down strikes" in France and the United States in the 1930s; it appeared again with the sit-ins of the 1960s and the squats of the 1970s and 1980s. For almost a century, protesters have used one or another form of the occupation.

Figure 1.1 tracks the appearance of the words used for the occupation of factories, university faculties, private dwellings, and public spaces from 1914 through 2008 in an Ngram analysis based on Google Books in English. The first form to appear in significant numbers was factory occupations, which peaked after World War I and then again in the 1970s. These are followed by sit-ins, which arose in the 1960s and never significantly declined but reappeared in large numbers around the turn of the century (Tilly and Tarrow 2007). Building occupations describe a more jagged line, first appearing in the Depression and then subsiding until the squatter movements that followed the 1960s. Only in the 1990s do the occupations of public space like OWS begin to appear in significant numbers in our Ngram tracking, and they continue to rise through the first decade of the new century. Although the Occupy Wall Street protesters added something new and fresh to the repertoire of contention, they were operating in a long and checkered repertoire of occupations.

## What Is Happening Here?

Readers may wonder why I have begun a book about changes in the language of contention with a potted history of the occupation. There are at least five things the story can help us see about the language of contentious politics.

First, words that emerge as symbols of contention are seldom invented on the spot: they have sources in ordinary speech, in popular folktales or music, commercial media or huckstering, previous experiences of war or conflict, and authoritative statements of law and policy. Though it had new and refreshing permutations, the term "Occupy" in Occupy Wall Street was part of a long linguistic narrative (Polletta 2006) that emerged out of an episode of contentious interaction almost a century earlier and evolved in response to changing strategic situations.

Second, as historian Daniel Rodgers writes, "though words constrain their users, hobble political desires, nudge them down socially worn channels, they are in other circumstances radically unstable" (1987: 10). Over time the meanings of words change, merge, divide, and diffuse, as the various forms of occupation in Figure 1.1 suggest. From its original connotation of the occupation of territory in war to occupations to avoid lockouts to the practice of peaceful nonviolence in the 1960s and, most recently, to dramatize inequality, the meaning of "occupy" has continued to evolve.

Third, changes in contentious language are "dialogic" (Bakhtin 1981; Steinberg 1995, 1999a): they are not simply dreamed up by political wordsmiths or dictated by courts or legislatures; they result from the thrust and parry of the political process and from the slower rhythms of political and cultural change (also see Freeden 1996). This construction and reconstruction of contentious language results from the interaction among actors in contingent action situations, using the stock of symbols available to elites as well as ordinary people. In ordinary times, elites possess power over language, but in critical junctures, ordinary people not only erupt on the stage of history but also gain the power to affect the language of contention.

Fourth, although we usually think of words as the expression of something, words themselves can mobilize, unite, divide, and even conquer. "Words are tools, often weapons," writes Rodgers. "[T]he vocabulary of politics is contested terrain and always has been" (1987: 11). When Italian university students occupied their faculties in the 1960s, they saw themselves as part of a story that had begun in Turinese faculties a half-century before but also in the occupation of Sproul Hall in Berkeley and Hamilton Hall at Columbia a few years earlier (Tarrow 1989). Like the terms "barricade," "strike," "boycott," and "revolution," which you will encounter in this study, the term "occupy" has brought people together in episodes of contentious collective action for at least a century.

Finally, some words survive and diffuse as symbols of contention while others disappear or are absorbed into ordinary language. "Occupy" has already been adapted to other settings (e.g., "Occupy Sandy" after the superstorm of 2012). The term will undoubtedly remain part of the repertoire of contention, but its meaning has already changed from its association with "the 99 percent." As words diffuse, their meanings expand and change: "occupy," for example, went from meaning a form of action to the name of the movement that employed it. This brings us to the repertoire of contention and its relation to the construction, the durability, and the diffusion of language, for language – no less than the forms of protest people use – is part of an ongoing and ever-changing repertoire.

## The Construction of Contentious Language

We owe the concept of the repertoire of contention to the work of Charles Tilly, as well as his systematic analysis of the words used to describe forms of contention (Tilly 1995a and b; 2008). In his archival work in France, Tilly noticed that a few central forms of action recurred over and over even though a much larger number were theoretically possible (Tilly 1986). From these forms of contention, he identified a "traditional" repertoire, made up of forms of action that were parochial, local, and direct, and a "modern" one, made up of forms of action that were indirect, translocal, and modular. In the former, attacks on bakers and millers, the tearing down of houses, and *charivaris* (or "rough music") were mounted by local actors against their direct opponents; in the latter, marches, demonstrations, and strikes were organized through associations that frequently targeted national institutions.

Tilly saw changes in repertoires occurring incrementally as actors improvise around the central core of known forms of action in response to different circumstances. In research extending his work, Tilly's student Takashi Wada has shown how British actors "either mastered a small number of forms of contention well (rigid users) or experimented with a large number of forms and became flexible users" (Wada 2009: 19). Seldom did they invent new forms of contention out of whole cloth; more often, they innovated on existing performances. In the culmination of his career – his magisterial *Contentious Performances* (2008) – Tilly systematized these findings and gave microscopic attention to the words that actors and observers use to describe collective actions. Tilly also saw some repertoires as strong or rigid and others as weak or flexible (2006a), a distinction we will return to.

For Tilly, it was only as major shifts in the economy and in state building presented new constraints and opportunities that fundamental changes in language repertoires occurred. These changes marked major stages in the construction, the durability, and the diffusion of new contentious language as well as the forms of action they described. But major innovations tend to cluster in critical junctures of contentious interaction: wars, revolutions, religious and nationalist conflict, and even in ordinary cycles of contention (Collier and Collier 1991). These "cycles of contention" are the sources of major changes in language as well as in the forms of contention (Tarrow 2012).

### Critical Junctures of Contention

When people are thrown together in new combinations against new or different targets under new configurations of opportunity and threat, they produce both new forms of action and the words to describe them. The barricade in the French revolutions; the sit-in in the American civil rights and the anti–Vietnam War movements; the occupation of central squares in the Middle Eastern and North African revolutions in 2011: these critical junctures give rise to new forms of action and affect the narratives that describe them.

Of course, this does not mean that contentious language emerges *only* within critical junctures. The French *charivari* was reproduced in North America in the form of the "shivaree," in which community members who violate community norms are humiliated and sometimes physically abused (Thompson 2009: 523). The boycott of slave-produced sugar was invented in England in the 1770s but was "named" in Ireland over an entirely different issue, as you will see. And the strike developed its characteristic routines and narratives over the century that followed its first naming (see Chapter 3). But critical junctures raise the awareness of the public, heighten the tension between authorities and claims makers, attract the attention of the media, and set off spirals of protest and response that lead to the invention of new forms of action and efforts to name and frame them (Snow and Benford 1992).

Some names for contentious interaction that emerge during cycles of contention rapidly disappear or are absorbed back into ordinary language. Take the term "male chauvinist pig": it was coined by a radical section of the feminist movement from the term "pig," a derogatory term for a police officer in the 1960s, combined with the term "chauvinist" for an arrogant male (Mansbridge and Flaster 2007). But even though the term eventually entered ordinary usage, it never stuck as a movement term as feminism entered a more institutionalized phase, as you will see in Chapter 5.

What are the characteristics of contentious words that do endure? One major feature is their ambiguity. Once invented, words for contentious politics are polysemic, and that makes their meaning both ambiguous and available: their ambiguity is part of what makes them modular and therefore available for repetition (Polletta 2006: viii). Ambiguity helps create coalitions, enabling groups "with very different agendas to come together in a common stance of indignation" (ibid., p. 19). Ambiguity also condenses meanings. Contentious words are what Edward Sapir called "condensation symbols," which grow in complexity with increased dissociation from their original usage (Sapir 1934: 493–4).

Take the concept of "occupy": it retains its underlying military meaning, and that makes it potentially violent; its use in the factories since World War I gave it a connotation of class struggle; and since the 1960s its use for nonviolent and participatory politics has given it an association with liberation, the very opposite of its original military connotations. But ambiguity and polysemity are only internal features of contentious language. Contentious words emerge through the interaction and constitution of contentious actors.

### Actor Constitution
Early in his career, Tilly ascribed major changes in repertoires to fundamental shifts in capitalism and state building (Tilly 1978). But these processes appeared, as it were, "offstage," in William Sewell's pithy critique (1996). There was something wooden – and almost detached from contentious interaction – in this structuralist trope. Later, together with this author and Doug McAdam, Tilly lowered his gaze from the macrostructural levels of capitalism and state building to the constitution of new actors through episodes of contention (McAdam et al. 2001: 315–21). In that work, we argue that political actors are not formed simply through the mobilization of resources or the response to political opportunities; they form by mounting a repertoire of collective action, both innovative and routine, in interaction with opponents, allies, and third parties (pp. 102–3).

But this is only the first stage of an interactive process that shapes (or reshapes) the emergent new actor. Imagine a simple two-actor contest between a challenger and an opponent: first, I take advantage of perceived political opportunities and threats to make claims on you or retreat in the face of your threats; second, I engage in a combination of routine and innovative collective actions, to which you respond, and I respond to your responses; third, I attempt to certify myself as a worthy, powerful, legitimate actor, to which you respond by calling me a terrorist, a thug, or someone who wants to exploit my followers. To this I may respond that you are nothing more than a corrupt coterie of corrupt exploiters who have been living off the people for decades. Within my hardening identity boundary, I work to frame a consensual appeal to hold on to and increase my support base, while maintaining a conflictual message across it.

The typical result of this process is the formation of a new actor category on the part of the crystallizing group, and a significant reconstitution of relationships among a broader set of actors comprising an emergent field of political contention. Out of these interactions a loose set of sites of contention are created that share a boundary. The initial symbols that form across that boundary – what Daniel Rogers calls "contested truths" – become part of an ongoing set of symbolic and behavioral relationships (Rogers 1987: 115–16).

We can see from this "standard story" that actors constitute themselves as part of a broad, dynamic, and interactive repertoire of contention that is both behavioral and discursive. To use a metaphor that Tilly employed to describe the repertoire of collective action, a repertoire is less like a completed symphony than like improvisational jazz; composers provide the initial line for a jam session, but the improvisations depend on a group of players over whom they have little control. These players interact with one another, with opponents, and with those they are trying to attract (1983: 463). Over time, new players move into the band, and others move out. It is through this process that new narratives are formed; reflecting on Tilly's work, John Krinsky and Ann Mische write that "meanings were created through interaction and transaction, via the claims and stories people direct at each other as part of these relations."[3]

Of course, once constituted, words for contentious interaction survive and diffuse because they come to be associated with past successes – or with past tragedies – the meaning of which actors understand and apply to their own circumstances. The French did not invent the term "revolution," but their revolution of 1789 endowed the term with a tissue of assumptions, expected forms of action and interaction, and a corresponding language. Aspiring revolutionaries around the world, when

---

[3] John Krinsky and Ann Mische have done a better job than anyone else in delineating the main lines of Tilly's interactive perspective, in "Formations and Formalisms: Charles Tilly and the Paradox of the Actor," *Annual Review of Sociology* 39: 1–28.

they adopted the term, fit their actions into the template of what they thought of as a revolution (Anderson 1991). Two major concepts help us see why some contentious words endure and diffuse, whereas others disappear or are absorbed into ordinary language. Those concepts are symbolic resonance and strategic modularity.

## Symbolic Resonance and Strategic Modularity

By "symbolic resonance" I mean the degree to which a particular term resonates with culturally familiar concepts (Snow and Benford 1988). Symbolic resonance is in part the result of the core meaning of a specific term; for example, the meaning of a "strike" or a "boycott" is largely the same in many countries (see Chapter 3). "Meaning comes about in both the individual psyche and in shared social experience through the medium of the sign," writes Bakhtin's interpreter, Michael Holquist (1990: 49; also see Krinsky 2008). Take the word "barricade": it has both dramatic and solidaristic implications (Traugott 2010). After 1789, in France, its symbolic associations led it to be repeated each time insurgents challenged authorities. In both 1848 and 1871, Parisians erected barricades (Gould 1995); as late as May 1968, cobblestones were piled up across the streets of the Latin Quarter against police charges. These charges seldom eventuated, and the barricades of 1968 had a largely symbolic function. "The place that any word or phrase has within such a system significantly determines its polysemy, how readily and to what extent it can be populated with multiple meanings," notes Marc Steinberg.[4] Since its invention in France, the barricade has gained a place in a larger system of meaning.

But the durability of a contentious term also depends on whether it can be adapted to different circumstances. By "strategic modularity" I mean the degree to which terms that emerge in one strategic context can be repeated without losing the strategic advantages they originally possessed. Strategic modularity also gives rise to actors who are organized, in part, to take advantage of these strategic opportunities and repeat, or modify, the original forms of action. Thus a union forms a "strike committee," appoints parade marshals to control unruly elements and negotiate with the police, and distributes handbills and banners to proclaim the purpose

---

[4] In a personal note to the author, commenting on an earlier version of this chapter. For Steinberg's most fundamental contribution to the dialogic understanding of contentious language, see his study of English working-class contention, *Fighting Words* (1999).

TABLE 1.2. *A Hypothetical Typology of the Durability of Contentious Language*

|  |  | Strategic Modularity | |
|---|---|---|---|
|  |  | *Low* | *High* |
| Symbolic Resonance | *Low* | Disappearance | Partial endurance |
|  | *High* | Moderate endurance | High endurance |

of the strike. These parade marshals may then become the military wing of the movement and drift off into armed violence, as some of them did in Italy in the 1960s. Occupiers appoint cleanup committees, run lectures and discussions at the site of the protest, and provide food and blankets to hungry and shivering protesters. Strategic modularity carries with it a host of practices inherited from the past and modified with practice.

Table 1.2 sketches the main argument of the book. It predicts different degrees of durability of contentious language as the result of the intersection of symbolic resonance and strategic modularity. Of course, "high" and "low" are crude measures, and the endurance of a contentious term may be high in one setting and low in another. Moreover, what is resonant to one group of actors may be a source of indifference to another, and what resonates with listeners in one period of history may fall flat in the next. Nor do we even have clear indicators that can measure these qualities or their underlying mechanisms with any precision. But these two terms provide us with a rough-and-ready baseline with which to assess why particular terms of contention survive while others either disappear or become part of ordinary language. They will also help us return, in the Conclusion, to contemporary contentious terms that may or may not find a permanent place in the repertoire of contention.

### Brokerage and the Mechanisms of Diffusion

The durability of contentious language is assisted within a particular setting by a common language, by forms of organization that "remember" it and are organized to repeat its use, and by routines of interaction with public authorities. But what of the diffusion of contentious language from one cultural and linguistic setting to another? In different countries, organizations have different traditions of protest; moreover, police and public authorities are used to dealing with protesters with different routines of facilitation and repression. Yet one of the striking findings of this study is the degree to which words for contentious politics *do* diffuse – sometimes amazingly rapidly – to other places, and even to places where languages, organizations, and public authorities vary widely.

Something concrete has to happen for contentious language to be diffused from one site to another; "brokerage" is the general process that brings this about. By "brokerage" I mean the process through which a third party acts to create a connection between two other actors who would remain unconnected except through the action of the broker (McAdam et al. 2001). The process of brokerage occurs through a number of alternative or simultaneous mechanisms: *communication agencies*, which publish and diffuse – often for commercial motives – information about what happens in one country to another; *halfway houses* (Morris 1984), organizations or institutions whose purpose is not protest, but which sympathetically diffuse information about protest to others; *movement missionaries*, activists who either deliberately, or as a side product of migration, bring contentious language from one country to another; and the *transnational organization of protest*, activities that transmit the language of contention to a number of countries through coordinated protest campaigns.

Although there were examples of such transnationally-coordinated protests as early as the nineteenth century, it is only since the 1990s that such campaigns have become common, animated by cheap international travel, the Internet, and the presence of a new stratum of "rooted cosmopolitans," who gain experience of protest in one setting and are equally at home outside their own country (della Porta 2007; Tarrow 2005). Diffusion is also effected by "connective action" – the coordination of contention among people who have never met but combine their actions through the new forms of social media (Bennett and Segerberg 2013).

### Diffusion and the Evolution of Meaning

As contentious words diffuse across borders, their meanings diffuse and evolve, too. Take the term "terror," which we examine in Chapter 2. Since the terrorist outrages of the first decade of this century, "terrorism" has become almost a synonym for all deliberately violent forms of politics by nonstate actors against the state or their political enemies (della Porta 2013: Ch. 1). But when it was first employed by the English Puritans five centuries ago, it had a mainly subjective meaning: causing dread.[5]

---

[5] According to http://www.etymonline.com, the use of the old Latin word "terror" as the "quality of causing dread" was found as early as the 1520s. In an online discussion, John

It was given an objective meaning only with the radical phase of the French revolution, but even then, there was no "systematic" use of the word (Martin 2006).

In the nineteenth century, terror*ism* – especially in southern Europe, Russia, and the Balkans – became a descriptive term used by *non*state political actors to characterize the violence they used or planned to use against the state. By the late twentieth century it changed yet again, to be used to describe acts of violence against large or significant sectors of the public (Chaliand 2007). By the tenth anniversary of the terrorist bombings of September 11, 2001, American public figures were implicitly returning to the original subjective meaning when they proclaimed proudly that Americans *had not been terrorized* by the massacres of that day. Around the modular core of the term "terrorism" a number of meanings radiated, changing in response to different strategic and cultural changes. Part of the effort of this book is to examine these variations and the political and social contexts that produce such changes in meaning.

### Culture or Strategy?

Are people who are employing words for contention responding mainly to strategic imperatives or to a cultural logic? For some writers, language is a tool employed strategically by organizers to mobilize followers around themselves and their goals. For example, Bert Klandermans's term "consensus mobilization" implies an active agent attempting to mobilize the consensus of prospective followers (Klandermans 1988). But for others, words for contentious politics arise out of the cultural situation in which actors find themselves; this was the way the "fighting words" described by Marc Steinberg emerged from the Spitalfields weavers' struggles in the eighteenth century (1995; 1999a).

Is it culture or strategy that determines which words people will use to describe their contentious actions? This book argues that the deployment and diffusion of contentious language respond to *both* cultural and strategic incentives through the constitution of actors who draw upon a battery of language to describe their identities, their claims, their opponents, and their forms of action. Changes in the culture of contention

Hall notes that "the modern idea of terror goes back at least to the Puritan revolution in England, a point made by Michael Walzer concerning the Puritans themselves, when he called The Terror 'the effort to create a holy commonwealth and to force men to be Godly.'" In parallel, Derrida has noted, Hobbes invoked terror as a principle basis of the commonwealth, "by the terror of some punishment." I am grateful to John Hall for these references.

result from newer actors adopting the language and the forms of action invented by previous actors, which are modified, ritualized, and in some cases institutionalized.

## Words as Expressions of Action and Words as Action

What role does language play in the survival and diffusion of a contentious practice? Or to put this differently, do words have an effect on contentious politics distinct from the structural factors from which they emerge? Would the Wall Street occupiers in 2011 have gained less attention had they failed to employ the resonant symbol of the "occupation"? What effect did the adoption of the slogan "pro-life," and the contrasting term "pro-choice," have on the appeal, respectively, of the pro- and anti-abortion movements in the United States, and why were these terms chosen over more direct signifiers? Did the expression "dirty Jew" simply animate anti-Semitic rioters to attack Jewish *shtetlach* (villages) in the late nineteenth century, or did the adjective "dirty" authorize violence against anyone who could be dismissed as unclean (see Chapter 7)?[6]

These questions go to the heart of our understanding of the relationship between language and collective behavior. What I try to show in this book is not that language drives action independent of other factors, but that it plays an important role in the construction, the endurance, and the diffusion of contentious politics. I argue that the effects of collective word making go well beyond its immediate outcomes to become part of the culture of contention; and the successful invention and diffusion of a term depends largely on the political context and the responses of antagonists, the press, and the authorities.

Such a combination of factors cannot be understood through linguistic analysis alone. We need to combine attention both to the meaning of words and to the strategic situations in which word workers find themselves when they employ them: to the actual *work* that words do in specific contexts (Rodgers 1987: 5). To do so, we must combine an ethnographic attention to the settings in which new contentious terms are invented with longer-term and comparative analyses of where they diffuse to and how well they endure. That means drawing not only on evidence about the words themselves but also on the political process of contention. Let us

---

[6] A brief history of this term of denigration will be found in Josh Lambert, "A Literary History of the Dirty Jew," on JBooks.com at http://jbooks.com/interviews/index/IP_Lambert_DJ.htm. Visited November 15, 2012.

turn briefly to the spectrum of approaches to the changing language of contention.

## A Multitude of Voices

I am far from the first to try to understand the language of contention, its duration, and its diffusion. Historians, political scientists, communications scholars, sociologists, and anthropologists have examined different aspects of how language emerges and is used in the process of contention. First in the field were historians from various countries; then political theorists and political scientists, moving beyond their traditional institutional preoccupations, began to focus on political culture and communications; more recently, innovative work has been done by sociologists of social movements; they have joined anthropologists, who have long experience in studying symbolism and ritual. What seems to be lacking is a systematic attempt to connect the language of contention to the material and structural settings in which it emerges, diffuses, and endures.

### Historiography and Mentalities

Since the 1960s, much innovative work has been done on the language of contention among historians of the United States, France, Britain, and Russia. Daniel Rodgers and Michael Kammen in the United States, Maurice Agulhon, Lynn Hunt, and William Sewell Jr. in France, Marc Steinberg for England, and Claudia Verhoeven for Russia have done original work in tracing the origins and the permutations of political language.

In his foundational book on the United States, *Contested Truths*, Rodgers followed the trajectories of seven keywords – "utility," "natural rights," "the people," "government," "the state," "interests," and "freedom" – through American history, particularly during periods when "the basic metaphors of politics were up for grabs" (1987: 11–12). Similarly, Kammen traced the permutations in the use of the term "liberty" from the colonial period to the twentieth century, with a unique display of the term's iconography (1987). It will not surprise American readers that the term could be arrayed on behalf of causes as different as a revolution against the British Empire, the defense of slavery, and the right of Americans to bear arms and avoid universal health care.

France has been a center of attention to the language of contention. Agulhon focused on the imposing figure of "Marianne" and on how that symbol evolved from the 1789 revolution, when it was adopted from Latin precedents, through the nineteenth century (Agulhon 1982a). For her part, though focusing more on physical symbols – dress, monuments, the body – than on words, Hunt showed how the French revolutionaries fashioned "costumes of revolt" and how these costumes affected the ways people behaved in revolutionary situations (1984; 1992). Sewell traced the itinerary of "corporatist" language from the Old Regime through the French revolutions of 1789 and 1830 to its transformation into the language of class in the 1848 revolution (Sewell 1980; 1986).

In England, following the pathbreaking work of E. P. Thompson (1966), attention centered on the formation of the language of labor. Those who followed in Thompson's wake strove to make fine distinctions between artisans and mass production workers (Calhoun 1982), sometimes centered on the appearance of a singular working-class language and culture (Briggs 1960) and sometimes linked to changes in politics and the state (Stedman Jones 1983). Marc Steinberg, drawing on the work of Bakhtin, showed how contentious language evolved out of changes in the structural situation of eighteenth-century English weavers (1995; 1999a).[7]

Most of these historians were deeply embedded in their own countries' histories and used concepts that were not always easy to apply outside their chosen territory. But starting in the 1960s, French historians began to array a term – "mentalities" – that could be applied to the histories of other countries just as easily. Interest in the concept reached its peak as the result of a particularly creative cross-fertilization among history, demography, and the social sciences (Ariès 1978, 403 ff.). One of the most refreshing characteristics of the new school was that it legitimated the use of a broader range of sources than was found in traditional historiography. Popular fêtes and carnivals, songs and canards, the cheap press, and data on people's eating habits, nutrition, and health, how they procreated – or tried not to – and to whom or to what they left their property when they died: all this became grist for the new historians' mill.

But the concept of mentalities was so broad that it was difficult to apply to particular episodes of contention.[8] The *Tresor de la langue française informatisée* defines mentalities as the "collection of the habitual

---

7 I am grateful to Marc Steinberg for his trenchant comments on an earlier version of this chapter, urging me to look more carefully into Bakhtinian linguistic studies. For an introduction, see Holquist, *Dialogism: Bakhtin and His World*.

8 Ariès, for example, devoted an essay of twenty-one dense pages to the concept of mentalities without ever hazarding a definition (1978, 402–23). Agulhon was scarcely less catholic, defining the field as no less than "the content of our knowledge, the way we represent reality, our sentiments – everything that is intellectual and everything that is psychological" (1986, 23).

manners of thinking and believing and the psychological and moral dispositions that are characteristic of a collectivity and common to each of its members" (author's trans.).[9] With so broad a definition, it is difficult to imagine anything that would not be part of a society's mentality!

The history of mentalities was almost inevitably understood to be the history of the lower classes, which ought to make the concept useful in studying popular contention (Agulhon 1986: 28). But the poor were largely illiterate until well into the nineteenth century, and the language of contention was mainly defined by elites, authorities, and clerics. How would the student of language know what peasants or workers called their protests when the words used to describe their actions came from official sources and were almost unfailingly negative? A broader question was how mentalities change: through social and economic change? The diffusion of learning and new modes of communication? Or through the actions of elites and ordinary people? The same question was faced by political scientists as they explored the concepts of ideology and political culture.

### Ideologies and Political Contexts

Ideologies have long been an intellectual stepchild of political theory, "appearing mainly as a peculiar and frequently unsavoury expression of distorted and power-serving political thinking" or "as a simply classificatory label for broadly based political belief-systems and the historical traditions in which they unfold" (Freeden 1996: 2).[10] This has obscured the fact that ideologies are built of some of the same concepts as political theories, but with a closer relationship to the political contexts in which they are arrayed. Words are the outward forms of concepts, so it is peculiar in some respects that political theorists have given so little attention to the language of contention. As Michael Freeden puts it, "[T]heory is to concepts what language is to words: an organizer, a regulator, a set of rules and uniformities, a grammar, a system" (ibid., p. 49).

It was Ferdinand de Saussure who first argued that theory cannot be separated from thought, or thoughts from the words that express them, but rather, in Freeden's words, "a linguistic sign connected sounds and

---

[9] "Ensemble des manières habituelles de penser et de croire et des dispositions psychiques et morales charactéristiques d'une collectivité et communes à chacun de ses membres." http://atilf.atilf.fr/dendien/scripts/tlfiv5/advanced.exe?8;s=3058255545.

[10] For the subhead of this section, I deliberately adopt the subtitle of Michael Freeden in *Ideologies and Political Theory* (1996: 48–60), who has carried out the most innovative work on the analytical study of ideology.

concepts, signifier and signified" (de Saussure 1983; Freeden 1996: 49). Saussure also argued that the linguistic meaning of a word depended on its relations with other words. Thus, "revolution," to which we turn in Chapter 2, takes its meaning from its obverse – "stability" – and relates conceptually to words like "movement," "violence," "anarchism," and "socialism" (Calise and Lowi 2010: 196).[11] The relations between these words define possible combinations (e.g., "socialist revolution," "revolutionary movement") in a synchronic system that affects the meaning of words even beyond the consciousness of individuals who use them. Thus, the Egyptian youths who rose up against the Mubarak regime did not need to know the grammar of the language *in toto* in order to use the term "revolution," as they did in 2011; the term contained its own combinatorial possibilities (Freeden 1996: 49).

Because the meaning of words, for Saussure, was based entirely on their relation to each other, his system was closed to contextual influences. That is the major limitation of the utility of Saussurian thought for the study of political language. "Political concepts exist in the 'real world' of time and space and their meanings derive in part, though not completely, from that world. More precisely, they derive from an interplay between thought and the facts of the external world," notes Freeden (p. 51). "Effectively, the continuity of an ideological tradition – which is assumed, rightly or wrongly, by the continuity of the words that denote those concepts – can only be put to the test by examining multiple synchronic states, over time and space" (p. 52). Political concepts are rooted in their contexts, and the history of these contexts "sticks" to them as they evolve through space and time: "concepts" are rooted in "contexts" and take something of those contexts with them as they diffuse.

### Political Culture and Political Communication

In the 1960s, Gabriel Almond and his collaborators introduced to the field of political science a new concept – political culture – to connect the social structural bases of politics to its institutional outcomes (Almond and Verba 1964, 1–3).[12] Their general argument was that around each

---

[11] Recently, Mauro Calise and Theodore Lowi, have ingeniously related a large number of central political concepts to a number of other concepts that are close to these concepts, in their innovative book *Hyperpolitics* (2010). Many of their concepts are institutional (i.e., "constitution," "legislature"), whereas others are more closely related to contentious politics (i.e., "movement," "terrorism").

[12] Only the briefest bibliography can be presented here. In addition to Almond and Verba (1964), the locus classicus for political culture studies is Pye and Verba, eds. (1965).

political system is a greater or lesser degree of consensus toward its legit-imating symbols and that citizens contribute to the maintenance of the system by their knowledge of and support for these symbols. The authors' more specific concern was with what they considered to be the culture necessary to *democratic* political systems, for which they deduced a con-struct they called the "civic culture," a mix of participant and supportive, as well as traditional and modern, values and orientations supporting liberal democratic practices (ibid., pp. 29 ff.).

The concept of political culture was revived and expanded in the 1980s and 1990s (Laitin 1988; Wildavsky 1987; Inglehart 1988, 1990), in part as a result of growing disillusionment with the microeconomic approaches that had become dominant in the field, and in part though exposure to the growing influence of anthropology and culture studies (Wildavsky 1987: 4–5; Inglehart 1988, 1203). This took the concept beyond the culture-bound parameters of "the civil culture," as described by Almond and his collaborators, and linked with more field-based work in political anthropology from scholars like David Laitin (1977, 1988) and James Scott (1976).

But like students of mentalities and ideologies, scholars of political culture had difficulty dealing with collective action. For some practition-ers, political culture was the sum of the politically relevant attitudes of the mass public and could best be measured by what they told survey researchers (Almond and Verba 1964; Inglehart 1977, 1990). For others, it was found in the beliefs of those who operated the political system, and this led to an emphasis on elite culture (Putnam 1971). But nei-ther approach developed a vocabulary to describe contentious interaction among political actors. Members of the mass public who expressed com-pliance in responding to surveys might go out on the streets to engage in highly contentious behavior. They might also choose from within a repertoire of cultural identities, depending on the others they face (Laitin 1988: 591). By asking them whether they approve of, or have ever partic-ipated in, unconventional behavior (Barnes et al. 1979), it was impossible to link specific actors to those they interact with, and over what claims.

Research into political communication could help to bridge the lacuna between words and actions found in the mainstream political culture tradition. Scholars working in this tradition have focused on persuasion,

Also see Almond, Flanagan, and Mundt, eds. (1973). For a historical retrospective and critique, see the papers collected in Almond and Verba, eds., *The Civil Culture Revisited* (1980).

symbolism, and narrative as ways in which elites and media communicate with mass publics and ways movements attempt to fashion new and creative stories to contest inherited constructions of reality. Behind their work is the concept of power and the ways social or cultural power shape the symbols and narratives of political communication.

In a series of works beginning in the 1960s, communication theorist Murray Edelman focused revealingly on the relations between symbols and politics (1964; 1971; 1977). Unlike the political culture adepts, Edelman focused on power and on the ways power shapes "the ultimately self-defeating logic of stereotypical political plots that bring old and simplistic formulas to bear on new and complex problems" (Bennett and Edelman 1985: 157). His work directed attention to hegemonic systems of culture, mass communications, and socialization. He was impressed – and discouraged – by daily life stories that "seem objective because they are confirmed time and again by self-fulfilling selection of documentary detail." But Edelman's pessimism did not prevent him from asking "whether political opponents are able to frame their analyses in ways that yield new insights, identify new points of struggle and consensus, and lead to new actions" (ibid.).

Edelman's work drew political scientists' attention from the dry statistics of political culture studies to the narratives that animate political debate, which – in his pessimistic view – often disguise ideology behind standard stories: stories such as, "The world is complicated, and so we should defer to elites who are in a position to understand it"; "welfare beneficiaries are taking advantage of a bureaucratized system and should not be encouraged to be lazy"; "the Soviet Union wants to conquer the world, and so domestic anticommunism is warranted." These stories obscure the recognition of the ambiguity and complexity that are necessary to the construction of creative solutions to societal dilemmas.

Edelman's work was mainly theoretical and had only a loosely empirical foundation, but William Gamson worked more closely with empirical materials, first with media sources (1992a) and then more ethnographically with participant observation of groups of ordinary citizens (1992b). Gamson's focus shifted back and forth creatively from the media, to social movements, to ordinary people, describing the "ideological packages" that appear to come together in political discourse (1988). He, too, was interested in power and worked to show how the representation of an event – for example, welfare policy or affirmative action – reflected the power relations involved in the interaction among contentious actors, the state, and the media (Gamson and Lasch 1983; Gamson and Modigliani 1987).

More recently, Francesca Polletta has followed in the tradition of Edelman and Gamson in her study of narratives of contention. In her book *It Was Like a Fever* (2006), Polletta tried to "shed light on the specific discursive mechanisms by which the canonical stories that make up a political common sense operate." She paid careful attention not only to meaning but also to what she calls "the social organization of the capacity to mean effectively" (p. xii). What makes a story "superior" is its resonance with other stories, central themes of political culture (Margulies 2013), and central myths of the people who use it.

Disadvantaged groups can use personal stories to "chip away at the wall of public indifference... elicit sympathy on the part of the powerful and sometimes mobilize official action against social wrongs," notes Polletta. But she is also convinced that the use of narrative has risks for such disadvantaged groups: first, the risk that standard stories "make it more difficult to tell a story of long-term endurance than one of short-term triumph" and, second, because "stories are differently intelligible, useful and authoritative depending on who tells them, when, for what purpose, and in what setting" (2006: 2–3). This may be another way of saying that the poor are dependent, at least in part, on the hegemonic culture that produces the language they are obliged to use in mounting contention, as both Gramsci and James Scott have argued (Gramsci 1971; Scott 1985, 1990).

Polletta may be more pessimistic about the constraints of language on contention than she needs to be. First, as Tilly wrote in an artful essay, some stories are superior to the standard stories that leap to the mind of social actors (Tilly 2006a: 171–2). Second, even though, in the short run, actors lacking cultural capital may be doomed to tell "standard stories," popular language can induce solidarity and provide signals to coordinate collective action. You will see examples of such popular language in Chapter 3, when I discuss the development of the term "working class" and the language of the strike. Finally, in the process of mobilization, challengers can develop new stories that open up new possibilities for action and constitute themselves as new actors, as Polletta's own stories demonstrate (2006: Chs. 6, 7).

The most important lesson from the work of Edelman, Gamson, and Polletta is that we can best understand the role of language in contentious politics by turning from the methodological individualism of the political culture tradition to the "social organization of how to mean effectively"

(Polletta 2006: Ch. 1), or, as Bennett and Edelman put it, to "how people in collectivities can best present and reconcile competing truths" (Bennett and Edelman 1985: 162). As they conclude,

> The seedbed of creative use and creative reception of narratives lies, we believe, in learning to recognize and appreciate the inevitability of contradictory stories, the multiple realities they evoke, and their links to the conditions of people's lives. (p. 171)

### Frames and Emotions

This takes us to the most influential work in the sociological study of contentious language: the theory of framing.[13] In a series of papers beginning in the 1980s, David Snow and his collaborators argued that there is a special category of cultural understandings – frames – that relate to collective action (see Snow et al. 1986; Snow and Benford 1988, 1992, 2000). Snow and his collaborators adopted Goffman's (1974) term "framing," which they defined as "schemata of interpretation" (Snow et al. 1986), to conceptualize how ideological meanings are proposed by movement organizers to would-be supporters. These authors argued that "by rendering events or occurrences meaningful, frames function to organize experience and guide action, whether individual or collective. So conceptualized, it follows that frame alignment is a necessary condition for movement participation, whatever its nature or intensity" (ibid., p. 464).

With their concept of "frame alignment," Snow and his collaborators related framing to a society's broader cultural understandings. They identified four types of alignment, which they called "frame bridging," "frame amplification," "frame expansion," and "frame transformation" (ibid.), which vary in the degree to which they rest, on the one extreme, on existing values and predispositions and, on the other, on alternative meanings that challenge individuals' beliefs and understandings of organizers' reading of the public's existing values and predispositions.[14]

---

[13] Once again, I cannot hope to summarize the vast literatures on these concepts. For a synthesis of work on framing through the turn of the century, see Snow (2004). For a brief introduction to the study of emotions and social movements, see Goodwin and Jasper (2006).

[14] *Frame bridging*: this is the least ambitious form of framing. It "refers to the linkage of two or more ideologically congruent but structurally unconnected frames regarding a particular issue or problem" (Snow et al. 1986: 467). *Frame transformation*: at the opposite extreme, when a movement wishes to put forward a radically new set of ideas,

Snow and his collaborators went on to examine the concept of "frame resonance," a term very close to the concept of "symbolic resonance" that I use in this study (Snow and Benford 1988). Snow and his collaborators argued that movement organizers construct symbol systems designed to attract supporters to their views, but they do not invent them on the spot. On the contrary, in all but the most transformational framing efforts, movement organizers attempt to relate their goals and programs to the existing values and predispositions of their target public. They are thus in a certain sense both consumers of existing cultural meanings and producers of new meanings.

The same cultural turn that spurred sociologists in the 1980s and 1990s to focus on collective action frames also contributed to the rediscovery of the emotions that trigger, accompany, and result from participation in social movements. Not that emotions were ever absent from accounts of social movement mobilization: but the exaggeratedly pathological depiction of emotions in social movements in the past put scholars off from putting emotions in the forefront of studies of social movements in the succeeding decades (Goodwin and Jasper 2006: 612–14). This was particularly true of work inspired by the rationalist paradigm (for example, see Olson 1986, Chong 1991, Opp 1989); but emotions were also given short shrift in the "political process" and "resource mobilization" approaches that emerged in the 1970s and 1980s.

By focusing more centrally on emotions, sociologists like James Jasper (1997), Ron Aminzade and Doug McAdam (2001), Jeff Goodwin, James Jasper, and Francesca Polletta (2001), Helena Flam and Debra King (2005), Deborah Gould (2009), and Erika Summers Effler (2010) revived attention to the emotional fabric of contention. Chapter 7 delves more deeply into this literature in examining the role of "love" and "hatred" in contentious politics. Only three comments are important to add here: first, there is seldom a one-to-one relationship between the emotions that underlie mobilization and their outward expression in contentious language; second, the emotions that animate participants in collective action

---

it must engage in "frame transformation," which implies that "new values may have to be planted and nurtured, old meanings or understandings jettisoned, and erroneous beliefs or 'misframings' reframed" (473). Between these polar types, two intermediate processes of frame alignment are identified. *Frame amplification*: this refers to "the clarification and invigoration of an interpretive frame bearing on a particular issue" (469). *Frame extension*: by this process, a movement attempts to "enlarge its adherent pool by portraying its objectives or activities as attending to or being congruent with the values or interests of potential adherents" (472).

may be different from those that are arrayed by the leaders who mobilize them because leaders are more likely to be doing "emotion work" than their followers; and third, some social movements are more constrained than others from emotionality by the "common sense" of their societies. We need to be cautious in assigning the same value to the language of emotion in all sectors of contentious politics.

### Ritual and Symbolism

I have left for last the contributions of anthropologists, but not because they are the least important: of all the social sciences. Anthropology has given the most attention to ritual and symbolism, both of which are communicated largely through language and are crucial to the processes of endurance and diffusion of contentious language. "Symbolism" I define, with Edward Sapir, as the use of language or practice "that is a substitute for some more closely intermediating type of behavior," and that "expresses a condensation of energy, its actual significance being out of all proportion to the apparent triviality of meaning suggested by its mere form" (Sapir 1934: 492).[15] Sapir distinguishes between "referential symbolism," by which he means symbols that refer directly to some object or some practice, and "condensation symbols," which combine a number of meanings and whose meanings increase the further the object or practice "travels" from its original form.

"Ritual" is a term of equally capacious meaning. The dictionary definition focuses on formal religious practice, but anthropologists have used the term more broadly. I define ritual, with David Kertzer, as "symbolic behavior that is socially standardized and repetitive" (1988: 9). Ritual action, for Kertzer, "has a formal quality to it. It follows highly structured, standardized sequences and is often enacted at certain places and times that are themselves endowed with special symbolic meaning." Ritual language is often repetitive and redundant, but it is precisely these factors that make it useful to channel emotion, guide cognition, and organize social groups (ibid.). Ritual has a double function: on the one hand, it is the social glue that holds society together, but, on the other, ritual practices bring together an opposition and authorize its actions.

Forms of collective action are ritualized as condensation symbols when they either have led to great successes or mark particularly dramatic

---

[15] Sapir's most important article can also be found online at www.broku.ca/Mead/ Project/Sapir/Sapir_1934_a.html. I am grateful to Lance Bennett for reminding me of Sapir's foundational contribution to the study of symbolism.

episodes of contention. It is at this point that these symbols become modular. Their repetition through successive cycles of contention both gives them symbolic resonance and demonstrates their strategic modularity. The language developed through these episodes communicates both the symbolic resonance and the strategic modularity of particular forms of contention.

Repeated collective actions like strikes, demonstrations, and May Day celebrations have a deeply ritualistic character, but the significance of ritual and symbolism can also be seen in the interaction between challengers and their antagonists in nonroutine interactions. Some opposition groups mimic the rituals and even the language of elites in order to mobilize supporters without threatening social order, as Communist officials did in organizing festivals around Catholic ritual forms in Italy (Kertzer 1990). Others invert the symbols of power by arraying the power of symbols, as the Polish opposition did in the rise of Solidarity (Kubik 1994). Jan Kubik found a whole repertoire of ritualistic phrases in the propaganda of Polish Communist elites (e.g., the frequent use of the adjective "certain," p. 47). It was often sufficient for Solidarity activists to employ a more natural language in order to contest the deadening hand of party orthodoxy. Kubik's work is a classic example of how symbolic resonance combines with strategic context to produce new words and new meanings for old ones in the context of contentious confrontations.

### Implications and Complications

As you have seen, language plays a wide range of roles in the work of historians, political scientists, sociologists, and anthropologists on contentious politics. Language can be studied in terms of its expression of societal mentalities and political cultures, its communication of key narratives, the frames and emotions it embodies, and its capacity to express rituals and symbols to prospective supporters as well as opponents and third parties. I hope it is clear by now that we can best look at the role of language in the process of contention as *relational*, *concrete*, and *dynamic* (Steinberg 1999: 5–6):

- It is *relational* in the sense that Bakhtin talks about language as relational: "It is composed of an utterance, a reply, and a relation between the two" (Holquist 1990: 38).
- It is *concrete* in the sense that it develops within specific communities "within the lattice work of daily life" (Steinberg 1999: 5).

• And it is *dynamic* in that it develops through an interactive process of contention with significant others (McAdam et al. 2001: Ch. 2).

What this means is that we will not fully grasp how contentious language develops unless we can root it in what Steinberg calls "loosely-coupled ensembles internally and in relation to dominant ideologies" (1999b: 7). This means that language can play several roles either in sequence or in combination: it is the vehicle through which new collectivities – especially those whose members are at some distance from each other – are formed; it is the means of communication between leaders and followers within these collectivities and between them and significant others; and it is the mechanism for the diffusion of contention from one group to another and from one place to another. Finally, and most important, it is the main marker we have to understand the historical evolution of contentious politics.

But there are complications. First, actors who use a particular language in emergent episodes of contention are influenced by a variety of cultural repertoires and ritual language, as well as by their immediate environments. Thus, as you will see in Chapter 3, the English working class was influenced by the English reformism, by Painite radicalism, and by Christian associationism before developing its own ideology and sense of its collectivity in the struggles of the 1820s and 1830s.

Second, movements that develop a particular language of contention in one historical juncture often retain that language and the emotions it communicates even as their situation changes and its attendant emotions have cooled or hardened. Think of the language of May Day, born as a language of struggle in 1880 but retained when the first of May had become no more than a day of ritual festivity (Tartakowsky 2005). The language of earlier critical junctures can also be revived by new actors who reject the ritualization of their movements, as striking workers revived the language of Maoism in a China that was fast becoming an authoritarian capitalist state (Hurst 2009). Most important, language that develops in particular "loosely-coupled ensembles" of conflict can be disseminated beyond the confines of the daily world of experience and struggle, potentially producing widening circles of common understanding (Steinberg 1999: 5). This is the most fascinating aspect of contentious language, but also the most difficult to understand. Much of this book is engaged with the diffusion of contentious language, with its domestication in new sites, and with ways the needs of actors in these sites affect its meaning.

There are some aspects of contentious language that I do not try to address in this book. First, I do not focus on the different tones of language as it is used in spoken form in particular contexts; the use of irony, sarcasm, and humor in public speeches I have not witnessed is beyond the capacity of the study. Second, I do not attempt a content analysis of speeches or writings; this would require a more formal – and less contextual – analysis than what I am equipped to carry out. Finally, I do not attempt to delve under the surface of public language to intuit what actors "really meant"; the book focuses on the collective expression of contentious language rather than on the many meanings that individuals may give to it.

Here are some of the main problems that I address in the book. Why do some terms that appear in contentious episodes survive beyond these episodes, while others – equally resonant at the time – either disappear or are absorbed into ordinary discourse? Why are some terms that emerge from activist language eventually normalized, while others are not? Whose language is more important in the survival and diffusion of contentious language – that of elites, commentators, or ordinary people? Does the repression of contentious language suffocate words that boil up from below, or does popular language eventually percolate into official usage despite attempts to repress it? Finally, how do changes in communication – the print press, radio and TV, and most recently the Internet – affect the rapidity of diffusion and the unity of meaning of contentious language?

There is no way that all these questions can be answered satisfactorily in one slim volume. By raising and illustrating them, I hope to elevate the language of contention to the same status in our armory of concepts as the forms of contention, the attitudes and attributes of activists, the organization and mobilization of movements, and the policy outcomes that have been the stock-in-trade of social movement scholarship over the past few decades. Most of all, I hope to explicate, more systematically than has been done before, the connection between contentious language and its material and structural settings. That will mean giving short shrift to certain structural properties of language – for example, its grammar, its syntax, its clarity or ambiguity. These are issues that have been treated extensively by other scholars; my hope in this book is to demonstrate how contentious language is formed in particular material and structural settings, when it endures, and how it diffuses.

# 2

# Revolutions in Words

As France's Old Regime was dissolving in the 1780s, a wave of violence spread across the country. Jean-Clément Martin puts this dramatically: from the autumn of 1788 to the spring of 1789, at least 289 *émeutes* occurred (Martin 2006: 52).[1] He writes,

> People living in the countryside intercept grain convoys, distribute the own-ers' stocks, and if challenged, stand up to the bailiffs and gendarmes, bran-dishing cudgels. In the urban market places, merchants are thrashed by the consumers who are suffering from the blockades of the food convoys. Women often play a leading role in this unrest. The whole country is beset with fear, with rumors... with terrors and plots. (ibid.)[2]

Was this the onset of a "revolution"? The term originally came from the revolution of the planets and in the eighteenth century came to be used for natural disasters, such as the great earthquake that devastated Lisbon in 1755. And the forms of contention that Martin describes drew upon

---

[1] The *Tresor de la langue française informatisée* finds the origin of the term "émeute" in the old French *esmote*, meaning "movement, explosion, outbreak of a war." In the Old Regime the term was equivalent to the modern English term "riot." Visit http://atilf.atilf. fr/dendien/scripts/tlfiv5/advanced.exe?8;s=2322938565.

[2] This, and all other quotations from the French in this chapter, were kindly translated by Susan Tarrow.

*Author's note*: I am grateful to Michael Dorf, Jason Frank, Michael Kammen, Jean-Clément Martin, and Lea Sgier for helpful comments on a previous version of this chapter and to Claudia Verhoeven for her help with the section on "terror." Too late to be effectively drawn upon for this draft chapter, I discovered the remarkable work on revolutionary language of Jacques Guilhaumou, *La langue politique et la révolution française* (1989), which goes much deeper than this chapter into the rich linguistic tapestry of the French revolution.

a well-known repertoire of collective action forms (Tilly 1986, 1995a, 1995b), including grain seizures, the burning down of houses, attacks on elites, *charivaris*, and a number of other familiar routines. But once the Old Regime began to dissolve, these multiple, and largely traditional, forms of contention were subsumed under a new and broader language: the language of revolution. Martin describes this crucial point:

> The French people's conviction that they have made *the* revolution explains why the positive aspects of the word obscure the multiple forms of violence that accompany it, since these are perceived as merely secondary, without any real significance. (2006: 67)

The new term "revolution" became the master frame over the next decade, a term that would inspire, aggregate, and legitimate many other forms of contention – violent and nonviolent – just as it was terrorizing those, from Edmund Burke (1986) to Alexis de Tocqueville (1955) to François Furet, who saw only its destructive potential (1989). "Revolution" revolutionized the language of contentious politics.

Of course, the term was already common in the eighteenth century in both the political sense of regeneration, cyclicity, and even of "palace revolutions," as well as in the biological sense of "natural" revolutions, such as the Lisbon earthquake (Miller 2011: Ch. 1). But the revolution in France became "The Revolution," both condensing and expanding the word into a new discourse of politics that subsumed previous forms of action under a new and more exciting umbrella. The word reached its most forbidding tones in 1792, when the king was imprisoned, the constitutional monarchy was overthrown, and the republic was founded. But it was when mass violence combined with political transformation – as it did with the taking of the Bastille in July 1789 – that the term "revolution" took on a constituent meaning that helped people around the world place their actions under a dignifying and energizing semantic umbrella for the next two centuries.[3]

The transformation in the meaning of the word "revolution" was not an isolated phenomenon. As France was engulfed by conflict, an entirely new language of contention began to appear: alongside traditional terms like *charivari*, *émeute*, and *émotion*, there appeared new words like *assemblée*, *Jacobin*, and *terreur*. As Maurice Agulhon observes,

---

[3] Specialists differ: Sewell (1990) places the onset of the revolution in its modern sense at the taking of the Bastille in July 1789; Martin places it at the arrest of the king and the formation of the republic in August 1792. As in most such controversies, the timing of the beginning – or the end – of a revolution depends on definitions.

"[T]he main effect of the Revolution was to take iconography out of the studios" (Agulhon 1982a: 13; also see Baker 1990; Miller 2011). These words did not disappear when the revolution ended; each time familiar forms of collective action began to look like what had happened in France between 1789 and 1799, they would reappear. This was what Tocqueville noticed in 1848, when he saw men systematically putting up barricades outside his house. "These barricades," he wrote, "were skillfully built by a small number of men who worked industriously – not like criminals fearful of being caught *in flagrante delicto*, but like good workmen who wanted to do their job expeditiously and well" (1992: 39). Revolution – and its component language – had become normalized.

The diffusion of revolutionary language is the first focus of this chapter; the second is the polysemic quality of words that arose out of revolutions. Three such terms will illustrate both points: "patriot" arose among a group of eighteenth-century English gentlemen intent on reforming the monarchy, but evolved into a term to mobilize rebels in both America and Europe; "convention" was used to attack legitimate monarchy in England, before becoming a form of governance in the French Revolution and a recurring institutional procedure in the United States; and "terror/terrorism" began as a form of state violence in France before evolving into its opposite – the use of organized violence to overthrow states – as the words diffused to eastern and southern Europe.

Before turning to these terms, I should mention a methodological problem for the comparativist who is interested in the diffusion of revolutionary language. Much of the evidence we will use comes from historians who specialize on a single country and often focus on a single revolution in that country.[4] This leaves us in the position of having to infer the diffusion of language from one revolution to another through the co-appearance of the same words, without direct evidence of actual connections between the actors who used them. But sometimes, as you will see, there *are* connective fibers, such as the evidence that revolutionaries from one country were reading about other revolutions; that they traveled from one country to another to spread the message of revolution; or that they labeled themselves heirs of other traditions by deliberately adopting their terms of discourse (Anderson 1991: 80).

---

[4] For example, Agulhon, in tracing the etymology of the Marianne symbol in French revolutionary iconography, returns to Roman antiquity and says nothing about the female symbol of liberty in the American revolutionary tradition. Compare the iconography in Kammen 1986, pp. 175–80.

Words, moreover, played a different role in different revolutions: there might have been an English revolution without the influence of Roundhead or Cavalier pamphlets (the Bible was something else again); but can we imagine the American revolution without the influence of Tom Paine's writings (1989) or of the deluge of pamphlets that Bernard Bailyn has collected from that revolution (Bailyn 1992)? Or can we imagine the radical phase of the French revolution in the absence of the press (Darnton and Roche 1989)? In the course of these episodes, pamphlets, broadsheets, newspapers, and the spoken word diffused and amplified the language of revolution. But if written words have had a different degree of importance in various revolutions, the history of revolution can be written through the diffusion and differentiation of contentious language, as words were hewn from the raw materials of revolutionary situations and changed as they diffused to new settings and different actors.

## Patriots

As the Old Regime approached its inglorious end, the term *patriote* began to be used to construct a linguistic boundary between supporters of the revolution and their enemies.[5] The word, of course, derives from the French *patrie*, which was at first used to designate the town or village where one was born and only later came to be refer to national loyalties.[6] Surprisingly, however, although the root of the term was French, in its political usage it made its way to the French revolution through a circuitous route.

We first find it in England as an adjective used for the Whigs who opposed Walpole's tenure in office after 1725. Even after these dissidents transmuted from "Patriot Whigs" into the Patriot Party, their goals remained largely negative, and the term was no more than an adjective. But when the term crossed the Atlantic after mid-century, probably through the medium of a newspaper, *The Craftsman*, it took on a more subversive meaning. The colonists who rebelled against British control called themselves Whigs because they identified with the Radical and Patriot Whigs in England, who favored more lenient colonial policies than

---

[5] Note, however, that the term *patriote* appeared in French political thought in the 1770s, when a part of a ceremony in the election of the king – which appeared to require the consent of the people – was suppressed. See Keith Michael Baker, *The Invention of the French Revolution* (1990: 110–111), for this episode.

[6] This and further French etymological information comes from *Le Trésor de la langue française informatisé* at http://atilf.atilf.fr/tlf.htm, visited August 22, 2011.

did the governing Tories. But they also called themselves "patriots," turning the British adjective into a noun to designate those who were willing to take vigorous action against the mother country. "Patriots," according to Gordon Wood, "were not simply those who loved their country, but those who were free of dependent connections" (Wood 2002: 94). Beginning with opposition to the Stamp Act and the non-importation duties in the 1760s, ordinary people began to organize themselves into "patriotic" associations to oppose British policies.[7]

Although the British usage had no particular social texture (in fact, the Patriot Whigs were mainly upper-class gentlemen), in America the term took on a popular ring – at least to their opponents. "The patriots, Tories charged, seemed to regard as important 'no law, no friendship, no alliance, no ties of blood,' and to be bent on dissolving all society 'under the specious show of an exalted kind of virtue'" (Wood 1991: 214).[8] Alongside rich landowners like John Adams and businessmen like John Hancock were the poor farmers who came down from the hills to join Washington's army.

After the American rebellion, the term "patriot" spread to the European reading classes through the press. In England, a radical journal called *The Patriot* was founded in Sheffield in 1787 (Thompson 1966: 151); in Germany, twenty-nine newspapers used the word "patriotic" on their mastheads; and the new American state constitutions were published in both France and Holland (Godéchot 1965: 44–5).

It was in the latter country that the term "patriot" made an appearance as the name for the movement that launched the Batavian revolution of the 1780s.[9] The American influence was felt in both high and low politics: high, when, in 1780, the Dutch were "dragged willy-nilly into war with England," because the colonists had negotiated a secret commercial treaty with the city of Amsterdam; and low, when the conflict elicited a pamphlet war between the Orangists, who favored peace with England, "and the

---

[7] The first to use the term "patriotic" were probably the mechanics of Philadelphia, who formed a Patriotic Society, the first nonreligious pressure group in Pennsylvania's history (Wood 1991: 244).

[8] In Robert Munford's Virginia play *The Patriots*, loyalists "betray their uneasiness with electoral developments in the colony, 'when coxcombs and jockies can impose themselves upon it for men of learning'" (Wood 1991). Quoted from the Boston *Evening Post*, April 13, 1767.

[9] The term "patriot" was first used by the Dutch during the war against Spain in the sixteenth century and referred – as in French – to "love of country." It was only during the Batavian revolution that it took on the meaning of an antiroyal revolutionary movement, as in America. See Schama 1977 and Philippa 2009.

so-called Patriots, who favored the American cause" (te Brake 1985: 203).

Ironically, it was John Adams, the American ambassador to the Netherlands, whose actions helped make the connection. Arriving in 1781, Adams formed an alliance with "a group of political dissidents who, like the American rebels, called themselves "patriots" (ibid.). These "patriots" launched a pamphlet war to insist on Adams's recognition by the court, which was stalling. His chief ally was a Dutch republican, J. D. van der Capellen, "an outspoken advocate of the American cause whose radical politics had gotten him expelled from the provincial Estates of Overijssel" (ibid., p. 203). With a clear republican reference, Van der Capellen published an attack on the House of Orange, *Aan het Volk* (To the People), urging the Dutch to

> take up arms, all of you, choose yourselves those who must command you, and proceed with modesty and composure, *just like the people of America* where not a single drop of blood was shed before the English attacked them, and Jehovah, the God of Liberty, who led the Israelites out of the house of bondage and made them a free people will surely support our good cause. (Quoted and translated by te Brake 1985: 204; emphasis added)

The French term *patrie* – via the English Whigs and the American revolution – returned to the European continent in revolutionary form in Dutch.

### Back to France

We do find the term "patriots" in French in 1771 in the polemics against the "revolution" of Louis XIV's minister, René Nicolas de Maupeou, who was trying to curb the power of the Parlement of Paris. By the 1780s the term began to invest official discourse.[10] This led to the fateful decision of July 5, 1788, "authorizing all Frenchmen to publish their views on the meetings of the Estates," an action that, in effect, cemented the party of the Patriots. Among these was the Marquis de La Fayette, who knew the term from his service in America, where he had served briefly in Washington's army; he may have popularized its use among his friends in the clubs that were pushing for the constitutionalization

---

[10] Palmer found a 1787 circular of the Academy of Chalons-sur-Marne offering a prize "for the best essay encouraging patriotism in a monarchy" (1940: 108). Godéchot writes that Loménie de Brienne, in 1788, "decided to support those who were beginning to be called 'Patriots' or the 'National Party' after the example of the American and Dutch revolutionaries" (Godéchot 1965: 85).

of the monarchy.[11] But we also find the term used by radicals, such as Robespierre, whose first pamphlet, in the spring of 1798, was called *Les ennemies de la patrie démasqués*. "A good revolutionary was called a patriot," writes Palmer, "and his qualities were called virtue, which meant public spirit and a love of his country" (Palmer 1940: 108). Later, the term took on a more militant meaning – including a willingness to take up arms on behalf of the *patrie*.[12] Interestingly, the word was used less as the revolution proceeded into its more violent phase, giving way more and more to words like "citizen" (see Chapter 6).

## Conventions and Contention

The term "convention" also traveled back and forth across the Atlantic and changed its meaning in different contexts. We encounter it in three completed revolutions and a failed one: the British Glorious Revolution of 1688; the American revolutionary and constitutional period; the French revolutionary Convention of 1792–4, and, briefly, in the Jacobin and Chartist movements in Britain in the 1790s and 1830s. There were differences even in the origins of the term: the English gentlemen who met in a Convention Parliament to overthrow a king were uneasy with the irregularity of the procedure they had used and never used it again; the Americans who used it to create a federal Constitution associated it with natural rights and conventionalized it; and the French, who thought they were copying the American model in calling a convention to write a constitution, actually produced an instrument of government.

### England: A Convention Without The People

The word "convention" has a long etymology in the English language, deriving from the Latin word *conventio*, meaning an assembly of people, which led to the medieval Latin term *conventus*, for coming together.[13] Thus, the term's contemporary double meaning: something is "conventional" when we expect it to happen; and "conventions" are regularly scheduled events at which decisions are made. But nothing could have

[11] Martin points out that in Paris, "[t]he Patriots were organized around the Société des trente" and that in Rennes, "the Young Patriote" organized against the aristocrats (2006: 55, 56).

[12] The *Trésor de la langue française* defines the term as "[o]ne who loves his country and is willing to take up arms on its defense." http://atilf.atilf.fr/tlf.htm, visited August 22, 2011.

[13] http://www.myetymology.com/english/convention.html.

been more irregular than the meeting of English parliamentarians in February 1689 outside Westminster when they voted to dethrone a king (Caplan 1988; Harris 2006). "So far as the English were concerned," writes constitutional lawyer Bruce Ackerman, "the 'Convention' was a name for a legally imperfect body, such as one or both Houses of Parliament meeting without the consent of the King" (1998: 1060–1). The Catholic James II was in flight; James's "loyal parliament" would not have agreed to his abdication; and the Pretender, William of Orange, had not yet arrived in London. The Protestant members of Parliament met in a "convention parliament" to ask William, along with his English wife, Mary, to take the throne.

But these English gentlemen, many of them peers, were uneasy about having seen King James off the premises and decided that "the Convention's work required ratification by a *legally perfect* Parliament, with William and Mary sitting in their proper place" (ibid., p. 1061). Anything less would have been illegitimate. And so, on February 23, 1689, William converted the Convention into a regular parliament, which duly chose him and Mary as dual monarchs and passed the Resolution of Right. Paradoxically, this "conventional" term was used in a most irregular way, which is probably why it largely disappears from British political discourse, with some exceptions, as you will see.

### The United States: Conventions with The People

Not so in the United States. Here, conventions – along with committees, popular juries, and crowds – arose as "a continuation of the revolutionary tradition of popular constitutionalism" (Frank 2010: 24; Wood 2002: 144–5). The patriots who called conventions as instruments of revolutionary transition in the 1770s did bow courteously in the direction of their British forbears (Frank 2010: 26). But in contrast to the reticence of the British to accord their convention legitimacy, it was the very illegality of the convention that gave it a superior claim. As Jason Frank writes, in America "it provided the theological supplement of that which is 'beyond' or 'prior to' the law" (ibid.).

The Articles of Confederation, which regulated the states' relationships until the federal Constitution was passed, required a unanimous vote of all thirteen states for their amendment. But the founders were not willing to follow this endless and possibly futile procedure: they "blandly excluded state legislatures from *any* role in ratification, and went on to assert that the approval of special constitutional conventions meeting in only nine of the thirteen states would suffice to validate the Convention's effort to speak for the People" (Ackerman 1998: 41). These conventions were extralegal but constitutive of the authority of the people.

Delaware and Pennsylvania were the first to call conventions to draft state constitutions, but neither document was submitted to the voters (Ward 1995: 277). It was Massachusetts, which had had a constitution since 1691, that submitted a draft constitution to the towns for approval in 1778. It failed for lack of a bill of rights, for its narrow representation, and for insufficient separation of powers (ibid.). It was John Adams who redrafted a new one, which was sent to the towns and approved in 1780. This was followed by Jefferson's *Notes on Virginia*, in which he argued that for government to be legitimate, "the people must delegate persons with special powers... special *conventions* to form and fix their governments" (ibid., italics added). The convention that produced the federal Constitution in 1787 was originally called only to resolve border disputes between a few states under the unworkable Articles of Confederation. When its delegates unexpectedly began to write a superlegal document, they created "a machine," in historian Michael Kammen's words, "that would go of itself" (Kammen 1987).

At the heart of this departure was not less legalism than in Britain; on the contrary, the majority of the delegates to the Philadelphia convention were lawyers. It was the growing conviction that claiming the "Rights of Englishmen" was not going to get them very far. By 1776, writes Daniel Rodgers,

> the claim that men were by original nature free and independent of each other... possessed of a fund of natural, original rights which their descendants could turn back to and reclaim whenever the scales fell from their eyes – all this (to the alarm of many of the more cautious patriots) reverberated up and down the colonies. (1987: 53)

"All power is vested in, and consequently derived from the people," the Virginia Convention of 1776 had proclaimed (ibid., p. 85). From that time onward, Americans embraced the convention as the mechanism through which natural rights would be brought down to earth. The illegality of the Philadelphia convention did not deter its members from making the claim – proclaimed in the Constitution's opening line – that they spoke as "We the People."

That claim came close to hoisting them by their own petard. For once having made the claim that they represented The People, the delegates had no choice except to consult them on the outcome of their deliberations. "Only in one extraordinary political act – the popular ratification of their constitutions – was the grandeur of the slogan of the people's sovereignty joined to a deed reflecting the grandeur of their words," writes Rodgers (1987: 86).

But ratification was a close thing, and it took all the eloquence of Hamilton, Madison, and Jay – plus a good deal of crude politicking – to entice the states of the South to enter the Union. And after that first "hazardous experience with constitutional plebiscites, the framers of American politics abandoned the gesture [of popular ratification] in ill-disguised haste" (ibid., p. 87). Here, unlike the case in Britain, calling a convention ensconced The People in power, effectively proclaiming "that a group of patriots in a Freedom Tavern might speak for the People with *greater* democratic legitimacy than any assembly whose authority arose only from its legal form" (Ackerman 1998: 1061).

The point is not simply that the Americans were more daring than their British predecessors; through the convention, Americans came to take the idea of natural rights so seriously that their founding document referred to "inalienable rights." Rather than being built on the idea of restoring historical rights – as in Britain – the convention became the act of a legally anomalous body that "paradigmatically expressed the higher-lawmaking will of the American People" (Ackerman 1998: 1061).

The tradition of using conventions to pass controversial or divisive changes continued through the nineteenth century. In the Jacksonian period, as the suffrage expanded and a new generation of leaders and voters arose, the constitutional acknowledgement of the sovereignty of The People was expressed in a wave of state constitutional conventions wedded to a rise in popular politics. "Turned loose in a constitutional convention," Rodgers notes,

> talk of the People served as a powerful instrument of constitutional dis-
> mantlement; on the stump the same words formed a powerful language
> of mobilization ... The rhetoric of a sovereign people, possessed of unitary
> will, and the practice of partisan political mobilization were two sides of
> the same phenomenon. (1987: 89)

The pace and the rhetoric of state constitutional conventions reflected both this wave of populism and its contradictions. "Between 1829 and 1880, it was an unusual political year that did not witness the calling of a revisory state constitutional convention somewhere in the United States," writes Rodgers (ibid.). "Between 1844 and 1853, when the convention era was at its apogee, more than half the existing states summoned a constitutional convention into being" (p. 94). Figure 2.1 traces the number of these state conventions and their geographic provenance: they came

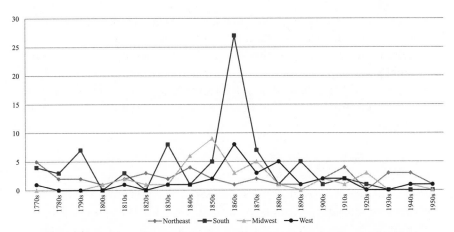

FIGURE 2.1. Number of State Constitutional Conventions, by Geographic Region and Decade. *Source*: Calculated by the author from Albert K. Sturm, *Methods of State Constitutional Reform*. Ann Arbor: University of Michigan Press, 1954, pp. 114–15.

from industrializing states of the Northeast; the slaveholding states of the South; the "old" new states of the Middle West, and the "new" new states of the West. "In the constitutional convention," concludes Rodgers, "that abstraction called the People found its reification" (p. 96).

But populism in America – as in Europe – had both a radical and an authoritarian face, and both were expressed in the use of the convention. Its radical face could be seen in Rhode Island, in what came to be called the Dorr War, when a constitutional convention was fed by a challenge by new men who had made money in the first years of the republic and demanded legislative representation for themselves and others like them (Rodgers 1987: 102–6). But in Kentucky, when western debtors pushed for a constitutional convention to challenge the power of the banks, the convention that resulted in 1850 actually occupied itself with passing a number of articles aimed at preserving slavery (ibid., pp. 97–9). The largest proportion of state constitutional conventions before the Civil War came from the South and were dominated by slaveholders whose leaders were fearful that an antislavery coalition would strip them of their property. When Lincoln's election seemed to guarantee such an assault, under the same natural rights doctrine that had inspired the Virginia Declaration of Rights in 1776, the slave states set in place a revolutionary government under the banner "We the people of the Confederate States" (ibid., p. 109).

That experience did not end the use of the convention to revise state constitutions. After the Civil War, "Northern efforts to appease

Southern demands were often expressed in proposals for extraordinary 'conventions.'" In response, radical Republicans "sought to discredit the very idea that 'conventions' might legitimately revise preexisting constitutional procedures" (Ackerman 1998: 1062, note 86). The ultimate fate of the convention was to descend into the most tawdry expression of conventional American politics: the presidential nominating convention (Chase 1973).

### France: In the Name of the People

Not so in France. If the English abandoned the use of conventions after 1688 and the American convention ended up a routine method for nominating presidential candidates, the French *Convention nationale* – at least in the short run – was the main instrument of a revolutionary government.[14] A few short years after the Americans organized the convention that would produce the federal Constitution, the French Provisional Executive Council "decreed election of a new constitutional assembly to be elected by universal suffrage," writes Godéchot (1965: 156), who links the choice of the term "convention" to its American predecessor (1968: 273–4). The Convention of 1792 was elected by manhood suffrage to abolish the monarchy, maintain the institutions that had been created by the Constituent Assembly, and write a new and more democratic constitution (Godéchot 1965: 160). That constitution would have established universal male suffrage, proclaim the right of self-determination of peoples, and affirm the social rights of the citizens (ibid., 165–6). But in the conditions of civil strife and external attack that the Republicans faced after 1792, the Constitution of the Year I (1793) was never put into effect, and the Convention became the country's legislative institution. It ordered the *levée en masse*, fixed food prices, voted the execution of the king, and established the institutions – the revolutionary tribunals and the Committee of Public Safety – that oversaw the Terror. It governed the country until the overthrow of the Jacobins in July 1794 (Godéchot 1968: 304–14, 376–85), and afterward, in its Thermidorian incarnation. What was intended as a temporary constitution-writing assembly like the Philadelphia convention turned into an institution of revolutionary governance that is best remembered for producing

---

[14] It is remarkable that, in their thousand-page *Critical Dictionary of the French Revolution*, published on the bicentennial of the revolution, François Furet and Mona Ozouf did not see fit to include an entry for "Convention," even though the convention was for some time the legislative body of the republic.

the much-reviled Committee of Public Safety. Yet as long as it remained in force, the Convention produced literally thousands of legislative decrees on virtually all subjects of public policy.[15]

### Radical Conventions in England

Britain's reactions to these revolutions were contradictory. We saw that the term "convention" tended to disappear in England as an official convocation after its brief employment to see one monarch off the stage and install William and Mary in 1688. But inspired by the American and French revolutions, the term reappeared in Edinburgh, first in 1792 and then a year later as an association of radical reformers. Thomas Paine, who had removed to England after the American revolution, with his *Rights of Man* (1989), helped inspire a Jacobin movement among British reformers (Thompson 1966: Ch. 5). Reform societies were formed all across the country, especially in London and the midlands, where rapid industrialization had both expanded and threatened an artisan class. It was a London radical, Joseph Gerrald, later arrested and transported to Australia, who popularized the idea of a convention, as "the only Means of Saving us from Ruin" (ibid., p. 793).

Responding to Paine's and Gerrald's call, the Scottish "Friends of the People" held a "National Convention" in Edinburgh in December 1792, by which time the French *Convention nationale* had been formed. "The proceedings of the Convention were moderate, if somewhat histrionic," notes E. P. Thompson (1966: 126). In the atmosphere of looming war and counterrevolutionary fervor brought on by the events in France, it was remarkable that it was able to meet at all.[16] It was no doubt the double association of the term "convention" with both the American rebellion and the French revolution that led to its repression and its failure to return in anything like the results of the American or French incarnations.

---

[15] Yet antirevolutionary historians like Furet and Ozouf do not even reserve a chapter for it in their monumental *Dictionnaire critique de la Révolution française* (1989).

[16] Even more provocative: in addition to the English delegates, there were observers from the United Irishmen – soon to launch an insurrection against British rule – and French forms of procedure and address were employed. Minutes were dated – "First Year of the British Convention." When Gerrard went on trial, he "appeared at the bar 'with unpowdered hair hanging loosely down behind – his neck nearly bare, and his shirt with a large collar, doubled over. This was the French costume of the day'" (Thompson 1966: 128).

With one major exception: in the spring of 1839, supporters of the People's Charter called a "General Convention of the Industrious Classes" in London. The effort failed, mainly because middle-class advocates of a charter that would expand the suffrage refused to support an initiative that would act as a rival legislative body threatening Parliament (Stedman Jones 1983: 161–2). By 1842, when a general strike was called, "the idea of an anti-parliamentary convention was conspicuously absent" (p. 162). The hope for a people's convention to demand the expansion of the suffrage disappeared, and the very idea of a convention setting itself up against Parliament only reappeared during World Wars I and II, in a short-lived effort of the British Left to rally the workers against the war. "Convention," in British history, remained the recourse of outsiders.

### Terror/Terrorism

Like many other revolutionary words, the term "terror" at the time of its first employment needs to be distinguished from its later usage. The first thing to understand about "terror" is that it was only one among the many forms of violent politics that began in France even before the seizure of the Bastille (Martin 2006: Ch. 1). The second is that the later construction of the term into "*the* Terror" was far more systematic than its actual use at the time. And the third is that it was only in the course of the nineteenth century that it gave way to the concept of "terrorism" – the action of nonstate actors against states and rulers.

No revolution is ever entirely peaceful, but in the French one, each phase of political evolution triggered numerous and interacting forms of violence. Some of these took the form of unorganized *jacqueries* (Kaplan 1982); others were organized urban *journées*, such as the so-called revolution of August 10, which led to the end of the constitutional monarchy; still others reached the level of counterrevolution and festered in particular regions for years (Tilly 1964; Martin 1998).[17] From 1789 on, writes Jean-Clément Martin, "[t]he country thus enters into veritable civil wars,

[17] Martin writes, "It is hard to find a political and ideological unity in the various forms of violence that took place. On the contrary, this violence was the result of political divisions and politicking, of local schemes and personal self-interest, as well as the maneuvers employed by different networks who wanted to win and merely to stay in power and stay alive" (2006: 213, author's trans.). Only by the greatest effort of reductionism or of ideological conviction could all these forms of violence be categorized as part of "the Terror."

TABLE 2.1. *Phases and Central Cleavages in the French Revolution,*
*May 1789–November 1799*

| Period | Central Cleavage |
|---|---|
| May 1789–July 1789 | Crown versus Third Estate |
| June 1792–January 1793 | Crown versus revolutionary regime |
| March 1793–December 1793 | Vendée rebellion; Mountain versus Gironde, Federalists |
| August 1799–November 1799 | Directory versus royalists versus Bonaparte |

*Source*: Charles Tilly (1993: 156).

unified by the cleavage which imposes itself between the revolution and the counter-revolution. Religious, social, regional and cultural antagonisms combined as authority dissolved and both legality and legitimacy were placed on the agenda" (2006: 12).

Overlapping with, but by no means identical to this state of social civil war were the ideological conflicts between warring parties that triggered each change in regime. Table 2.1, drawing from Tilly's work, summarizes these cleavages.

It was only during the most radical phase of the revolution, under the influence of the Parisian *sans-culottes* and the Jacobins, that an organized process of repression began, before the Jacobins themselves fell victim to it (Gough 2010: Ch. 8).[18] This is quite different from using the term "terror" to designate *all* forms of violence in the course of the revolution, something that conservative users of the term tended to do. As Martin writes, "[F]or many historians, the terror is taken to be the very essence of the revolutionary period" (2006: 8).[19] The term "terrorism" was not current at the time and was constructed only later by critics of the revolution to designate its "original scandal" (Martin 2006: 8).

Contemporary students of "terrorism" – like many students of the French revolution – disagree over the scope of the term, to the point

---

[18] Martin (2006: 64) quotes the Abbé Gregoire before the Assembly, who seems to use the term "terror" in its modern sense: "Let us teach the French people around us that the terror is not waged against us." But the term's use to mean state-sponsored terror appears later only in the revolution.

[19] For example, François Furet, the dean of the revisionist school of French historians, argued, in brief, that before becoming a set of repressive institutions used by the republic to liquidate its adversaries and establish its domination on the basis of fear, the Terror was a characteristic feature of the mentality of revolutionary activism (Furet 1989: 137).

that Tilly, in his book *The Politics of Collective Violence* (2003), discarded it altogether because of the futility of distinguishing it from other forms of political violence. But the term spread remarkably quickly in the nineteenth century, with the growth of gunpowder, bomb-making capacity, and cheap travel and communications. Terrorism, as we use the term today, is the deliberate use of political violence by nonstate actors, in contrast to the deliberate use of violence by a state against its opponents.[20] How this change in definition took place is an important reflection of the intersection of linguistic concept and political context.

### From State Terror to Terrorism

In the middle of the nineteenth century, the Italian Mazzinian Carlo Pisacane coined the term "propaganda of the deed" in a political testament published after a failed assault on the southern Italian town of Sapri. Pisacane never used the word "terrorism," but his term "propaganda of the deed" diffused rapidly across anarchist circles in Europe, mostly from west to east (Chaliand 2002). In Russian, it seems to have been first used in the "French" sense by the exiled Social Democrat Alexander Herzen to criticize the policies of Peter the Great. A figurative usage came from Russian conservatives in the 1860s, who condemned radicals like Chernyshevsky, who was said to have "terrorized" young minds with his novel *What Is to Be Done?* (Verhoeven 2008: 101), published in 1863.

In the same decade came the first serious attempt at tsaricide, by a penniless aristocrat, Dimitrii Karakazov. Karakazov's attempt on the tsar came to be considered the "prologue" to revolutionary terrorism.[21] But the term seems to have come from an activist of the people's will, Nikolai Morozov, who published a pamphlet called "The Terrorist Struggle" and from G. Tarnovsky, who wrote "Terrorism and Routine," both in 1880. The term passed into common usage as *terrorizm* when the group that successfully assassinated Tsar Alexander in 1881 identified themselves as "terrorists" (Verhoeven 2008: 100–1).[22] At that point, terrorism took

---

[20] In their study of the conceptual structure of terrorism, Mauro Calise and Theodore Lowi identify linkages to both state terror ("totalitarianism," "authoritarianism") and nonstate ones ("anarchism," "revolution"). See *Hyperpolitics* (2010: 202).

[21] In a personal communication, Claudia Verhoeven reports that in his writings Karakazov used the term "factual propaganda," which suggests at least that he had heard of Pisacane, who first used the term "propaganda of the deed" in 1857, but neither, to my knowledge, ever referred to themselves as "terrorists."

[22] I am grateful to Claudia Verhoeven for help in tracking down this Russian itinerary. For a detailed analysis of the Karakazov episode, see her *The Odd Man Karakozov: Imperial Russia, Modernity, and the Birth of Terrorism* (2009).

on its modern meaning: "[a] policy intended to strike with terror those against whom it is adopted" (OED 1971: 216).

Russian terrorism had a double goal: first, to terrorize those in power; and second, to demonstrate to the people the power of the deed. Albert Camus, in his play *Les Justes*, captures this double goal, in the words of one of the members of a revolutionary socialist group that is planning to execute a grand duke:

> All of Russia will know that Grand Duke Serge has been executed by a bomb by the combat group of the Revolutionary Socialist Party to hasten the liberation of the Russian people. The imperial court will also learn that we are determined to exercise terror until the land has been returned to the people. Yes, Stepan, the hour approaches. (Camus 1977: 19)

Because terrorism was adopted by individuals and small groups and did not require a formal organization, its diffusion was easier in authoritarian settings than were the more organized tactics of its Socialist and Social Democratic competitors. The Russian model diffused broadly to areas where capitalism had barely penetrated largely peasant societies – to southern Italy, Spain, and the possessions of the Ottoman Empire. Through immigration, it spread to the United States, where President William McKinley fell to a bullet fired by anarchist Leon Czolgosz in 1901. It was at this point that the original French meaning of terrorism declined, and the second usage – the employment of methods of violence by nonstate actors to strike terror amongst their opponents – became dominant.

And what of France, the country to which we owe the original concept of terror as state violence? Even there, despite its original experience, it is the second meaning – the use of organized violence by nonstate actors – that has come to dominate the culture, especially in the past decade. Figure 2.2 demonstrates that *terrorisme* steadily increased in French culture, whereas the French original – *La Terreur* – at first remained steady and eventually began to decline.

Like "patriot" and "convention," "terror/terrorism" never lost its original connotation of organized violence, but its meaning in any particular country or epoch changed with the political context to which it diffused. And even though "patriot" was available to any number of liberal and conservative groups (think of the "tea party patriots"), and the convention was adopted in America to choose party candidates, "terror/terrorism" expanded so widely in its meanings that it became available to denote any form of organized violence.

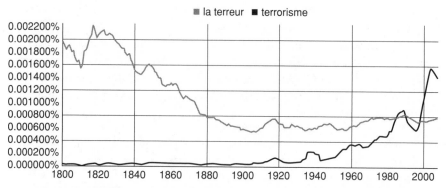

FIGURE 2.2. "La Terreur" and "Terrorisme" in an Analysis of French Book Publishing, 1800–2008. *Source*: http://books.google.com/ngrams.

### 1688/2011

This chapter has not claimed to be a history of either the origin or the diffusion of revolutionary practice, or even of the three terms – "patriots," "conventions," and "terror/terrorism" – that I have examined here. My goals have been more modest.

First, I have tried to show how words employed by revolutionaries often emerge from ordinary language and routine politics. The French word *patrie* meant a village long before it came to be the root of "patriotism." When eighteenth-century country gentlemen in England used the term "patriot," they were trying to draw a boundary between themselves and the foreigners who had come to England with the Hanoverians under the corrupt regime of Horace Walpole. Neither the French nor the English were attempting to produce a template for American, Dutch, or French rebels to use in contesting monarchy in the name of republicanism. By the time the term returned to France during the heady days of the Revolution, the term *patriote* had come to mean, first, those who wanted to bring about constitutional change and, second, the opposite of the hated term *aristocrate*.

Second, I have tried to show how, after being employed successfully in one revolution, terms like "patriots," "conventions," and "terror" diffused elsewhere – and changed in meaning as they crossed the Atlantic or headed to eastern and southern Europe. The American patriots who called constitutional conventions were certainly thinking of the Convention Parliament – at least at first; the French Republicans who elected the *Convention* in 1792 to write a new constitution had in mind the Philadelphia convention, which had produced its own constitution only a few years earlier; and the English reformers who called a "National Convention" in Edinburgh in 1793 were merging both the American and the French uses of the term. As for the Russian terrorists of the 1870s, their call for purification through the execution of elites had more than a whiff of the Jacobins' reign of virtue.

But, third, after being liberated from their origins, these words took on different meanings as they intersected with new political contexts. Take the convention: a hesitant and illegal expedient to get rid of one king and welcome another in England under the mantle of natural rights, it became a font of supralegal authority in America, and a revolutionary institution in France. As for terrorism, we know how much more lethal and more widespread that practice became when it spread beyond its specific origins in France.

Finally, terms that arise in revolutionary times not only travel but also inspire and mobilize. This was true of the words we have examined, and it is still true today. Consider some of the words that emerged in Tunisia and Egypt during the first half of 2011; they diffused rapidly to electrify other parts of the Arab Middle East and North Africa:[23]

- *baltagiyya*: this Egyptian word of Turkish origin was used to describe the armed thugs who were sent to intimidate the protesters in Tahrir Square; it then spread to Bahrain, Morocco, and Yemen to describe plainclothes police and thugs who were sent to repress the protesters.
- *"ash-sha'b yurid isqat an-nizam"*: "the people want the overthrow of the regime"; it spread across the region from Egypt.
- And, of course, there was the term Tahrir Square itself, a name that protesters tried to use in renaming spaces of occupation throughout the region.

If these terms diffused faster than the older words examined in this chapter, that may have been the result of the media, the Internet, Facebook, and Twitter. One thing is already becoming clear: the new digitized forms of personal communication that transmit contentious language move messages faster, further, and more telegraphically than was the case with older expressions such as "convention," "patriot," and "terror." It is too soon to tell whether these terms will have the same endurance, because both endurance and diffusion depend on the symbolic resonance and strategic modularity of contentious language, and for that it is too soon to tell.

---

[23] I am grateful to my colleague David Patel for calling my attention to these phrases.

# 3

# Words at Work

This chapter analyzes the language of contention that emerged from labor conflict. It begins with two of these words: sabotage and striking. It then turns to the broader issue of the formation of the working class in England, made famous by E. P. Thompson and a number of historians and sociologists. The third part moves from England to France and the United States, where similar histories of class formation can be found. The fourth part reflects on the decline of class language in contemporary politics. The underlying theme of the chapter is the strong influence of the political context both on the construction of class conflict and on the constitution of the working class. I begin with a form of contention that, like many others, emerged from a specific conflict between workers and their employer in the context of a political crisis – the boycott – and then became modular.

## Boycotting Colonel Boycott

> boycott (*tr*): to refuse to have dealings with (a person, organization, etc.) or refuse to buy (a product) as a protest or means of coercion to boycott foreign produce.[1]

Colonel Charles Boycott was the land agent for Lord Erne during the Irish land wars of the 1870s and 1880s. Charles Parnell, an Irish politician,

---

[1] http://www.thefreedictionary.com/boycott, visited August 29, 2012.

*Author's note:* Comments were made on an earlier version of this chapter by Eitan Alimi, Michael Hanagan, Ira Katznelson, Joe Margulies, Bill Roy, and Marc Steinberg. Lance Compa offered bibliographic help.

had called for reform of the extortionate rents that Irish farm workers were forced to pay their absentee English landlords. When Boycott refused, he was chosen as the target of the new policy, designed to put pressure on greedy landlords by ostracizing their agents and avoiding the violence that had often broken out during the land wars. When Boycott's workers refused to work in the fields as well as in his house, and when even the local merchants refused to trade with him, he was completely isolated (Marlow 1973). The term "boycott" was invented after this episode to designate the refusal to deal with a person or organization. What was not expected was that the term would diffuse far and wide.

Boycott's isolation was local, but the first national use of the boycott in Britain was the boycott of slave-produced sugar in the 1780s. It depended on preexisting networks of Protestant dissenters and the provincial press to urge supporters to sign mass petitions to Parliament. Without naming it, Americans had been practicing something like the boycott since the late eighteenth century. For example, the now doubly famous term "tea party" was only the most clamorous episode in a long series of attempts to limit trade with Britain by refusing to buy British goods. In the non-importation agreement signed in 1774, colonial representatives opposed the Stamp Act of 1765, the Townshend Acts of 1767, and the recent Coercive Acts (Wood 1991). Antislavery advocates used the strategy again in the 1830s, when the National Negro Convention encouraged a boycott of slave-produced goods.

What was remarkable in the Irish case was how rapidly both the term and its practice spread after it was used against Colonel Boycott. News of the practice spread ahead of its use: Colonel Boycott worked for an English lord, so it was not surprising that the *London Times* would editorialize, "The people of New Pallas [in Ireland] have resolved to 'boycott' them [the landlords] and refused to supply them with food or drink." The term spread rapidly across the Atlantic. On November 16, 1880, the *Chicago Daily Tribune* both reported on the new technique and shrewdly noted its strategic advantages:

> Boycotting is a new term added to the popular vocabulary of Ireland, after the manner of "bulldozing" and other similar additions to the American terms now passing into general use. Boycotting, though a peaceful means of coercion, is perhaps a more efficient mode of intimidating than actual violence. It is a means within the letter of the law, and, involving no violence or breach of the peace, cannot be put down by force nor punished as a legal offense. (p. 4)

TABLE 3.1. *Diffusion of the Term "Boycott" from Ireland to Various Languages*

| | |
|---|---|
| English (UK) | *boycott* |
| English (USA) | *boycott* |
| Dutch | *boycot* |
| French | *boycottage* |
| German | *boykott* |
| Italian | *boicottagio* |
| Portuguese | *boicote* |
| Spanish | *boicoteo* |
| Swedish | *bojkott* |

*Sources*: Unless otherwise noted, all translations for this and other words analyzed are from publicly available online dictionaries.

The term then spread to France, Spain, Italy, Portugal, and elsewhere and was adopted in a similar linguistic form in each of these countries, as Table 3.1 shows.

Why did a term derived from an obscure man's name spread so rapidly and so far beyond the farm workers who had employed it against him in a British colony? The term had no particular symbolic importance and no connection to an existing discourse, but the tactic was strategically modular: it could be applied to a variety of targets by a variety of actors and organizations without incurring the violent reaction of the authorities. In Poland in the 1930s it was used by the government to boycott Jewish-owned businesses; in California in the 1950s it was employed by farm workers' sympathizers against grape growers (Ganz 2009); after the creation of the state of Israel it was used by Arab governments to boycott Israeli-made goods. Its strategic modularity more than made up for the symbolic poverty of the term.[2]

The term "boycott" gave rise to antonyms. When recent consumer movements wanted to show preference for a particular producer, they engaged in a "*buy*cott." Terms like "girlcott," "procott," and "anti-boycott" came next (Friedman 1996). This was followed by a complete inversion of the boycott strategy – the "carrotmob": "carrot" to mean

---

[2] But there are objective limits to the strategic use of the boycott: when an environmental group proposed to boycott goods produced by *maquiladora* (foreign-owned) factories, following the example of the earlier California grape boycott, their Mexican counterparts could not see people in a poor country like Mexico complying (Williams 2003).

support for a particular product, and "mob" to mean a group."[3] Carrot-mobs began to appear in the United States in the 1990s but then spread to Western Europe, where they gained popularity among Finnish and German consumer groups (ibid., 219–20).

Note that in its diffusion over the past century or so, the essential logic of the boycott did not change; but it did shift from a tool of workers against their employers to a much broader range of actors: environmentalists, consumers, Poles, Arabs, and many others. The shift reflects not only the flexibility and ease of understanding of the boycott but also the weakness of workers in the market: they could not, on their own, consume enough to make the boycott an essential tool of contention. But there were some tools that did correspond to workers' structural position, and they mark the rise and fall of "the working class."

## Worker Forms of Contention

Workers have always employed a broad repertoire of contention, as we can see from the time-series data collected from English press sources by Charles Tilly for the period from 1758 to 1834. Workers struck, turned out, destroyed machinery, demonstrated, met, and tried to control the means of production (Steinberg 1999; Tilly 1995a and b). Using Tilly's data set of contentious gatherings for the period from 1758 to 1834, Takeshi Wada plotted the different forms of action he studied.[4] Tilly enumerated hundreds of discrete forms of collective action from many different published sources, forms that he eventually aggregated into a few verb forms, such as "move," "attack," "meet," "bargain," and "control." Wada's analysis of Tilly's data shows that almost every form of action that Tilly enumerated increased in its usage during the 1820s and 1830s.

During the 1758–81 period, when the Industrial Revolution was winding up, workers employed a number of forms of action that Tilly summarized as "move" (i.e., marches, demonstrations, turnouts). During the years of war with France, when the Combination Acts and a generally

---

[3] Where the "buycott" – like the boycott – is carried out independent of the action's target, carrotmobs actually involve cooperation with the firm or business that is targeted (Hoffman and Hutter 2012).

[4] I am grateful to Professor Wada for carrying out this statistical analysis on my behalf. See his "Demonstrating Repertoires of Contention" (2009) and his "Modularity and Transferability of Repertoires of Contention" (2011) for a more sophisticated use of this data set.

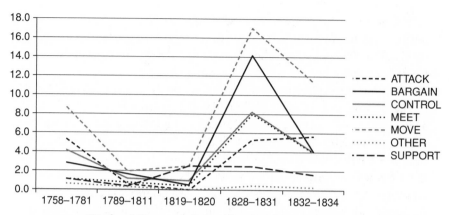

FIGURE 3.1. Workers' Forms of Contention in Four London Counties between 1758 and 1834. *Note*: The WORKERS category includes "workers," "backlegs," "labourers," and "weavers." *Source*: Original Tilly "BRIT" data set, kindly provided by Takeshi Wada.

repressive atmosphere strangled contentious action, there was a precipitate decline in the use of "move" forms. But during the run-up to the reform act in the 1820s and the early 1830s, workers were "moving" at a greater rate than at any other time in the seventy-six-year period Tilly studied. But as Figure 3.1 shows, they were also bargaining with their opposite numbers, meeting and controlling others, and engaging in violent forms of conflict. As you will see, this period of heightened political conflict was key in the constitution of something we can reasonably call "the working class."

Especially before procedures for collective bargaining began to develop, workers were quite violent on behalf of their claims. In his collaborative work with Chris Tilly, Charles Tilly observed that workers confronting ruthless employers have from time to time

> beaten them, killed them, sued them, run them out of town, broken their plant windows, smashed their machines, thrown garbage at their houses. Attacked their families, occupied their offices, torn up their papers, appealed to their competitors, seized control over their enterprises, performed humiliating ceremonies, sung demeaning songs, presented petitions, posted anonymous handbills, sabotaged production, solicited intervention from priests, quit jobs en masse, formed competing cooperatives, held material or equipment hostage, and otherwise harassed owners. (Tilly and Tilly 1998: 239)

The Tillys did not try to make accurate counts of the number of worker actions during the period they studied, but from other accounts, such as those of Thompson (1966) and Steinberg (1999a), we can see the centrality of work to the expanding language of contention. This was particularly clear in the appearance of two modern forms of conflict – sabotage and the strike. Both sabotaging and striking were invented in the factory and spread from there to the streets, and from early industrializers like England and France across the world.

### Luddites and Saboteurs

As mechanical looms spread across the English midlands early in the nineteenth century, handloom workers began to engage in the practice of machine breaking, giving rise to what was probably the first cross-territorial campaign of collective action of the English working class: Luddism. "Luddism proper," writes Thompson, "in the years 1811–17, was confined to three areas and occupations: the West Riding, South Lancashire ... and the framework-knitting district centered on Nottingham and taking in parts of Leicestershire and Derbyshire" (Thompson 1966: 521–522). As mechanical looms spread, the masters managed to ram through Parliament bills that ended age-old protective legislation on the workers' behalf. The weavers responded with a campaign of machine breaking under the umbrella of a fictional leader, Ned Ludd.

To the weavers, "Ned Ludd was the defender of ancient right, the upholder of a lost constitution," writes Thompson (p. 530). Between March 1811 and February 1812, croppers, framework knitters, and stockingers began a campaign of frame breaking that destroyed hundreds of looms (ibid., p. 535). But they also engaged in more conventional forms of action. In Leicester, for example, "[i]t was thought necessary to put ourselves under the broad Sheild of the Law and solicite the Concurance of the Magistrates of the Borough" (quoted in ibid., p. 535). Luddism was deeply political in both its inspiration and its methodology (ibid., p. 557).

The term "Luddism" has survived, but its original meaning of breaking or damaging a machine has given way to mean any form of opposition to industrial or technological change. More recently, it has come to be used as a mild term of disparagement for someone who lacks elementary computer skills. For example, a popular retort to someone struggling to operate a new smartphone or refusing to buy the latest gizmo might be, "You're such a Luddite!"[5] But unlike the equally obscure term "boycott," "Luddite" failed to diffuse outside England in its original

---

[5] Go to http://www.thefreedictionary.com/Luddite for both definitions. Visited August 29, 2012. Also see Tom Di Castella in "Are You a Luddite?" for the BBC Online Magazine at http://www.bbc.co.uk/news/magazine-17770171, visited April 21, 2012.

meaning. Not so the term invented for the same practice across the English Channel.

In 1801, French inventor Joseph-Marie Jacquard invented a new textile loom that used a series of punched cards to control the pattern of longitudinal warp threads depressed before each sideway passage of the shuttle. On later machines these cards were joined to form an endless loop that represented the "program" for the repeating pattern of a carpet. By 1812 there were eleven thousand such looms in France, and they were introduced into many other countries. Punched cards were the basis of the massive gray counter-sorters that made tiresome work for a generation of social scientists who cut their teeth on computerized data analysis in the 1960s. But in the nineteenth century, the jacquard loom threatened the work of thousands of skilled weavers, many of them silk workers in Lyons, who responded by throwing wooden shoes – *sabots* – into the works. The result was the French term *sabotage*. By the middle of the nineteenth century, the malicious damaging or destruction of an employer's property had come to be called "sabotage" all over Europe – very rapidly and with almost no change in spelling, as Table 3.2 shows.

Sabotage was an effective way of stopping production when an employer either was irretrievably evil or refused to negotiate and before the strike was invented or could be used effectively. But it had a self-defeating quality, especially after assembly line methods were introduced: even damaging a single machine or phase of the assembly of a product would halt production and throw workers out of a job. Like boycotts, which spread outside the working class, even as sabotage declined in the factory, the term expanded into wartime efforts to undercut an enemy's infrastructure by bombing or mining installations. And, like

TABLE 3.2. *Diffusion of the Term "Sabotage" to Specific Languages from France*

| | |
|---|---|
| French | *sabotage* |
| Dutch | *sabotage* |
| English (UK) | *sabotage* |
| English (USA) | *sabotage* |
| German | *sabotage* |
| Italian | *sabotaggio* |
| Portuguese | *sabotagem* |
| Spanish | *sabotaje* |
| Swedish | *sabotage* |

the "boycott," it developed antonyms. For example, by the late 1970s, inspired by a book by the American anarchist/ecologist Edward Abbey (2000), the variant "ecotage" appeared among American and English activists to describe the destruction of property to protect the environment (Plows et al. 2004). From local efforts to jam wooden shoes into a weaving frame, sabotage became a staple of a broad range of contentious politics. But at the same time, it was giving way to the repertoire that became the central recourse of workers and others attempting to use their place in the productive process to increase their leverage: the strike.

### The Strike and the Grève

"Strike!" is a dramatic term that also contains a call to action. As strikes spread across England's industrial heartland and were violently repressed, and as they moved from the individual firm to entire sectors of industry, the term came to carry a symbolic freight that could inspire workers and terrorize opponents. But first the strike had to spread, a process that took two main linguistic trajectories: the Anglo-American term "strike" and the French word *grève*. The two terms have almost exactly identical meanings but had diverse origins and followed different trajectories across borders. One followed an arc to northern, central, and southeastern Europe, while the other spread southward through Romance language countries to the Mediterranean and eastward to Turkey.

In the *Concise Oxford Educational Dictionary*, the ninth meaning of the term "strike" is given as "[a] concerted suspension of work on the part of a body of workers, for the purpose of obtaining some concession from the employer or employers" (p. 3094). Similarly, the *Robert Micropoche* defines the term *grève* as a "voluntary and collective work stoppage decided by the employees to obtain material or moral advantages" (author's trans.).[6]

But the origins of the two terms were very different. Although the word "strike" first appeared in English to mean "hit" in the twelfth century, it came to mean a suspension of work only when eighteenth-century sailors in the port of London "struck" (i.e., lowered) the sails of their ships as a sign of their unwillingness to work, in a 1768 dispute with shipowners (Linebaugh and Rediker 1990: 240; Tilly and Tilly 1998: 239). Striking the sails was an effective way of stopping a ship without destroying

---

[6] A "cessation volontaire et collective de travail decidée par les salariés pour obtenir des avantages matériels ou moraux (Robert Micropoche, p. 504).

the means of production: according to historian Tony Taylor, "[A] ship whose sails had been 'struck' was effectively crippled," and no one knew this better than the sailors who "struck" in the port of London in 1768.[7]

This was no chance occurrence. Merchant sailors were among the most radical workers on the Atlantic trade run: "During the twenty years that preceded the strike of 1768, merchant sailors in the Atlantic trade had become increasingly combative," writes Taylor. And according to Marcus Linebaugh and Peter Rediker, sailors were involved in frequent riots on both sides of the Atlantic (Linebaugh and Rediker 1990: 227). Many had been radicalized in the famous campaigns on behalf of the imprisoned radical John Wilkes; others took part in actions against the horrendous conditions on British ships when they reached the less restrictive atmosphere of colonial America; still others seem to have been aware of the growing tension between Britain and its colonies, much of which centered on the Atlantic trade route.

Note that although the term "strike" still had a nautical connotation in 1768, from another report it is clear that it soon came to be mean a collective withdrawal of labor in general. Taylor cites an excerpt from the *Newgate Calendar* about the tumults of the same year:

> These disgraceful tumults, and the lenity, or as some would have it, the timidity of government, spread disaffection into *all classes of mechanics*, who, thinking the time at hand, when they might expect what wages they pleased, and perhaps beyond their masters' profits, *struck their work*. (cited in Taylor, p. 3, italics added)

From the "concrete community" of sailors in the particular context of a ship, the strike was "disseminated beyond the confines of the daily world of experience and struggle" of the sailors, "producing a widening circle of common understandings" (Steinberg 1999a: 5).

The French term *grève* also spread from the particular conditions of its origins to a general term of contention. The word itself derives from the Gaulish word *grava* for sand or gravel, and referred to the sandy area (now the Place de l'Hôtel de Ville) on the banks of the Seine, where unemployed workers would gather to seek work unloading barges that brought provisions up the river. From this, both the terms *faire grève* (to go on strike, 1834) and *gréviste* (striker, 1872) derived.

---

[7] Taylor's colorful narrative is found in a release of the Australian National Centre for History Education at ww.hyperhistory.org/index.php?option=displaypage&itemid= 746&op=page.

But before it came to mean the collective withdrawal of labor, to be *en grève* meant to be seeking work, like the unemployed men hanging around on the sandy area on the Seine looking for a day's employment (Tournier 1992).

As with the term "strike," the acceptance of the term *grève* did not develop without a struggle. In Maurice Tournier's account, strikes were at first characterized as "debauchery," "illicit assemblies," "cabals," "plots," "tricks," "desertions," and "coalitions" by the authorities in order to deny their legality (1992: 24–38). It was only as workers created national forms of organization that the term *grève* – like the practice of the strike – was grudgingly accepted and generalized. By the late nineteenth century, legal authorities were comfortably using the term and striving to regulate its practice, sometimes cooperating with workers' *services d'ordre* (parade marshals assigned by the unions to keep strikers in order).

Note that although "going on strike" is frequently connected with large-scale industry and mass production, neither sailors on the Atlantic trade run nor poor Parisians looking for a day's work were "workers" in mass production industry. Moreover, the two terms spread more along lines of north/south diffusion than along the lines of industrial take-off. "Strike" and its various derivatives spread first to agrarian America and to the rest of the English-speaking colonies and former colonies. It then diffused to Northern and Central Europe by way of Germany and Austria (*streik*), then to Hungary (*sztrájk*), and from there to the Balkans (*strajk*).[8] *Grève* spread from France to Romance language-speaking countries like Portugal (though not to Spain or Italy) and Romania, and – of all places – to Turkey, where it displaced the perfectly serviceable Ottoman term *tatil-i esgaal*.[9] The diffusion of the language of the strike had less to do with the pathways of mass production than with cultural or political ties. Figures 3.2 and 3.3 summarize the trajectories of the two terms "strike" and *grève* across various countries in Europe and in some of the countries that Europeans colonized.

---

[8] In a personal communication, Aida Hozic notes that the etymology of the word in Serbian and Croatian dictionaries refers to German and English as sources. But it is most likely that the word came to the Balkans via the Austro-Hungarian Empire, given the degree to which Serbia and Croatia were dependent on it and the role of German as a lingua franca in the empire in the late nineteenth century.

[9] I am grateful to Berk Essen for pointing this out to me. The choice of the French root *grève* may have had more to do with the fact that many Turkish intellectuals had studied in Paris than with the diffusion of industry to Turkey.

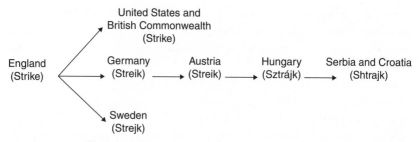

FIGURE 3.2. Diffusion of the English word for "strike" to Northern, Central, and Southern Europe

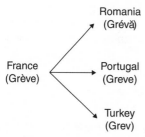

FIGURE 3.3. Diffusion of the French Word *Grève* to Central and Southern Europe

## The Differentiation of the Strike Repertoire

Strikes spread quickly and everywhere because they gave workers strategic opportunities – stopping production, but also localizing contention within the factory, where it could be contained, negotiated, and ultimately institutionalized. As the strike developed its characteristic forms, early variants, such as the "turnout" – the participation of entire communities in support of strikers – tended to disappear. Although unions could control the actions and the militancy of their worker members, the same was not true for wives, children, and families in the communities; as strikes were organized for whole sectors of industry across a national territory, local turnouts became unwieldy and inefficient. Only in tight-knit communities like the mining towns of the North Country did community participation – especially that of women – retain a role in industrial conflict (Beckwith 1996).

Even after the strike became the core of the working-class repertoire, it was accompanied by other forms of action that tended to be encapsulated within the language of the strike. Consider the phenomenon of the "mass strike" as described by Rosa Luxemburg:

Its use, its effects, its reasons for coming about are in a constant state of flux... political and economic strikes, united and partial strikes, defensive strikes and combat strikes, general strikes, of individual sections of industry and general strikes of entire cities, peaceful wage strikes and street battles, uprisings with barricades – all run together and run alongside each other, get in each other's way, overlap each other, a perpetually moving and changing sea of phenomena.[10]

"Mass strikes" contained within them a broad spectrum of other forms of action. A good example was the period of widespread labor conflict in the 1870s, which Americans called "The Great Upheaval" (Brecher 1972: Ch. 1). It began unobtrusively in the little railroad town of Martinsburg, West Virginia, where the B & O railroad had a depot. When the firm's management announced a 10 percent cut in the railwaymen's wages, "men gathered around the railroad yards, talking, waiting through the day. Toward evening the crew of a cattle train, fed up, abandoned the train, and other trainmen refused to replace them" (ibid., p. 1). From Martinsville, the strike spread to other divisions of the B & O, to other rail lines that had been cutting wages, and then to other industries in neighboring Pennsylvania, Ohio, Maryland, New York, and Kentucky, and eventually as far as Texas. Everywhere it was met by police, militias, regular army troops, and the hostility of management and politicians. It eventually forced timorous union officials and party leaders to take notice.

Like other mass strikes, the "great upheaval" was accompanied by a wide range of organizing activities, public meetings and marches, organized and unorganized violence, and, here and there, attempts to negotiate settlements and manage the railroads by the workers themselves. Table 3.3 codes the behaviors of participants from the outbreak of the first Martinsburg agitation to the strike's end from Brecher's narrative. It shows that "striking" was only one of the many things that workers and townspeople did during this "general strike." "Strike!" was at the core of the language of contention, but as in England in the late 1820s and early 1830s, the repertoire of American workers in the 1870s was much broader than striking.

Each new wave of industrial conflict led to the invention of new forms of struggle and new language to describe them. The 1960s produced a new wave of contention all over Europe (Crouch and Pizzorno, 1978) in

[10] Rosa Luxemburg, "Massenstreik, Partei und Gewerkschaften," pp. 437–38, translated by J. P. Nettl (1966: 500).

TABLE 3.3. *Terms Used in Jeremy Brecher's Narrative of the "Great Upheaval" of 1877*

| Terms Used | N | % |
|---|---|---|
| Strike | 18 | 15 |
| General strike; mass strike | 7 | 5 |
| Turnout | 5 | 4 |
| March | 19 | 16 |
| Meet | 14 | 11 |
| Organize | 5 | 4 |
| Occupy | 7 | 5 |
| Obstruct; blockade | 10 | 8 |
| Self-manage | 4 | 3 |
| Persuade, fraternize | 5 | 4 |
| Force concessions | 2 | 2 |
| Burn, destroy, seize | 8 | 6 |
| Attack | 13 | 11 |
| Other | 2 | 2 |
| TOTAL | 119 | 96 |

*Note*: Percentages are rounded to the nearest percent. I have coded the events "general strike" or "mass strike" only when there was evidence that an entire community participated in the strike.
*Source*: Coded by the author from Jeremy Brecher (1972: Ch. 1).

which workers joined students in industrial conflict that – like the "great upheaval" – expanded outside the factory. As the strike wave reached its peak, workers employed demonstrations, mass meetings, violence against factory managers, and occupations as part of their strike repertoire. Table 3.4 summarizes Italian strikers' nonstrike forms of behavior from my study of Italian protest data (1989). The table shows not only the wide range of nonstrike actions strikers used but also the year – 1969 – when virtually all the forms identified peaked, at the height of the "hot autumn."

Like boycotts and sabotage, strikes spread beyond the working class. In Italian newspapers of the 1960s, one could read about striking by students, farmers, public employees, hospital patients, sellers of contraband cigarettes, and even prostitutes (Tarrow 1989). Part of the reason is that the term communicates a known and easily understood sequence of actions to a dispersed and not normally activist population. A second reason is that – like "revolution" – the word has become a linguistic umbrella that makes it simpler to communicate than other terms. But a final one seems to me to be the most important: the word "strike" calls

TABLE 3.4. *Italian Strikers' Use of Nonstrike Forms of Action by Year,*
*1966–1973*

| Form of Action | 1966 | 1967 | 1968 | 1969 | 1970 | 1971 | 1972 | 1973 |
|---|---|---|---|---|---|---|---|---|
| Public displays | 31 | 28 | 78 | 107 | 97 | – | 78 | 74 |
| Assemblies | 10 | 15 | 40 | 69 | 84 | 59 | 43 | 33 |
| Routine actions | 13 | 15 | 37 | 59 | 88 | 77 | 87 | 14 |
| Confrontations | 32 | 15 | 52 | 118 | 72 | 70 | 31 | 33 |
| Violent clashes | 20 | 5 | 33 | 18 | 23 | 34 | 16 | 15 |
| Property attacks | 12 | 4 | 13 | 28 | 19 | 12 | 3 | 8 |
| Attacks on persons | 2 | 3 | 4 | 19 | 9 | 10 | 4 | 6 |
| TOTAL | 120 | 85 | 257 | 418 | 392 | 372 | 262 | 183 |

*Source*: Author's data coded from *Corriere della Sera*. Reported in detail in Tarrow (1995).

up a host of historical experiences and symbolic meanings that inspire
people, coordinate their actions, and give them the impression that they
are acting on behalf of a collectivity well beyond themselves. But what is
that collectivity? This takes us to the language of class.

## The Construction of "The Working Class"

"Workers of the World Unite!" These familiar words – with which Karl
Marx and Friedrich Engels hoped to inspire a still-to-be created working
class – have echoed through the past 160 years in the discourses of Socialists, Communists, Social Democrats, and Anarchists (Marx and Engels
2012: 72–3). Marx and Engels went on to claim that "[t]he history of all
hitherto existing society is the history of class struggles."

Since Marx and Engels wrote, social scientists have considered the
language of class to be a traditional possession of the workers. But such
a connection is far from inevitable, and, in fact, the term "working class"
appeared in popular discourse only well after the Industrial Revolution
began. Moreover, as E. P. Thompson and others have argued, the concept
was not "natural" or especially "industrial": it was constructed out of
collective action and crystallized through political conflict. As Gareth
Stedman Jones puts it, "[I]t was not consciousness (or ideology) that
produced politics, but politics that produced consciousness" (Stedman
Jones 1983: 19).

### The Background
The term "class" in the sense of a social formation first appeared in the
eighteenth century among middle-class Frenchmen unhappy with their

place in the estate system (Perrot 1986: 95). Only later was the term applied to workers. Not only that, from the eighteenth century onward there were three different representations of class: as a seamless hierarchy of fine-grained positions, a system of ranks or orders that were not necessarily in fundamental conflict with one another, and an "us versus them" model that underlay Marxist representations. The term "class" was used in all three representations but held different meanings.[11]

It is tempting to think that the term "working class" emerged with the Industrial Revolution, but it didn't. As late as 1816, William Cobbett was still addressing "Journeymen and Labourers'" (cited in Thompson 1966: 235). Asa Briggs traces the emergence of the term to the 1830s (1960: 51–3). Briggs was essentially correct: the use of class language in England began to increase only in the 1820s, and it rose rapidly after 1825 through the middle of the 1840s, as you can see from British published sources traced from a Google Books search in Figure 3.4.

The United States was slower to adopt the term "working class." In 1833, in his famous "We have borne these evils far too long" speech, Seth Luther still referred only to "the producing classes."[12] And when he criticized the upper classes for using the term "lower orders" to describe the workers, he could only conclude, "Let us be determined no longer to be deceived by the cry of those who produce nothing and who enjoy all, and who insultingly term us – the farmers, mechanics, and laborers – as

FIGURE 3.4. "Working Class" in British Books, 1800–1850. *Source*: http://books. google.com/ngrams.

---

[11] I am grateful to Marc Steinberg for pointing this out to me. For Steinberg's foundational contributions, see Steinberg (1999a).

[12] From Luther's "Address to the Working Men of New England." The speech is available at http://books.google.com/books?hl=en&lr=&id=PHdGAAAAYAAJ&oi=fnd&pg=PA6&dq=seth+luther&ots=aZJYeam2cl&sig=v954XItBM894A4giHuvBSIp7N4A.

the lower orders" (p. 240). The term "working class" had not yet taken hold of the imagination of workers' representatives.

Most dictionary definitions of the term "working class" are ambivalent about its boundaries. Does it refer to a section of society that is defined by what it isn't – i.e., not the middle or the upper class? A population group defined by its engagement in manual labor? A group that works only in industry? Or, more narrowly still, only to workers in mass production – the "proletariat"? Does the term refer to the place of workers in the social structure, to their ways of life, their dispositions, or their characteristic forms of collective action? It is probably all four, as Ira Katznelson argues (Katznelson 1986: 14–22), depending on the context in which the term is employed, who uses it, and which actors are seen as its opponents.

## Thompson and After

The start of the modern debate about the working class was the towering contribution of E. P. Thompson.[13] Unlike most Marxists in the 1950s, who were deeply wedded to a materialist epistemology, Thompson delved into the cultural formation of the working class (1966). His basic thesis was not novel, especially to those who had read the early Marx, with the latter's distinction between a "class in itself" and a "class for itself." But whereas most Marxists and some of their ideological opponents – such as Weber – saw working-class consciousness resulting from material conditions (see the discussion in Katznelson 1986: 7; Trigilia 2011), Thompson saw class as a "process." He began his classical study by positing that

> Class happens when some men, as a result of common experiences (inherited or shared), feel and articulate the identity of their interests as between themselves, and as against other men whose interests are different from (and usually opposed to) theirs. The class experience is largely determined by the productive relations into which men are born – or enter involuntarily. Class-consciousness is the way in which these experiences are handled in cultural terms: embodied in traditions, value-systems, ideas, and institutional forms. (1966: 9–10)

---

[13] The debate triggered by Thompson's book has engaged the efforts of many historians, political scientists, and sociologists, all of whose work cannot be summarized here. This discussion is based on the contributions of Asa Briggs (1960), Craig Calhoun (1982), Eric Hobsbawm (1984), Ira Katznelson and Aristide Zolberg and their collaborators (1986), William Sewell Jr. (1980), Margaret Somers (1992), Gareth Stedman Jones (1983), Marc Steinberg (1995, 1999), and Chris Tilly and Charles Tilly (1998).

It did not take ordinary workers long to describe their employers, not as individual oppressors but as a "they" (ibid., pp. 206–7). Workers also rapidly came to understand the importance of "combination" – both among the employers who oppressed them (ibid., p. 200) and among themselves (p. 238). The wartime repression of 1798–9 made this dichotomy all too palpable. Thompson finds workers using the concept of "monopoly" quite early in the Industrial Revolution. Even in the 1790s, reformers such as John Thelwell railed against monopoly: "the hideous accumulation of capital in a few hands" (ibid., p. 185). Workers also quickly developed a concept of the alienation of labor: "labour is always carried to market by those who have nothing else to keep or to sell, and who, therefore, must part with it immediately," wrote one spokesman (ibid., p. 297). Most important, workers developed a labor theory of value well before Marx and Engels did: "Capitalism," said a Manchester silk weaver, "I can make out to be nothing else but an accumulation of the products of labour" (ibid., p. 297).

Yet it was only in the late 1820s and early 1830s that workers and those who claimed to represent them converged on the idea that there was a unified body of men (women were something else again) who could be called "the working class." Why did this take so long, when the ravages of the industrial system were evident to all? One possible reason was the vast internal differences in industrial structure, region, and craft in early industrializing England. There were also profound differences between "honourable" and "dishonourable" trades (Thompson 1966: 261–2; 279–81; Steinberg 1999a: 26–7); between native-born and Irish workers; and, increasingly, between skilled craftsmen and mass production workers (Calhoun 1982).

Yet these differences were still great in the 1830s – when class language developed – and even in the 1840s, when there was a stalwart working-class movement: the Chartists (Stedman Jones 1983).[14] New divisions also developed later in the century, producing new trades and new forms of sweated and semiskilled labor. If there were divisions in the working population both before and after the formation of the concept of a single working class, then we cannot use the structural divisions in the working population to explain when class language was adopted. So how and why did "class formation" happen when it did? I argue that the language of the working class was formed out of the conflict over the suffrage in the late 1820s and early 1830s.

---

[14] Even in that period, the Chartists frequently referred to what we would call the working class as "the people." I am grateful to Marc Steinberg for pointing this out.

## The Political Crystallization of "Class"

Thompson saw class formation resulting from two processes: first, from the development of an identity of interests among diverse groups of workers and against the interests of others (Thompson 1966: 807); and, second, from the growth of forms of political and industrial organization that drew them together – the trade unions, friendly societies, educational and religious movements, political organizations, and periodicals. But to understand why the 1820s and 1830s were pivotal, we need to add a third factor, one for which Thompson's book provides much evidence but less theory: the interaction between workers, the state, and the reformist middle classes.

We can understand this process better by introducing two related terms from the social movement vocabulary: *diffusion* and *scale shift* (Givan, Roberts, and Soule 2010; McAdam and Tarrow 2005). Typically, class language spread *horizontally*, from areas and sectors of advanced industrialization to secondary areas of new industry, from large firms to smaller ones, and from regions of early industrialization to more recent ones. This is what I am calling "diffusion." There is no doubt that such a lateral process of class formation was at work in England in the 1820s, as mass industry swept away handcraft production. Class language also diffused "dialogically" as workers developed a language of class in interaction with their economic and social "others" by reacting to the values of political economy that were being imposed on them. Political economy was the dominant genre of the age, as Polanyi eloquently described it (2001).[15]

But it was not only through horizontal interaction between workers and managers that the language of class crystallized. Both class language and workers' consciousness developed *vertically* through the struggle over the franchise. As the debate over the vote heightened and as middle-class allies of the working class defected to support a suffrage expansion that would exclude them (Thompson 1966: 820), workers increasingly saw themselves as their own advocates. As Bronterre O'Brien, editor of the *Poor Man's Guardian*, wrote of the 1832 reform act, "We foresaw that its

---

[15] This explanation has been most forcefully put forward in Marc Steinberg's *Fighting Words*. "A vital strand," Steinberg writes, "was the language of the free-born Englishman appropriated from the constitutional rhetoric of the rulers and turned as a weapon against them" (1999: 18). This was a language that had already been used by Painite radicals in the 1790s (Thompson 1966: Ch. 4). But in conflict with the aggressive expansion of "political economy," workers in the 1810s and 1820s moved beyond Painite radicalism to use the moral language of the past against the "linguistic capital of Smithian political economy" (Steinberg 1999a: 19; Thompson 1966: 272–3).

[the suffrage reform's] effect would be to detach from the working classes a large portion of the middle ranks, who were *then* more inclined to act with the people than with the aristocracy that excluded them" (quoted in Thompson 1966: 821). The sharpening of class language among the working class was the result of a shift in scale to national politics.

### Actor Constitution

Let's look back at Wada's reanalysis of Tilly's 1758–1834 data on British "contentious gatherings" in Figure 3.1. There was plenty of industrial and religious conflict during this period (Tilly 1995a and b), but the struggle over how far to extend the suffrage was at the core of conflict. "The debates over the reform bill," writes Thompson, "increasingly turned upon the definition of class" (1966: 812). "To step over the threshold, from 1832 to 1833," he writes, "is to step into a world in which the working-class presence can be felt in every county in England and in most fields of life" (p. 807). It was politics – and not economics – that crystallized the appearance of class as the common metaphor of self-description of workers and artisans despite their divergent statuses, sectors of industry, and ethnic backgrounds.[16]

Thompson ends his story soon after the 1832 reform act was passed, but the interaction between class formation and political conflict did not end there: it was in the name of class that the Chartists would take up the cause of electoral reform, deliberately framing it as a class issue. "In radical terms," writes Stedman Jones, "in 1832, 'the people' became the 'working classes'" (1983: 104). By the same token, "the middle classes had ceased to be part of the 'people'" (p. 105). Until their disappearance in the 1840s, the Chartists arrayed the language of class as a weapon in seeking the vote for workers. The "working class" was constituted as a political actor through the struggle over the suffrage.

### Variations on an English Theme

To be sure, each country had its own path to the development of working-class consciousness. But each was shaped by workers' relationships to

---

[16] Many other scholars offer evidence for such a political conflict argument. For example, although he gave more systematic attention to language than his predecessor, Stedman Jones adopted a politically inflected standpoint on class (1983: 19). Although he was influenced by the dialogic approach of Bakhtin (1981), Marc Steinberg gave a great deal of attention to the vertical dynamics of struggle between workers and Parliament (1995; 1999: 5).

political conflict. France and the United States – so different in the timing and the type of industrialization – both illustrate a similar political construction of the working class as you saw in England.

In the United States, the concept of the working class was heavily shaped by the dichotomization of political and industrial conflict. Because workers received the franchise before industrialization and mass immigration, it was electoral districts and electoral competition that shaped their mobilization into politics, competing with their sense of class membership in the factory (Katznelson 1981; Bridges 1986; Shefter 1986).

In the factory – particularly in the mechanized mills and mines of the East and the Midwest – class conflict led to frequent and violent altercations with management (Brecher 1972). But where workers had the vote and immigrants were absorbed into citizenship by urban machines, these machines could win elections only by forming cross-class alliances in the name of solidarities other than class – solidarities such as race, ethnicity, religion, or patronage (Shefter 1986). In different forms and certainly with different outcomes than the British one, the American political struggle shaped and constrained the concept of the working class.

In France, despite its very different pattern of industrial development (agricultural and small-scale production of finely made goods, rather than mass production), "it was in the social and political struggles following the July 1830 revolution . . . that the artisans of Paris, Lyon, and other French cities transformed their corporate understanding of labor into class consciousness," writes William Sewell (1980: 59). As the editor of the working-class paper *l'Atelier* wrote thirty years later,

> We all contributed to the journal, *l'Atelier*, to show to the workers from every trade that it brought together that a tailor using his needle, a typographer lining up his little lead letters, deserved, just as much as a baker, a woodworker, or a tanner the respectable title of worker. (quoted by Rancière 1981: 57)

Rebuffed under the Orleanist regime of the 1830s and 1840s by its middle-class officials, the workers "responded by developing a new political and organizational language that met the regime on its own chosen terrain: the discourse of liberty" (Sewell 1986: 60). French workers in the early 1830s adopted a language of labor-based value, declaring that labor alone supported all of society. They "fortified this conclusion by changing the usage of a cluster of important revolutionary words: 'aristocrat,' 'privilege,' 'servitude,' and emancipation,' among others" (ibid.). Sewell writes,

These unsuccessful risings broke the élan of the workers' movement and government repression soon drove its remnants underground. Yet the transformations of the 1830s created the intellectual, linguistic, and organizational space on which the subsequent workers' movement was built. *These transformations established for the first time a class-conscious discourse and institutional practice that was further elaborated by workers over the following decades.* (1986: 64, italics added)

The linguistic "transformations" that Sewell describes took place as the result of a successful bourgeois revolution and a failed series of risings against the government that resulted from that revolution. "At least in the French case," Sewell concludes, "'class consciousness' has been largely independent of economic structures and . . . the expression of class consciousness arose precociously in that country, as early as the first half of the nineteenth century." In this development, "the impact of political factors and events, more particularly of the revolutions of 1830 and 1848, was decisive" (1986: 93).

This is not to argue that the workplace, the pub, the chapel, the café, the volunteer fire brigade, and the working-class neighborhood did not matter in the maturation of the concept of the working class. As both Agulhon (1982b) and Hoggart (1961) have shown, these institutions were sources of the *content* of working-class consciousness. But because every such context was decidedly "local," and workplaces, trades, and skill hierarchies were and remained enormously fragmented, it took a shift in scale to national-level politics for class consciousness to take shape. It was the political struggle that crystallized the variegated conflicts of the workplace into a unified concept of class. This fusion was reflected in class practices that developed through contention with the workers' antagonists in the workplace and elsewhere – practices such as the boycott, the breaking of machines, and the strike.

But that was then, and this is now. The years following World War II were years in which scholars saw great changes in the economies of Western societies, changes that affected the integration of the working class (Franklin et al. 1992; Clark et al. 1993; Mayer 2012). Although theorists like Rolf Dahrendorf saw this as the result of an "institutionalization of class conflict" (Dahrendorf 1959), Alessandro Pizzorno saw class giving way to "individualistic mobilization" (Pizzorno 1964), while John Goldthorpe dismantled the concept of class into its occupational components to better measure the affluence that characterized the early postwar period (Goldthorpe 1963). The question that remains for us is, What happened to the language of class?

## The Political Deconstitution of "Working Class"

One outcome is that the use of the term "working class" – which, as you have seen, emerged early in the Industrial Revolution – has declined in political discourse all over the West. It was never very widespread in the United States, where it fought an uphill battle against ethnicity, race, and the general aspiration to join the middle class. But even in European countries, where class was historically an important marker in electoral politics, the sense of belonging to the working class has declined, even among people whose professional and personal background would suggest otherwise. This was especially clear in countries, such as Germany, whose slate was nearly wiped clean of class politics by fascism and anticommunism; but it was also true of France, where the "old" cleavages continue to shape political contention (Kriesi et al. 1995).

Table 3.5 summarizes forty years of survey research in France on "subjective class" – that is, the sentiment of belonging to a particular social class – from the work of Guy Michelat and Michel Simon based on data collected by the French polling firm SOFRES. Three things should be noted about these findings. First, the sentiment of belonging to a social class or group in general has not declined, as the figures in the final line of the table show; although there was a decline in subjective class early in the new century, the proportion of French citizens expressing a class sentiment was actually slightly higher in 2010 than it had been in 1966! Second, the major shift is not from "class" to "nonclass" but

TABLE 3.5. *Subjective Class in France, 1966–2010*

| Subjective Class | 1966 | 2001 | 2002 | 2010 |
| --- | --- | --- | --- | --- |
| Bourgeoisie | 4 | 2 | 2 | 3 |
| Directors | – | – | 0 | – |
| Executives | 1 | 3 | 3 | 2 |
| Middle classes | 13 | 27 | 22 | 38 |
| Shopkeepers | 1 | – | 1 | 1 |
| Working class | 23 | 9 | 14 | 6 |
| Workers, salaried | 3 | 2 | 2 | 1 |
| Peasants, farmers | 3 | 1 | 1 | 1 |
| The poor | 3 | 1 | 1 | 2 |
| Others | 8 | 6 | 5 | 10 |
| Total % naming a class or group | 61 | 54 | 53 | 64 |

*Note*: The table measures the proportion of the surveyed population with the sentiment of being part of a particular social class or group, 1966–2010.
*Source*: Guy Michelat and Michel Simon (2011: 139). Adapted with permission.

from a working-class to a middle-class identity. Third, the decline of class sentiment cannot be explained by the "objective" decline in the size of the French working class; when Michelat and Simon measured objective class membership through respondents' biographies, the decline of subjective class was actually greater among those with higher objective class membership (Michelat and Simon 2011: 139). Even in "old social movement" France, the sentiment of belonging to the working class has declined, even when subjective class was compared to citizens' positions in the stratification system (ibid., p. 140).

Survey research might be considered a thin way of measuring the importance of working-class identification. But "working class" has been declining in popular culture as well. Consider the Ngram analysis shown in Figure 3.5 of the terms "working class" and "middle class" in the English language since 1900: both terms rose to a peak in the 1930s – as we would have expected in a period marked by Depression and class conflict – and again in the 1960s, in response to the radical movements of that decade. But in the years since the 1970s, both terms have declined sharply in public usage.

The culture of class has also declined in political music. When William Roy collected data for his study of the folk music of progressive movements, he found that work songs were an important source of political music making in the nineteenth century as well as in the first half of the twentieth century. The use of music to create and enhance solidarity reached its peak in 1930's and 1940's America, when singer-songwriters

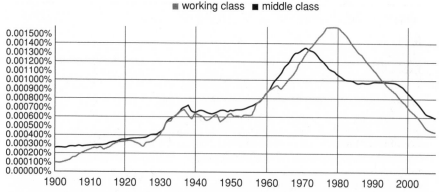

FIGURE 3.5. "Working Class" and "Middle Class" in British and American Books, 1900–2008. *Source*: http://books.google.com/ngrams.

such as Woody Guthrie, Pete Seeger, and Lee Hays began collecting and revising folk songs. "Capitalism," Roy argued, "could be fought through the form, not just the content, of the music, implying a double role – to create working-class culture and to facilitate those workers' development of their own culture" (2010: 127). But most interesting, it was not the music that the working class listened to but the kind of folk music that, in Europe, was associated with ethnic minorities that became the stock-in-trade of the Left in the 1930s.[17] Roy writes,

> Work songs included the musicking found in many occupations that involved clusters of workers engaged in repetitive and tedious activities, most notably sea men, loggers, miners, field hands, railroad workers, and cowboys...towards the end of the nineteenth century and into the early decades of the twentieth century a broad range of union organizations, independent collectors, and others began to gather them into songbooks and collections.... unions often embraced songs that voiced grievances and rallied for solidarity. (2010: 71–2)

Music was also an important source of inspiration for activists in the civil rights, antiwar, and New Left movements of the 1960s. But in contrast to the earlier period, when work was the origin of the language and cadence of protest music, in the 1960s, it was the music of the church, with its leader–response format, that inspired the civil rights movement. It was at mass meetings resembling the old religious revival meetings that the call-and-response format was most common (ibid., pp. 185, 199). Between the 1930s and the 1960s, the working class largely disappeared from the musical genre of the Left.

Class continues to underlie political discourse, but often in semidisguised or allusive forms. In the 1960s, it was under the rubric of a "war on poverty" that President Lyndon Johnson took on the task of improving the lot of workers and others; in the 1970s, sociologist William Julius Wilson titled his controversial book *The Declining Significance of Race* (1978) – and not the "increasing significance of class," which is what he meant by it; when New York officials wanted to put welfare clients to work, they called it "workfare" (Krinsky 2008); when Republicans today criticize welfare benefits to the poor, they talk of "entitlements," and not

[17] This may have had something to do, Roy points out in correspondence with the author, with the fact that the Communist Party of the Soviet Union was showing at least rhetorical support for minority cultures and for the folk culture they produced. I am grateful to Bill Roy for this and other comments on this chapter.

class benefits;[18] and when one of the veterans of the "workerist" strand of Italian radicalism – Toni Negri – wanted to write about the people, he felt it necessary to switch his discourse from "workers" to "multitudes" (Hardt and Negri 2004), to the confusion of almost everyone.

What is it that has pushed social class from the center of political and cultural discourse? Just as the political agitation of the late 1820s helped give British workers a sense of their unity and their distance from the middle class, it may be the changing context of political opportunities and costs that has driven class from the repertoire of contemporary politics. We can see hints of this change in both institutional and movement politics. In institutional politics, traditional "cleavage studies" took social class as an independent variable and deduced from it electoral alignments and party strategies (Lipset and Rokkan 1967). But it is equally likely that party leaders who were schooled in class dialectics chose to structure their appeals around the symbols of class and, to some extent, created attitudinal cleavages around them. Recall Stedman Jones's aphorism about the 1840s: "perhaps it was not consciousness (or ideology) that produced politics, but politics that produced consciousness" (Stedman Jones 1983: 19).

We see this decline of class language in all sectors of the Left: Communist, Socialist, and liberal. Responding to what they saw as the trends in postwar capitalism, the Communist parties of postwar Europe soft-pedaled the use of class language when they remembered that the "class-against-class" dialectics foisted on them by Stalin was a deadening discursive move and a deadly political one (Hellman 1975). The parliamentary social democratic parties came to understand the same lesson, but by another route: the working class would never become the majority of the population, and so without an interclass strategy, or one that submerged class within alternative discourses, these parties knew that they would never come to power (Przeworski and Sprague 1986). And when President Obama wanted to address working Americans during the election campaign of 2012, he described them as "middle class."

Since the 1980s, parties of the Left and center Left have been on the defensive against insurgent Right-populist parties that appeal to the working class – and to the unemployed – on the basis of xenophobia, antipolitics, anti-elitism, and, in the United States, religion (see the review

---

[18] The evolution of the usage and the connotations of the word "poverty" are also interesting. For an example, see Martin Ravaillon (2011). I am grateful to my colleague Nicolas Van de Walle for calling this interesting study to my attention.

in Mayer 2012). It may not be the statistical decline of the mass working class that has taken class out of the discourse of the party system, but the strategic decision of party leaders and intellectuals to abandon the language of class for less polarizing symbols (Hellman 1975). In a suggestive analysis of the Hungarian party system, Zsolt Enyedi (2005) showed that parties are potentially able to cross cleavage lines, restructure relations within the party system, and create new associations between party preferences, sociostructural categories, and attitudes.

But what of the non-institutional movements of the Left? Here, too, we find a loss of faith in the potential of class as a symbol with which to mobilize a mass following. With the extended prosperity of the postwar years, scholars and political actors in advanced Western societies came to believe in postcapitalism, postindustrialism, or the replacement of class cleavages by ideological ones (Drucker 1993; Inglehart 1977, 1990; Kitschelt 1994). The new movements of the 1960s and 1970s left class in an ambivalent position: some observers thought those movements had transcended class as an organizing principle and substituted life concerns instead (Offe 1985); others saw the (largely middle-class) student movement as the successor to the working class (Touraine 1971); and still others insisted on the continued centrality of the working class (Crouch and Pizzorno 1978; Tronti et al. 1978).

The deconstitution of the term "working class" toward the end of the twentieth century may also have had an effect on the language of worker contention. Because the word "strike" has such a strong historical association with "class" and class conflict, unions as well as others may have become reluctant to utilize it, preferring such neologisms as "job actions" and "industrial conflict." Just as the development of the strike helped constitute the working class in the nineteenth century, its deconstitution may have helped the use of the word and the practice of the "strike" to go into decline.[19]

The economic crisis that exploded in 2008 in the United States and spread to Europe and elsewhere has led to deep misery on both sides of the Atlantic. Yet not even the Occupy movement that emerged in lower Manhattan on September 17, 2011, against the abuses of Wall Street revived the language of the working class; that movement came to be known not through its social components, but through the form of action its militants favored – the "occupation." Of course, the

---

[19] This hypothesis was suggested by Joseph Margulies, after reading an earlier version of this chapter.

word comes from the occupation of factories dating from the end of World War I, so it has a working-class allure; but as for its social basis, the movement was deliberately vague. Populist terms like "the poor," "the people," "citizens," and, increasingly, "the 99 percent" dominated the movement's mission statements, but few of them contained the words "working class."

Should we be surprised at this change in the discourse of popular movements? I think not. Just as the language of class emerged from the political struggles of the 1820s and 1830s, a new political language may be emerging from the economic crisis and political struggles of today. When Occupy activists spoke of the "99 percent," they were trying to invent a new political language that connected to the broader discourse of a society that thinks more readily in terms of statistics than of classes. They may not have succeeded, but they helped produce a new concept of the use of public space that – like "boycott," "sabotage," and "strike" – may endure beyond the end of the movement they created.

# 4

# Race and Rights

Harvard professor Henry Louis Gates Jr. was tired. It was the middle of July, 2009, he had just returned from a trip to China, and the front door of his home wouldn't open. With the help of his driver, Gates forced it open. At the same time, a passing senior citizen told Lucia Whalen, who lived across the street, that two men were forcing open Gates's door. Not recognizing Gates or his driver, Whalen called the Cambridge police, making clear that she doubted whether an actual crime was in progress.

Sgt. James Crowley, a Cambridge native who had previously worked for the Harvard police, answered the call. He walked up the steps, saw Gates on the phone inside, and asked him to step outside. Gates replied, "No I will not!" When Crowley explained that he was answering a report of a break-in in progress, according to the police officer, Gates heatedly exclaimed, "Why? Because I'm a black man in America?" After a number of such exchanges Crowley put Gates under arrest. He was transported to a Cambridge police station in a police cruiser and booked for disorderly conduct.

Race was never far from the surface of the encounter: when Whalen called the Cambridge police, the dispatcher asked her several times if the men who had forced open Gates's door were "white, black, or Hispanic." According to Charles Ogeltree, Gates's attorney and a Harvard law professor, Crowley was obviously offended by Gates's belligerence, but his report reflected both "his presumption that a criminal act was taking place" and skepticism about Professor Gates's actual identity (Ogletree

*Author's note*: I am most grateful to my friends Doug McAdam and Rogers Smith for comments on an earlier version of this chapter.

2010: 31). Gates, for his part, felt he was being unfairly targeted in his own home because of the color of his skin.

But also not absent from the encounter was class. Gates is a Harvard professor and no ordinary one: the author of numerous books on black American history and literature, he has been the recipient of many honorary degrees, hosted a popular PBS series on race, and is a (moderate) advocate for black rights. His belligerent reaction to Crowley's presence on his porch may have reflected his public and academic reputation as much as outrage that he was being targeted in his own home.

The story did not end with Gates's release. On July 22, when President Barack Obama was asked at a news conference what he thought of the incident, he responded that he did not know the details of the story but that "the Cambridge police acted stupidly." "There's a long history in this country of African Americans being stopped disproportionately by the police," he continued. "It's a sign of how race remains a factor in this society."[1] But Crowley was a well-respected officer with a history of opposition to racial profiling and was following standard procedure: the police, as well as much of the white public, were outraged at Obama's jumping to conclusions: in a stark warning of things to come, Crowley's union warned the president that he would "regret the remarks he made."[2]

The media had a field day with Obama's mistake. Gates was interviewed numerous times, the TV pundits discussed the case widely, and an independent Harvard panel issued a report that distributed blame on both sides.[3] Retreating from his press conference statement, the president invited Crowley and Gates to the White House for what came to be called the "beer summit." The incident was soon buried under far more pressing business, especially the Affordable Care Act, which the president was hoping to shepherd through a reluctant Congress, but the importance of the Gates story went well beyond either partisan politics or the behavior of Officer Crowley and Professor Gates.

While many liberals jumped to Gates's defense, some Americans reacted negatively to Obama's intervention: in a Pew Research Center poll reported on July 30, 41 percent of the sample and 45 percent of white non-Hispanic respondents disapproved of the president's handling

---

[1]  www.nytimes.com/2009/07/23/us/politics/23gates.html, visited August 25, 2012.
[2]  www.boston.com/news/local/breaking_news/2009/07, visited August 25, 2012.
[3]  www.thecrimson.com/article/2010/6/30/report-police-gates-com, visited August 25, 2012.

of the dispute, as opposed to 22 percent who approved.[4] A few responded
with classical biological racism: a few days after Obama's intervention,
Justin Barrett, an officer of the Boston police department, sent a racially
charged e-mail to *Boston Globe* columnist Yvonne Abraham following
her July 21, 2009, column about Gates's arrest, referring to Gates as a
"bumbling jungle monkey."[5] Barrett's e-mail went viral, and he was
quickly told to turn in his badge. Many whites thought that Obama was
behaving like an arrogant elitist.

There were, of course, aspects of the story that were atypical: Gates's
prestige and sense of his own importance; the uncertainty and ambiguity
of the eyewitness report; Crowley's insistence that Gates show his identification in his own home; and Obama's inexperience as a recently elected
president. But the story also introduces four key aspects of America's
racial relationships: first, although biological racism has been in decline
for some time, it has far from disappeared (Kinder and Sanders 1996:
Ch. 5), as you will see later in this chapter.[6] Second, the question of
"who is black," which I review later, underlines the broad range of issues
that are still interpreted within a continuing racial framework (King and
Smith 2011). Third, a key turning point is the construction of new black
identities in the twentieth century, the topic of a later section in this chapter. But most important, I argue that every expansion of rights to black
Americans, from the Reconstruction amendments to the civil rights legislation of the 1960s to the election of a president of color in 2008, has
triggered a countermovement often couched in the language of rights.[7]
Race and rights are the point–counterpoint of American history.

What does any of this have to do with language? In the United States,
even issues that have nothing ostensibly to do with race are structured
along the lines of racially constructed alliances. As Desmond King and

---

[4] www.people-press.org/2009/07/30/obamas-ratings-slide, visited on August 25, 2012. It
should be noted that the president's previously very high ratings were declining in general
at the same time.

[5] http://www.boston.com/news/local/massachusetts/073009_barrett_email_text/, visited
March 17, 2013.

[6] For example, in an Internet search carried out in 2012, Seth Stephens-Davidowitz found
a high proportion of Google searches that included the word "nigger(s)." Many of these
were searches for "nigger jokes" and may not have been more lethal than the Polish
jokes or blonde jokes that circulated in previous decades. But when Stephens-Davidowitz
compared the frequency of Internet searches for "nigger(s)" by state, he found a strong
geographic correlation with voting against Barack Obama in the 2008 election.

[7] For simplicity and consistency, I use the term "black Americans" throughout this chapter
except when characterizing the language of one or another writer or group of writers.

Rogers Smith write, even in the current era, "the politics of the nation's racial policy alliances has generally focused on the claims of those characterized as 'white' and those categorized as 'black', with those persons and groups not placed in either category still treated according to how closely they appeared to policymakers to resemble one or the other side of the white/black dichotomy" (King and Smith 2011: 21).

## Race Talk

Race talk has been at the heart of the "American Dilemma" since the founding. "Slaves were property under state statutes," notes James Oakes, but the Constitution never referred to either slaves or property. "Instead the Constitution recognized slavery only as a servile status – 'persons held in service' – not as a right of property" (Oakes 2012: 9). That verbal distinction was a fig leaf for the founders, but it turned out to be important later, when it was mobilized by abolitionists to argue that while "property in man" was a state decision, the natural law principles of the Constitution made "freedom national" (ibid., 14).

As in the case of many other forms of contentious language, words for race are politically constructed and shifted with the historical context. Although the Constitution did not speak of Negroes, or blacks, or people of color, their weight in the population was a critical issue to the founders and the solution they devised to bring the southern states into the Union. The infamous "three-fifths rule" and the giving of every state the same number of seats in the Senate were ultimate sources of the breakup of the Union. Similarly, none of the three Reconstruction amendments – the Thirteenth, Fourteenth, or Fifteenth – mentions these terms, although Section 1 of the Fifteenth declares, "The right of citizens of the United States to vote shall not be denied or abridged by the United States or by any State on account of race, color, or previous condition of servitude."[8] But every advance in rights for black Americans was marked by changes in language (Smith 1997: 9). The rising use of the term "nigger" after Reconstruction reflects this checkered history.

### *"Nigger" and How It Changed*
The term "nigger" seems not to have originated as a racial slur, but, according to Randall Kennedy, who has documented it, the word "took

---

[8] http://constitutioncenter.org/education/educators/learning-resources/primary-and-secondary-sources/the-reconstruction-amendments.

on a derogatory connotation over time." "No one knows precisely when or how *niger* turned derisively into *nigger* and attained a pejorative meaning," he points out. "We do know, however, that by the end of the first third of the nineteenth century, *nigger* had already become a familiar and influential insult" (Kennedy 2002: 4–5).

During slavery, plantation owners seem to have used the terms "Negroes," "blacks," "servants," and "slaves" indifferently to designate their chattels but almost never – at least in their letters and writings – did they employ the opprobrious term "niggers."[9] Jefferson seems to have always referred to his slaves as his "servants." It would have contradicted the elaborately paternalistic constructions of southern slaveholders to have referred to their slaves as "niggers."

Not so for the lower classes. "The yeomen used it more frequently and the poor whites almost invariably," writes Eugene Genovese (1972: 437). But the word was ambivalent and was used on both sides of the racial divide. The slaves, according to Genovese, "referred to 'nigger quarters,' 'nigger meetings,' 'nigger preachers,' and even 'nigger dogs'" (ibid.). The term may even have had an affectionate usage among the slaves, with meanings that varied "from tenderness towards a loved one to a replica to the white man's usage." But by accepting the word and varying its meaning, Genovese argues, "the slaves went far toward denigrating themselves and accepting the white man's version of them" (ibid., p. 438). In this respect, as in many others, the Civil War was a watershed, for white as well as black Americans, as the following episode illustrates.

### From Contrabands to Citizens

In May 1861, not long after Virginia seceded from the Union, three escaped slaves crossed the James River to Fort Monroe, near Hampton, asking for their freedom from the fort's new commander, General Benjamin Butler (Goodheart 2011: Ch. 8). The recently elected president, Abraham Lincoln, had denied any intention to end slavery in the South, and the Fugitive Slave Law of 1850, reinforced by the Supreme Court's decision in the case of *Dred Scott v. Sanford* (60 U.S. 393) (1857), mandated returning the slaves to their master. But Butler – who had been in command for only a day – decided to keep them, especially since they had revealed key military intelligence about Confederate forces.

---

[9] For the writings of pro-slavery advocates, see Faust (1981) and Gordon (2003: Ch. 2). Slaveholder correspondence is quoted extensively in Genovese (1972).

When a Confederate officer rode up to the fort to politely ask Butler for the slaves' return, he replied, "I mean to take Virginia at her word, as declared in the ordinance of secession passed yesterday. I am under no constitutional obligation to a foreign country, which Virginia now claims to be." When the officer objected that the Union claimed that Virginia could not secede, Butler declared, "I shall hold these Negroes as *contraband of war*, since they are engaged in the construction of your battery and are claimed as your property" (Goodheart 2011: 314, emphasis added).

Butler may have used the term "contraband" tongue-in-cheek to refer to three human beings, but the word stuck. By the end of 1861, when thousands of African Americans crossed the Union lines seeking their freedom, many commanding officers offered them their freedom. Not only that, Butler's term "contrabands" for escaped slaves spread through the press and among the black population of the South seeking freedom (ibid., pp. 324–5, 329–30). "'Superintendents of contrabands' were created wherever the Union army triumphed and journals published pictures of contrabands being mustered to go off to aid the Union army" (Du Bois 2005: 34–5). "Never was a word so speedily adopted by so many people in a short time," wrote one Union officer (quoted in Goodheart 2011: 329).

Lincoln's 1863 proclamation and the Thirteenth Amendment legalized the actions of the Union officers who had taken in escaped slaves, and the term "contrabands" was soon displaced by "freedmen" and "freedwomen," the words used for former slaves during Reconstruction. But Butler's language demonstrates the ambivalence of white northerners toward the former slaves; even in the act of offering them their freedom, Butler – who was no racist – referred to black people as a form of property.

### Postbellum Naming

No one is named in a vacuum, and a combination of state and federal policy, social and cultural practice, and political struggle brought changes in what the former slaves were called. From chattel slaves, black Americans in the South were now suddenly citizens, and from workers who had been restricted to the most subservient roles in society, they could now legally compete with poor whites for jobs. During and immediately after Reconstruction, they could vote and run for office, while "poor whites lacked the power resources needed to bring about the kind of institutional changes that would have improved their economic lives, namely, segregationist laws restricting black competition" (Wilson 1978: 54).

But even though granting black Americans the vote was "the very least a guilty nation could grant a wronged race," "Negro suffrage ended a civil war by beginning a race feud" (Du Bois 2005: 52).[10] When the Republicans retreated to their regional redoubts in the North and West, the white South set about rolling back the gains of Reconstruction. This involved not only passing electoral laws that effectively disenfranchised the black electorate but also mounting a more general countermovement that set out to denigrate the former slaves' human capacities and even their very humanity, using the language of "scientific racism" after the 1890s.

The result was an increase in racist language and the development of "a new breed of southern politician, whose style combined the evangelistic fervor of the southern preacher with the racist rhetoric of the upcountry hillbilly" to articulate the feelings and represent the interests of working-class whites (Wilson 1978: 56). "It is one of the paradoxes of Southern history," writes C. Vann Woodward, "that political democracy for the white man and racial discrimination for the black man were often products of the same dynamics" (1971: 211). One reason for this was the changing economy of the former slave states.

### Economic Competition and Racist Language

Not only were southern blacks given political rights by Reconstruction, but they could also now compete in the labor market with lower-class whites (Wilson 1978). Of course, something like 80 percent of all southern workers until the early twentieth century still worked in agriculture, and blacks were at the lowest level of what remained a semifeudal system of oppression and debt peonage. But class-based segregation also grew as industry began to appear in the South, attracted by its lower labor costs and plentiful labor supply. With industrialization came the first attempts to unionize the southern workforce, and with that, employers' use of poor and unemployed blacks to replace white workers trying to unionize. Had black and white workers been able to cooperate, the history of the region would have been very different. The Populists tried briefly to forge

---

[10] Du Bois's essay "Of the Dawn of Freedom" remains one of the most balanced analyses of the promise and the pitfalls of Reconstruction. First published in the *Atlantic Monthly* in March 1901, it appears as Chapter 2 of *The Souls of Black Folk* (2005: 29–58).

an interracial coalition in the 1890s, but racism was a tool that could be used to divide the working class as nowhere else in the country.

Economic competition led to increased physical abuse, mainly from lower-class whites. In her analysis of county-level data in Georgia in the 1890s, Sarah Soule found that rates of lynching grew with economic competition (Soule 1992). Before the war, lynching had been used mainly against whites by other whites; but in the last sixteen years of the nineteenth century, the vast majorities of the victims were black (Wilson 1978: 59). The same period also saw a decline of upper-class paternalism toward "our respectable and well behaved colored people" (Woodward 1971: 257, quoted in Wilson 1978: 58).

This brought a diffusion of the N-word to all classes of white southerners. Southern congressmen and judges had no inhibition against using the word in public. When Gunnar Myrdal traveled through the South in the 1940s, he found few whites who were uncomfortable using it. And when Kennedy carried out a Lexis-Nexis judicial search through 2001, he found the word "nigger" in 4,219 reported state and federal court decisions, compared to "kike" in only 84, "wetback" in 50, "gook" in 90, and "honky" in 286 (Kennedy 2002: 32). Symbolically, the term "nigger" "seeped into practically every aspect of American culture, from literature to political debates, from cartoons to song" (ibid., pp. 6–8).

It was not only in the South that economic competition produced verbal denigration of black Americans. It is well known that white ethnic groups such as the Irish and the Jews gained social status in part by invidious comparison with their black fellow citizens (King and Smith 2011: 21). Northerners took a long time to accept the former slaves as citizens or even, in some cases, to see them as fully endowed human beings. In popular culture, blacks were frequently portrayed as lazy, childlike, unteachable, and comical. That did not prevent employers from employing them as scabs, a practice that helped keep wages down in southern mills and coalfields and fed into working-class racism.

Since the civil rights movement, the use of the term "nigger" has become increasingly rare in public – and probably private – discourse, but the Internet has provided a channel for classic white racism to be expressed anonymously. In a Google Insight search carried out between 2005 and 2012 for "nigger(s)" and for "hate/kill nigger(s)," the results were ominous: although one of the peaks in these searches was linked to comedian Michael Richards's racist outburst at a Los Angeles nightclub in 2005, and another came from Texas governor Rick Perry's "nigger rock" incident in the 2012 Republican primary campaign, both Obama's

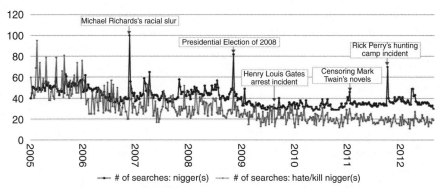

FIGURE 4.1. Racial Events and Internet Searches for Racist Terms, 2005–2012. *Source*: http://www.google.com/insights/search/. *Key dates:* Nov. 20, 2006: Michael Richards's racial slur (http://www.tmz.com/2006/11/20/kramers-racist-tirade-caught-on-tape); Nov. 4, 2008: Presidential Election of 2008; Jan. 16, 2011: Censoring Mark Twain's novels (http://www.nytimes.com/2011/01/16/opinion/16moore.html); Oct. 1, 2011: Rick Perry's hunting camp incident (http://www.washingtonpost.com/national/rick-perry-familys-hunting-camp-still-known-to-many-by-old-racially-charged-name/2011/10/01/gIQAOhY5DL_story .html).

election and Gates's arrest were associated with increases in such Internet traffic. Figure 4.1 traces the incidence of Internet searches for "nigger" from 2005 to 2012.

## Race and Republicanism
At the elite level, the dynamics of post-Reconstruction southern politics produced a revival of the reasoning that white southerners had employed before the Civil War to defend slavery and justify racial hierarchy. It was a language that came straight from the classical republican tradition, translated into racial terms. In this view, because whites possessed the requisite merit to govern and recently freed and mainly illiterate ex-slaves did not, black Americans could not be expected to exercise the same rights as whites. This belief helped justify rolling back Reconstruction in terms of the vote, education, and states' rights.

The Fifteenth Amendment gave the former slaves the right to vote in 1870. This forced the South to square white supremacy with black voters, even as they qualified it by drawing on the rhetoric of republicanism. "In resolving this conundrum, the champions of the New South accepted the liberal principle of universal adult male suffrage" (Margulies 2013: 46). Political participation, whites insisted, drawing on the classic republican synthesis, "required a virtuous citizen who could take the needs of the entire community into account" and must therefore rest "with men of wealth, character and intelligence" (ibid.). If African Americans would simply place themselves under a benevolent "white tutelage," they could gradually be equipped for the demands of responsible citizenship. When that day came, the vote would be theirs. "Of course, most white southerners were confident such a day would never come and were not at all troubled by this lacuna in their argument" (ibid., pp. 46–7). Separate but equal education was justified by the same reasoning. Because blacks lacked the virtues and merits of whites, putting them in competition with whites would put them at a disadvantage that they would never be able to overcome. "This 'reality' created an obligation to shelter African-Americans from a race they could never win; in African-Americans, it created a sense of gratitude (or so whites believed) that they had been spared the humiliation of beginning a hopeless contest. In both, it created a shared preference for segregation" (Margulies 2013: 47). Of course this argument did not justify separate eating, transportation, and sanitary facilities, but this was a subtlety that the ideologists of white supremacy preferred to pass over. Once the separate but equal doctrine was formulated, it could be justified for every aspect of southern life.

The most important facet of white racial ideology – states' rights – also came out of the republican tradition. Since the nullification crisis of the 1830s, the South had claimed that southern states had the right to nullify abusive federal policies such as the "tariff of abominations." On that occasion, South Carolina went so far as to begin military preparations to resist federal forces. The crisis had nothing to do with slavery, but henceforth, states' rights became the central plank in the South's defense of its peculiar institution. Southern congressmen defended the poll tax against northern attempts to end the practice with reference to the Constitution's reservation to the states of all powers that are not explicitly given to the federal government (Margulies 2013: 51–3). Throughout these debates, the republican language of civil virtue justified attempts to whittle away the rights that the war and the Reconstruction amendments had given black Americans. The extension of rights to blacks by the Civil War and Reconstruction led to a countermovement against those rights couched in the language of republicanism.

### Who's Black?

Americans often think that the South's racist practices were overcome by northern and federal opposition, but the definition of who is black has been constant and has in fact expanded in one important respect: the South's naming practices conquered the rest of the country.[11] The definition of who is black percolated from the practices of the South to the country in general. The state legislatures, the courts, and the Census Bureau helped construct a homogeneous black American identity.

State legislatures were a major source of symbolic racism in denying black Americans equal rights – for example, in the widespread banning of racial intermarriage. As late as the 1950s, half the states – many of them outside the South – still had antimiscegenation laws. It was only in 1967 (*Loving v. Virginia* 388 U.S. 1) that the Supreme Court struck down Virginia's "Racial Integrity Act" of 1662. Map 4.1 reveals the number of states that at any time had antimiscegenation laws and the dates when these laws were either overturned by the courts or revoked by state legislatures.

The courts were a potent source of racist language. When Federal Circuit Court judge Thomas Brady learned, in 1954, of the Supreme Court's decision to desegregate southern public schools (*Brown v. Board of Education of Topeka, Kansas* 347 U.S. 483), he fulminated that he "and the South would fight and die for the principles of racial purity and white womanhood rather than follow the Supreme Court's decision" (Davis 2001: 17). As James Davis writes sardonically, "It was, of course, centuries too late to keep the races pure in the South" (ibid.). Mississippi senator Theodore Bilbo had an answer to Davis's jibe: although he admitted that white men had over the years "poured a broad stream of white blood into black veins," that did not make white women "any less pure" (quoted in Williamson 1980: 138).

Keeping white women pure and winking at the "broad stream of white blood poured into black veins" could be reconciled only by constructing a binary division between whites and nonwhites, regardless of the complexion of the latter. In the early decades of colonial settlement, especially in the Upper South, biracial unions were predominantly between poor whites and black slaves. Later, it was in the black belts of the Deep South that white plantation owners were the main source of miscegenation with black servants. Whatever the source, before the Civil War an increasing proportion of the black American population was not black but various shades of brown (Williamson 1980: Ch. 3). Although mixed-race individuals were present in both the enslaved and the free black population,

---

[11] This section leans on the historical analysis of F. James Davis, *Who Is Black? One Nation's Definition* (2001), on Joel Williamson's *New People* (1980), and on Kim Williams's *Mark One or More* (2006).

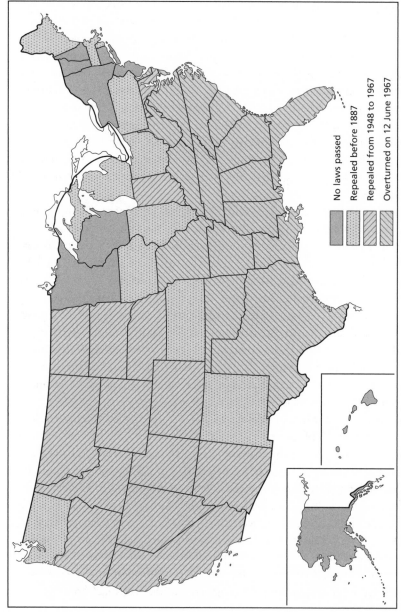

MAP 4.1. U.S. States, by Date of Repeal of Antimiscegenation Laws. *Source:* http://en.wikipedia.org/wiki/Antimiscegenation_laws_in_the_United_States.

Legend:

No laws passed
Repealed before 1887
Repealed from 1948 to 1967
Overturned on 12 June 1967

mulattoes constituted a higher portion of the latter group as a result of manumission, escaped slaves, and, after the Civil War, migration from the North.

White southerners had always struggled with the problem of how much white blood would allow someone to claim to be white. This varied from state to state and even from city to city within the same state, and there was at first no fixed rule about where the true color line lay (Davis 2001: Ch. 2). For example, New Orleans, where there was a major infusion of French-speaking immigrants after the Haitian Revolution, recognized mulattoes as a distinct group. Charleston was not very different. To many white southerners, mulattoes seemed like a useful buffer group between themselves and the slave population; indeed, some of them became landowners and purchased slaves of their own.

All this began to change in the 1850s. The source was the growing regional tensions between North and South. This was the decade in which white southerners began to feel themselves under assault from abolitionism and antislavery, from dissent by nonslaveholding whites, from free blacks, and from their own slaves. "They were fearful too," writes Joel Williamson, "of the possibility of conspiracy between slave Negroes and free Negroes." "Miscegenation was wrong and mulattoes must be made black, both within slavery and without" (1980: 74). This fear coincided with the erection of an ideology of southern culture that justified slavery for black Americans as a "protection" for their innocence and weakness but saw no justification for people of mixed race.

The Jim Crow period, which codified racial lines through a series of "Black Codes," essentially closed off sexual commerce between whites and blacks in the South. But the mulatto population continued to grow, mainly through intermarriage between blacks and mulattoes. "Experts" such as Josiah C. Nott were convinced that the progeny of interracial unions were weak and would live shorter lives (Williams 2006: 23). Nott predicted a decline in the number of mulattoes. But the censuses from 1870 through 1910 showed both an increase in their number and in their proportion of the total nonwhite population. By 1918 the Census Bureau had "accepted the estimate that three-quarters of the Negro people in the United States were indeed of mixed ancestry" (Williamson 1980: 111–12) and gave up the "decades-long search for evidence that mulattos were susceptible to early death" (Williams 2006: 23).

The figures admittedly were unreliable, but the fact that the government was naming and distinguishing among mulattoes (one-half black), quadroons (one-fourth black), octaroons (one-eighth black), and pure-black Americans tells us how obsessed many white Americans were with the color line. There was even a tendency among some social scientists to predict a progressively "whitening" trend in the Negro population, with lighter-skinned males "moving up" the color line through marriage with lighter-skinned females, and the most light-skinned males moving out of the black population altogether by marrying white women.[12]

The Census Bureau gave up measuring degrees of color in 1920, and the long-term trend toward a homogenization in the naming of the black American population continued. In 1962, Lerone Bennett estimated that the vast majority of American blacks were racially mixed (1962: Ch. 10). In the 1990s, Davis estimated that at least three-quarters of all American blacks had some white ancestry, except in the most isolated areas of the Deep South (2001: 21). But the recognition that not all nonwhite Americans were the same color, and that an increasing proportion were not black, did not produce gradations of acceptance by white Americans. On the contrary, the postbellum period was accompanied by the generalization of the "one-drop rule," which adopted the definition of black Americans from southern practice. With respect to who is black, it was the South that conquered the North.

### The One-Drop Rule

Some former slave countries, such as Brazil, recognize gradations of color informally but impose or allow no legal differences, even though status differences among people of different colors are substantial and structural (Marx 1998: Ch. 7). In others, such as South Africa under apartheid, a distinct "Coloured" population developed early and was frozen into a legal status slightly above that of blacks but well below that of whites (ibid., Ch. 5).[13] Among countries with substantial mixed populations, it was only in the United States that all persons with any black ancestry were assigned the status of the subordinate group. The one-drop rule appeared explicitly in the South at the end of Reconstruction, when seven states adopted it by defining as Negro anyone with *any* black ancestry. Other southern states – for example, Virginia – took longer to adopt the rule but had accepted it by 1930 (Davis 2001: Ch. 4). It was accepted

---

[12] Williamson (1980: Ch. 3) surveys this fascinating trend among social scientists. The key contributors were Ralph Linton, Melville Herskovits, and Gustavus Steward. The main dissenter from this "assimilationist" consensus was Gunnar Myrdal.

[13] There are other combinations. Davis enumerates and describes seven variants in a careful comparative analysis (2001: Ch. 5).

nationally when federal courts began to take "judicial notice" of state practice.

The capstone of the one-drop rule came with the infamous case *Plessy v. Ferguson* (163 U.S. 537) in 1896. *Plessy* is usually remembered for having legitimated the doctrine of "separate but equal" in public accommodations and schools, and that was its most nefarious effect. But the Court also denied white status to Homer Plessy, who had used his seven-eighths white ancestry to justify sitting in the white compartment of a railroad car. "Without ruling directly on the definition of a Negro," writes Davis, "the Supreme Court briefly took what is called 'judicial notice' of what it assumed to be common knowledge: that a Negro or black is any person with any black ancestry" (Davis 2001: 8; Harris 2010). This has been the consistent doctrine of the federal courts, even when it found that black ancestry was less than one-eighth of a person's background. As late as the 1980s, the federal and state courts were still arguing over what degrees of whiteness permitted people to call themselves white (Davis 2001: 9–11). But these white-led institutions were not alone. From the Civil War on, lighter-skinned black Americans who came south to work in Reconstruction began to take on leadership roles in the black community and eventually merged with that community (Davis 2001: Ch. 6). This does not mean that black Americans were unconcerned with complexion: some upper-status black Americans prided themselves on the fact that their "blue veins" could be seen through their skin and formed exclusive clubs that set them off from the rest of the black community (Lacy 2007: 12). Middle-class families like Gates's in West Virginia were deeply aware of each other's color, and of whether they had "good" – that is, straight – hair (Gates 1994). But the implicit racism of the one-drop rule had its ironic counterpart in the growing racial solidarity among Americans of color. We can see this in the restless search of black Americans for what to call themselves.

## The Self-Construction of Blackness

> My grandfather was colored, my father was Negro, and I am black. (Henry Louis Gates's personal statement for his Yale application in 1969, in Gates 1994: 201)

Because most of them were illiterate, we do not know very much about how the slaves referred to themselves before the Civil War, but we do know that black abolitionists used a variety of terms for their community, ranging from "Africans" to "colored people," to "Negroes," to "blacks." David Walker's *Appeal to the Colored Citizens of the World* referred to black Americans as "coloured," "people of color," and "Africans." Robert Young's *Ethiopian Manifesto* used "black," "black Africa," "African slave," "degraded sons of Africa," and "Ethiopian" (Gordon 2003: 87).[14] Early organizations of free blacks used the words "colored" and "Negro" to describe black Americans: in 1826, the Massachusetts General Colored Association was formed, a few years before the 1830 launch of the National Negro Convention.[15] "Freedmen" and "freedwomen" had a brief life on the public stage during Reconstruction, but when the federal government ended Reconstruction in 1876, these terms disappeared.

Poor rural blacks accepted the linguistic conventions that oppressed them; as late as 1901, in his travels through the South, W. E. B. Du Bois met black farm workers who routinely referred to other black Americans as "niggers" (Du Bois 2005: 74). As late as the 1950s, Gates quotes his relatives in rural West Virginia as referring to other black Americans as "niggers," too, but not always in a flattering manner (Gates 1994).[16] During the civil rights era and afterward, "nigger" became a term of casual endearment among some black Americans. As Davis writes,

> Traditionally an insult, *nigger* can also be a compliment, as in "He played like a nigger." Historically a signal of hostility, it can also be a salutation announcing affection, as in "This is my main nigger." A term of belittlement, *nigger* can also be a term of respect, as in "James Brown is a straight-up nigger." A word that can bring forth bitter tears in certain circumstances, *nigger* can prompt joyful laughter in others. (Davis 2001: 37)

### The Seasons of the "New Negro"

But as the one-drop rule left no mediating space for individuals of mixed race, and as racial solidarity began to grow within this boundary, there were increasing efforts to find a name for black Americans that would express both intraracial solidarity and freedom from the naming practices

---

[14] Walker's 1830 essay was republished by Hill and Wang in 1965. Young's *Ethiopian Manifesto* is most readily available in Sterling Stuckey's *Ideological Origins of Black Nationalism* (1972).

[15] Stuckey also claims that in the North, as late as the 1820s, black Americans were referring to themselves as "Africans" or "free Africans" (Stuckey 1972: 88), but I have found no other evidence for his claim.

[16] See the quotations on pp. 35, 37, 39, and 44 of Gates's evocative book. The fact that Gates titled his autobiography *Colored People* tells us what respectable southern black families liked to be called.

of whites. First in this progression of self-naming experiments was "new Negro." Before the terms "blacks," "African Americans," and "people of color" entered the American lexicon, educated blacks began to call themselves "Negroes," but not without a certain uneasiness. "Negro," after all, was a white person's term, and it carried with it "the image in the popular American imagination of the black as devoid of all the characteristics that supposedly separated the lower forms of human life from the higher forms" (Gates and Jarrett 2007: 3). This is what gave rise to efforts to construct the trope of the "new Negro."

The first use of this term seems to have been religious and educational. Reverend W. E. C. Wright used it in 1894 to point with pride to the effects of "Christian education in making a new Negro" (republished in ibid., p. 23). Education was also at the core of the term as it was used by the most prominent black American of the turn of the century: Booker T. Washington. Washington thought that black Americans should not aspire for political rights or for higher education but should combat the sloth and ignorance bred by rural peonage by learning crafts and trades (Washington, Williams, and Wood 1969). "The more practical education is the better, especially as the tendency of modern industrialism is more and more towards specialization in all departments of learning and activity of whatever sort" (Gates and Jarrett 2007: 36). The "new Negro," for Washington, was a teacher, and preferably not a teacher in the abstract reaches of higher education but a teacher who would train young blacks for trades and crafts.

In these early usages, there was already an ambiguity. Wright used the "new Negro" trope both as a mass phenomenon that would eventually transform the "old Negro" and to refer to a sector of the black population that was "pushing out into the remoter public school districts of the Black Belt" to educate the old Negroes (Gates and Jarrett 2007: 24) and represent black Americans to the white community. He proudly quoted one southern white who said to another of a black man who had been educated in a missionary school, "It was all I could do to keep from saying 'mister' to him" (ibid., p. 24). We find the same duality between elites and masses in Washington's employment of the term: he used it to mean mass racial "uplift," but he was also insistent on the need to create a vanguard that would eventually lead black Americans through their efforts to educate themselves.

The most devastating critic of his approach was Du Bois, who saw Washington's program as practically accepting "the alleged inferiority of the Negro races" (Du Bois 2005: 73). Du Bois's was a model for mass uplift: yet in criticizing Washington's accommodationism, he called for a new black leadership – a "talented tenth: As he wrote in *The Souls of Black Folk*, 'what can be more instructive than the leadership of a group within a group?'" (ibid., p. 66). Through higher education, the talented tenth would bring enlightenment to the mass of the black population (pp. 144–5).

After the First World War, Du Bois used the term new Negro in *The Crisis* to call for returned black soldiers not only to "return from fighting" but also "to return fighting" on behalf of democracy (quoted in Gates and Jarrett 2007: 6). The political inflection of the term was best encapsulated in Hubert H. Harrison's call for a "Race First" philosophy: "The new Negro race in America," he wrote, "will not achieve political self-respect until it is in a position to organize itself as a politically independent party" (ibid., p. 8).

Both Du Bois's political inflection of the term and Harrison's expansion of it to refer to "the new Negro race" were populist; not so was the use of the term by its most distinguished advocate, philosopher Alan Locke, who used it to apply to an intellectual and cultural elite working in and around "the Harlem Renaissance" (Locke 1983). Locke was not apolitical, as has sometimes been claimed; but by shifting the focus of the term "new Negro" from political radicalism to artistic achievement, he narrowed it socially to an elite of artists, writers, and cultural entrepreneurs, and geographically to the buzzing cauldron of talent in the Harlem of the 1920s.

Of course, Locke gestured toward the black masses, too – for example, when he recalled that "a main change has been, of course, that shifting of the Negro population which has made the Negro problem no longer exclusively or even predominantly Southern" (Locke 1983: 5). But when he wrote of the shift in the "life-attitudes and self-expression of the Young Negro, in his poetry, his art, his education and his new outlook" (ibid., pp. 4–5), Locke was changing the focus from the broad black masses of city and countryside to the formation of an intellectual elite.[17]

In one sense, Locke and Du Bois were on the same page: in their discovery of the potential links between black Americans and people of color around the world. In the preceding decade, Marcus Garvey had called for a worldwide alliance of people of color; Locke wrote of the

---

[17] I do not mean by this that Locke was apolitical, only that his concept of the political was far more cultural than that of Du Bois. For example, whereas Du Bois thought of art as an arena for propaganda, Locke thought that the political impact of the black artists lay in the recognition of the creativity of their work. For a sensitive examination of the political theory of Alan Locke, see Michelle Smith's "Beyond the Watch and Guard of Statistics: Race, Art and the Political Theory of Alan Locke" (2010).

"new internationalism" of black Americans, which he saw as "an effort to recapture contact with the scattered peoples of African derivation" (Locke 1983: 15). Du Bois went further, calling for solidarity among "the millions of black men in Africa, America, and the Islands of the Sea, not to speak of the brown and yellow myriads elsewhere" (Du Bois 2005: 7).

Internationalism was what distinguished Du Bois from the mainstream of the civil rights movement after the war, when leaders such as Martin Luther King Jr. focused the energies of the movement entirely on the United States and black internationalists were isolated into an internationalist – and radical – ghetto (Rana 2010: 329–36). When King used the term "new Negro" in 1957, it was in a purely domestic sense – for example, when he commented on the decision of *Brown v. the Board of Education of Topeka, Kansas* (347 U.S. 483, 1954) to force the desegregation of public schools. "Along with the emergence of a 'New Negro,'" he wrote, "with a new sense of dignity and destiny, came that memorable decision of May 17, 1954" (King 1957: 27).

But in 1954, King was still groping for a new language and a new identity. It was from the younger, more militant groups like Student Nonviolent Coordinating Committee (SNCC) and Congress of Racial Equality (CORE), interacting on a daily basis with white racism and with each other, that a new culture of blackness was born. The negative side was the increasing signs of antiwhite resentment that appeared in the movement after white activists began to join it in the early 1960s (Carson 1981: Ch. 8); but the positive side was noticed by activists like John Lewis in the spring of 1964. "Something is happening to people in the Southern Negro community," he wrote.

> They're identifying with people because of color... They're conscious of things that happen in Cuba, in Latin America, and in Africa. Even in SNCC... there have been great changes going on. There's been a radical change in our people since 1960; the way they dress, the music they listen to, their natural hairdos.... I think people are searching for a sense of identity, and they're finding it. (quoted in Carson 1981: 101)

With the Montgomery bus boycott in 1956, this new identity began to diffuse across the South. In a statement in March 1956, King asserted a new definition that resonated with the trope of the new Negro:

> Our non-violent protest in Montgomery is important because it is demonstrating to the Negro, North and South, that many of the stereotypes he has held about himself and other Negroes are not valid.... In Montgomery we walk in a new way. We hold our heads in a new way. (King 1957: 27)

"Figures associated with the campaign – most notably King – were engaged in 'signifying work'" (McAdam et al. 2001: 319).

## Constituting a New Black Actor

The civil rights movement was more than an effort to change the bus seating laws in Montgomery and elsewhere; it was an expression of a new collective identity in the making. The "new Negro" was a linguistic step in this progression, but it was too genteel, too "white," and too resonant of the past to make a permanent impression on the new black middle class. As this new consciousness percolated out of the South to more radical black militants in the North, a new language began to diffuse within the black American community. "Those cats gave us Negro," declaimed radical minister Franklin Florence in 1968, referring to white people. "[B]ut since we speak English, baby, we're going to be black in English. They can't get 'nigger' from that like they could from 'Negro.' Now they will have to be satisfied with our blackness" (quoted in Smith 1969: 8–9).

Few black Americans would go as far as Franklin wanted in rejecting the language that was imposed on black Americans after slavery. But in place of "Negroes" and "colored people," the dominant descriptor for the race has become the simple term "blacks." As Franklin hoped, the use of the traditional term "Negroes" has declined, except for a brief revival in the 1960s; the more ambiguous term "colored people" has also fallen into disuse, except nostalgically (Gates 1994); and the anodyne "African Americans" never made it very far beyond the academy, as Figure 4.2,

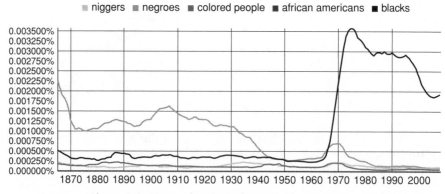

FIGURE 4.2. Alternative Terms for Describing Black Americans in Books in English from an Ngram Analysis of Google Books in American English, 1860–2008. *Source*: http://books.google.com/ngrams.

based on an Ngram analysis of Books in American English, shows.[18] The preferred term for black Americans in American culture today has become "blacks" or "black people."

The late 1960s was the take-off point for the new locution, both as a noun and as a modifier. The slogan "black power" for a time animated different sectors of militant black opinion; groups like the Black Panthers and the Black Muslims grew up on the extremes of militant black circles; and collections of writings like Middleton Harris's *Black Book* (1974) and Martin Bernal's *Black Athena* (1987) were avidly read by young black Americans.[19] When the term was first publicly used by Stokely Carmichael in 1966, it simultaneously electrified black youth in the North and frightened the more moderate civil rights leadership in the South. Doug McAdam writes, "No single phrase in the history of black struggle in the United States better captures the close connection between language and contention than 'black power.'"[20]

The new term encapsulated the shift from the integrationist civil rights language, which was largely welcomed by enlightened white opinion, to a new and more threatening language that had the perhaps unintended effect of splitting most white liberals from the movement. Following Davis, we might see this linguistic shift as the final success of the one-drop rule; we could also see it as part of the rise to consciousness of people of color around the world, including many whose complexion is far from black; or we could see it – as Franklin did in the 1960s – as the belated assertion of self-naming among a group whose names and imputed characteristics were foisted upon it by its oppressors. All of these influences probably played a role in the adoption of the new language, but they elide what seems to me the most important impulse that came

---

[18] I used "black" as an adjectival modifier for "people" in the analysis in Figure 4.2 because using "blacks" as a noun would not have allowed the Ngram search engine to discriminate between the use of the term to designate black Americans and other uses of the term. The term "African Americans" is used without a hyphen, but the results did not vary significantly when it was hyphenated. The variant "Afro-Americans" did not produce significantly different results.

[19] Bernal was neither black nor American, but a British sinologist who became fascinated with the contributions of African and Asian civilizations to Greek – and thus European – civilization. For a brief analysis of why the book made such a splash among black Americans and others, see Rodgers (2011: 115). For a critical response, which, however, largely ignores its impact on the black community, see Lefkowitz and Rogers (eds., 1996). Full disclosure: Bernal is a former colleague of the author's at Cornell.

[20] In a personal communication to the author. See McAdam's *Political Process and the Development of Black Insurgency, 1930–1970* (1999 [1982]: Ch. 4), for this period.

out of the civil rights movement: the attempt to create a sense of racial solidarity.

### Activating Rights Through Protest

The early successes of the civil rights movement rested on symbols and strategies that did not require supporters to depart from traditional and widely shared American values. The concept of rights and the attendant one of opportunity were deeply embedded in the black middle class, the movement's main constituency in the South, providing a language and a grammar that allowed the movement to mediate between its black constituency and the white liberal "conscience constituents" who bolstered it from the outside based on their own understanding of rights.

But the black middle class also shared a culture of quiescence that was nurtured by the black church and by a comfortable – if segregated – community life in the towns and villages of the South.[21] Despite the role of King and other ministers in leading the movement in the region, the majority of black churchmen were deeply conservative and nurtured careful ties with their white counterparts. To deal with this obstacle, rather than impose a frame of daring and risky activism around the acquiescent culture of southern blacks, the movement's leaders elaborated a frame of peaceful civil disobedience within the most traditional institution they possessed – the black church – using the language of rights. Traditional solidarities could thus be transformed into campaigns of peaceful civil disobedience on behalf of rights, both individual and collective.

The second half of the 1960s marked a dramatic shift in the strategy of peaceful civil disobedience. Both in the South and in the cities of the North, collective action took more-assertive forms, exploding into violence in cities like Los Angeles and Newark and drawing on the rage and frustration of urban black youth. But it also marked the constitution of a new collective actor – blacks who were proud of their race, rejected the integrationism of the mainstream civil rights leaders, and tried to create a new culture of black pride and separation.

The effort to create intraracial cultural solidarity was successful, at least in part: we see it in the extraordinary commercial successes of Alex

---

[21] Nowhere better than in Gates's autobiography, *Colored People*, do we find a moving document of the loss of community represented by integration, when the local mill owners in his hometown canceled the "colored pic-a-nic" for fear that they would be cited for segregation. "Who," he asks, "wanted to attend the mill picnic with the white people, when it meant shutting the colored one down" (1996: 211).

Haley's family history, *Roots*, or of more significant literary works by Alice Walker and Toni Morrison; in the growth of a black periodic press, including journals like *Black Enterprise* and *Jet*, joining the more derivative *Ebony* on the newsstands; in public opinion polls showing a high level of racial solidarity among black Americans; in the rise of successful local electoral coalitions that led to the electoral conquest of a number of majority-black cities; and, finally, in the growing solidarity of black voters in support of black candidates in national elections, culminating in the election of President Barack Obama in 2008.[22]

But we also see it in the extraordinary shift in ordinary black Americans' attitudes toward their own race and their skin color: whereas Gates and his family had prized lighter skin and "good hair" when he was growing up in the 1950s, in the 1960s black families began to name their children in ways that deliberately set them off from white naming practices.[23] "Black is beautiful," Afro hairdos, the adoption of "black English": these symbolic artifacts marked a reaction at the mass level against traditional black integrationism, and an attempt to fashion a new black identity.

But the effort to create a peoplehood in as heterogeneous a population as black Americans has had divisive as well as solidary effects. First, as in the early "new Negro" trope, there was an important strain of moral regeneration in the rise of black consciousness in the 1960s and 1970s (Rodgers 2011: 120–1). Think of the Black Muslims, who demanded an exemplary code of personal behavior of their devotees, or the theme of male responsibility in the Million Man March of the 1990s. Behind both of these was the baldly stated assumption that black Americans – especially males – were seldom either exemplary or responsible.

Second, as increasing numbers of black Americans took advantage of the new educational and professional opportunities that opened up in the wake of civil rights, many elite descendants of the "new Negro" became detached from what William Julius Wilson called the "black underclass" (1987). In *The Declining Significance of Race* (1978), Wilson

---

[22] According to the Pew Research Center, 95 percent of black voters cast their vote for Barack Obama. For these results, go to http://pewresearch.org/pubs/1209/racial-ethnic-voters-presidential-election, visited August 25, 2012. But black candidates do not always run racialized campaigns, and black voters sometimes reject the way black candidates use race in their campaigns. For a review and an innovative empirical test, see Christopher Stout's "Do Voters Prefer Post-Racial Black Candidates?" (2012).

[23] I am grateful to Doug McAdam for this information, drawn from his original research with Steven Levitt on black naming practices in California in the 1960s.

had argued that the new direction of American industrial capitalism was largely responsible for the poverty of black America, and not the racism inherited from the Jim Crow era. In *The Truly Disadvantaged* he now focused on the costs of the industrial divide to those who were hit hardest by it. That book not only revealed the economic plight of inner-city blacks but also implicitly underscored the growing detachment of the middle-class sector of the black community from its roots. The divide was geographic as well as sociological: with each ratchet of economic decline for their poorer counterparts, blacks who had successfully entered the middle class fled from the inner-city ghettos, first to the outer boroughs of the cities and eventually to the suburbs, leaving the inner city divorced from its "talented tenth."

Divisions also arose among the black elites and intellectuals who had seemed so solidary during the 1960s and 1970s. First came the divisions in the civil rights movement between its largely nonviolent, Christian-inspired institutional wing in the South, and the more militant groups that developed, largely in the North. Then divisions exploded between men and feminist women in the black intellectual community (Rodgers 2011: 139–40). These tensions exploded during the controversy over Clarence Thomas's nomination to the Supreme Court, when Thomas was accused by a former aide, Anita Hill, of sexual harassment. Like Thomas, a certain number of black Americans were convinced by conservative arguments that the civil rights struggle had been won. Thomas had always been suspicious of racial preferences and thought it was time for black Americans to be governed by the same rules as other Americans. A larger number, while voting solidly Democratic, turned away from active engagement in politics altogether. Only the election campaign of Barack Obama in 2007–8 reawakened widespread black political participation.

These divisions in the black community had three main effects: first, with the decline of the civil rights movement's mass base, the more progressive civil rights movements like SNCC and CORE withered away or drifted into sterile sectarianism; second, the rare (but highly publicized) conservatives like Thomas, and more moderate (but culturally conservative) Christian groups undermined the solidarity of black Americans; third, in the academy, black power movements that were born with a radical mission were transformed into black studies programs that began to play the same academic games as those played in white-dominated academic fields (Rojas 2007). These trends left the field of black movement politics to the traditional civil rights groups, which gravitated into the hands of professional administrators who saw their job as ensuring foundation and middle-class support, protecting the gains of the past, and holding off threats from "outsiders."

### "Mark One or More"

One such "outsider" was the briefly influential "multiracial movement," made up of congeries of small local and regional groups, many of them representing individuals in mixed-race marriages, who were interested in the creation of a multiracial census category (Williams 2006).[24] Coming largely from mixed-race suburban districts, these groups were able to gain the support of a number of liberal state legislators (ibid., Ch. 4). But at the national level, they were stymied by the opposition of major civil rights groups such as the National Association for the Advancement of Colored People (NAACP) (ibid., pp. 126–30). The logic of their opposition was that the creation of a multiracial category in the census would draw population statistics away from the black community, thereby reducing the amount of federal funding for programs of interest to their constituents (ibid., p. 25).

As the conflict heated up, Democratic members of Congress were pressured by their allies in the civil rights community to retreat from the issue. Ironically, the movement's major support came from members of what King and Smith call the "Color Blind Alliance" of Republican officeholders, conservative think tanks and advocacy groups, and especially from Speaker of the House Newt Gingrich, who quickly saw that the creation of a multiracial category would split the civil rights coalition and help the future chances of the Republican Party (Williams 2006: 54–5; King and Smith 2011: 209). Opposition came from most Democratic Party officeholders, many civil service members, the liberal media, and most nonwhite advocacy groups (ibid., p. 210).

In the end, after long study and even longer polemics, symbolizing the poor policy outcomes that King and Smith see resulting from the clash between rival race-conscious alliances, the Census Bureau created the compromise category "Mark More Than One," which gave voters the chance to express their identities – more than fifty different ones.[25] Because of the confusion and dispersion thus created, the census changes

---

[24] I adopt for this section the title of Kim Williams's important study of the multiracial movement of the 1990s and her analysis of the changes in the census in the 1990s (2006). Also see the more recent discussion in King and Smith (2011: 203–13).

[25] For the breakdown of the twelve combinations of ethnic identities comprising more than 100,000 people, see Williams (2006: 115). The remaining forty-five combinations are not listed in the table.

did not have a significant impact on elections or federal funding. Marking "more than one" may have provided the government with a measure of the growing diversity of the American population, but it did little to provide an identity for the increasing number of children of black–white marriages.

Between the 2000 and 2010 censuses, however, there was a dramatic increase in the number of Americans – particularly younger ones – who claimed a multiracial identity. In 2010, more than nine million Americans were self-identified as belonging to two or more racial groups, and the number who checked both "black" and "white" grew by 134 percent, as calculated by Jennifer Lee for the Russell Sage Foundation. Figure 4.3 records the changes between the 2000 and 2010 censuses. But despite these dramatic changes, and the effects of the new census category on some government programs (Hochschild, Weaver, and Burch 2012: 61), American policy coalitions continue to divide along racial lines (King and Smith 2011).

### Race-Based Coalitions and Movement–Countermovement Interaction

Fifty years after the civil rights movement and the extension of voting rights to black Americans, most white Americans support racial equality, and there is a widespread belief across the United States that racism has

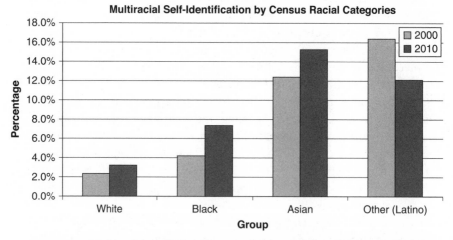

FIGURE 4.3. Multiracial Self-Identification in the 2000 and 2010 Censuses. *Source*: Jennifer Lee, "A Post-Racial Society or a Diversity Paradox?" http://www. russellsage.org/research/post-racial-society-or-diversity-paradox. Reprinted with permission from the Russell Sage Foundation.

declined (Kinder and Sanders 1996).[26] In this view, the persistence of racism is "an anomaly," a view most closely associated with Gunnar Myrdal's epochal *American Dilemma* (1944; also see Hochschild 1984: 5 for a critique). Few Americans today openly use the language of racism. But American politics is divided profoundly along the lines, not simply of race, but of race-based policy coalitions: a "color blind individual rights-based coalition" and a "race-conscious collective-rights coalition" (King and Smith 2011). Racist language plays no role in the dialectic between these two coalitions. In fact, as Michelle Alexander writes, "In the era of colorblindness, it is no longer socially permissible to use race, explicitly, as a justification for discrimination, exclusion, and social contempt. So we don't" (Alexander 2010: 2).

Documenting this shift, Donald Kinder and Lynn Sanders wrote in the 1990s, "Racial prejudice today is not what it once was; its public expression and private language are different now from what they were in the age of slavery" (Kinder and Sanders 1996: 94). Similarly, Joseph Margulies writes, "attachment to the raw racism of the Jim Crow era has all but disappeared" (2013: 70). Public opinion polls provide evidence for the change, from the sharp decline in the number of people who believe black Americans are inherently inferior to the more recent rise in the percentage of people who support racially mixed marriages.

But the surveys also show that there has been a growth of "symbolic racism" since the end of the civil rights era.[27] In place of the naked insults of Jim Crow era biological racism, a coded language has developed to silently label black Americans as undeserving beneficiaries of government largesse. As Rodgers observes,

> States' rights, law and order, the rights of private property and free association; family breakdown, crime, poverty, neighborhood schools, and bussing; the tyranny of government bureaucrats and liberal social engineers and the overreach of activist judges: into these code words conservative anger at the destabilization of the racial order flowed. (Rodgers 2011: 127)

The election and reelection of a mixed-race president in 2008 and 2012 did not still the voices of symbolic racism. On the contrary, on the Right – and not only the lunatic right – Obama has been condemned as

---

[26] This section is in debt to the fundamental contributions of Rogers Smith (especially 1997 and 2010), Daniel Rodgers (2011: Ch. 4), and King and Smith (2011).

[27] The debate over symbolic racism can be traced from McConahay and Hough's pathbreaking article (1976) to Sears and Henry (2005), with a good deal of debate and disagreement in between.

a Muslim, as a noncitizen, as a president who has taken America away from Americans, as someone who does not share American values, and even as someone who was not born in the United States. Although the assertions of the "birther movement" – which insists, against irrefutable evidence, that Obama was born abroad – is the most bizarre of these claims, more typical was the claim of former New Hampshire governor John Sununu during the 2012 election campaign that the president should learn about "Anglo-Saxon values."[28] The tea party, which emerged in response to Obama's election, has been marked by racist innuendos, too. When Theda Skocpol and Vanessa Williamson (2011) studied the attitudes of tea party members around the country, the one feature of their attitudes that they encountered more than any other was hatred for Barack Obama. Matt Barreto and Christopher Parker see this movement in a broader framework as the heir to the "paranoid style in American politics" (2013).

The most worrying issue in the current racial scene is not the invention of new racist language but the way in which the language of individual rights is used against the collective rights of black Americans. We often think of rights in a defensive form, as weapons used only "to protect and uplift the vulnerable." But political actors have also used rights offensively: "to batter despised communities, demolish existing institutions, and smash opposing ideas" (Bob 2011).[29] You saw earlier how the expansion of rights to blacks in Reconstruction was met by an ideological offensive based on classic republican principles; in the decades since the civil rights movement, a less lethal strategy based on individual rights has been mobilized to limit the reach of affirmative action and other civil rights–based policies, both in the courts and in representative institutions. This has been the ideological discourse behind a real countermovement, one that has been gathering steam since the 1960s but that took on new life with the Obama election and can be seen in such moves as efforts to restrict the vote of racial minorities and the poor in the 2012 elections.

---

[28] To be fair, Sununu was speaking to a British audience. The exact quote was, "We are part of an Anglo-Saxon heritage, and he [Mitt Romney] feels that the special relationship is special," the adviser said, adding, "The White House didn't fully appreciate the shared history we have." For this and other racially tinged Romney campaign remarks, go to http://colorlines.com/archives/2012/08/get_ready_to_debate_obamas_american_identity_again.html, visited August 25, 2012.

[29] I draw here, with permission, on Clifford Bob's research proposal, "Rights as Weapons in Political Conflict," presented at the Institute for Global and International Studies, George Washington University, March 2012.

In this episode, Republican officials showed that they were not above replaying the strategy of the Jim Crow era poll tax.

The backlash against the civil rights gains of the 1960s under the Nixon administration is well known, and under the Reagan presidency, the "southern strategy" that Nixon fashioned came into its own. Was this a reversal of the rights gained by black Americans in the 1960s? Not quite. If we look at the language of the countermovement against civil rights since the 1980s, it is not biologically racist, nor is it even a thinly disguised "symbolic racism." Instead, it has been the formation of a race-biased but rights-based "color-blind alliance" that has worked within institutions to whittle down the gains of the civil rights movement (King and Smith 2011). In Daniel Rodgers's words,

> It was the rapidity with which conservative intellectuals and policy makers who had once defended the historical and social necessity of racial distinctions moved to embrace as their own the language of equal individual changes that had once seemed so threatening. (Rodgers 2011: 127)

"This reversal on the field of rhetoric was not an idle matter," notes Rodgers, quoting a report of the conservative Heritage Foundation. "For twenty years, the most important battle in the civil rights field has been for the control of the language" (2011: 127). From the 1980s, when Ronald Reagan began the replacement of moderate-to-liberal judges with conservatives, the courts and the conservative think tanks have responded to the collective claims of the civil rights movement with the language of individual rights. "Liberals, they contended, were the new *Plessy*ites, defending collective privileges against the claims of individual merit.... A 'color-blind' America became the conservative project's goal" (ibid., pp. 128–9). The project reached its most dramatic expression in the Supreme Court's decision in the case of *Regents of the University of California v. Bakke* (438 U.S. 265) in 1978.

Here was a term – "color-blind" – that the Right wrested directly from the civil rights movement. King's anodyne sentence about individual rights (his hope that one day his children would "not be judged by the color of their skin but by the content of their character") is endlessly quoted in the white media, but his more stirring language from the same speech about the Negro being "an exile in his own land" is generally forgotten. King's praise of the "marvelous new militancy" in black America and his metaphor that African Americans and their allies had come to Washington to cash a "promissory note" at the "bank of justice" has also largely been forgotten (Rodgers 2011: 128; King and Smith 2011: 9–10). Both in the courts and in representative institutions, conservatives have fashioned a language of rights that largely ignores the *collective* nature of the rights demanded and won by the civil rights movement.

The adoption of the language of individual rights against the gains of the civil rights movement did not come all at once. At first, Republicans were silent when "white citizens councils" were formed to oppose school integration in the South. Then, in the wake of the ghetto riots under Nixon and Agnew, the GOP developed a "law and order" strategy. But echoing the more general turn toward the market in American thought, the Right eventually developed an individual-rights-oriented doctrine of color-blindness to push back against the gains of black Americans. "On the new constitutional plane," writes Rodgers, "only individuals entered the law" (2011: 134). In this spirit, the Supreme Court "moved towards progressively more narrow terrain, stripping race of more and more of its historical and institutional dimensions, contracting its social presence" (ibid., p. 135).

We usually think of movement–countermovement interaction as a struggle at the level of collective behavior (McAdam 1983; Meyer and Staggenborg 1996). But contentious interaction takes place at the symbolic and semantic levels as well. The conservative right's offensive to whittle down the gains of the civil rights movement took place at both levels: through the political offensive summarized as the Republicans' "southern strategy," and through the rhetorical individual-rights-based offensive of the courts. Rights have become a key axis of political conflict in a decades-long interaction between movement and countermovement.

## Conclusions

In their excellent study *Creating a New Racial Order* (2012), Jennifer Hochschild, Vesla Weaver, and Traci Burch see the outlines of a transformed racial order emerging in America. They are not utopian: Chapter 1 of their book points to the many obstacles to racial transformation (pp. 17–18). The book closes with a number of creative policy proposals that would advance the authors' goal of a new and fairer racial order in America (Ch. 7). Although I share the hopes of Hochschild and her collaborators, I think we are a long way from a transformation of the American racial order, as suggested by the story of Professor Gates and the Cambridge police as well as the more general structuring of American politics across the lines of King and Smith's two race-based policy coalitions (King and Smith 2011: Ch. 1).

It all begins with language. Think of the common classification of our first mixed-race president: although he has occasionally joked about being a "mutt" and makes no bones about his mixed racial background, Barack Obama is overwhelmingly classified as black both by both friends and enemies. Moreover, there is a tendency to interpret Obama as "arrogant," "elitist," and "detached," reactions we saw in his mistimed intervention in the arrest of Henry Louis Gates in 2009. Although the term "uppity nigger" was not publicly used to describe Obama's intervention in the Gates case, it was not far from the resentment of white Americans who thought he was arrogant to claim that the Cambridge police could have acted "stupidly."

Is the American population truly transforming? It is certainly true that interracial marriage has been increasing and that 16 percent of new marriages by blacks were to nonblacks (Hochschild et al. 2012: 61). But only 9 percent of whites marry outside their race, and of those who do so, the largest proportion are white males who marry Asian females. White females are about half as likely to marry black males, and half again as many white males are likely to marry black females (ibid., p. 62).

Moreover, although the debates triggered by the multiracial movement produced the addition of a new census category, that category was *not* multiracial, as advocates had hoped it would be, but the compromise solution of inviting Americans to "mark more than one" (Williams 2006: 113). And although many educational institutions – such as the Scholastic Aptitude Test (SAT) – have adopted a multiracial option on their application forms, as of 2011 most states had still not adopted the federal government's "mark one or more" classification (Hochschild et al. 2012: 59). Given the long history of racial thinking and race language in the United States, it will be a long time before the American racial order is transformed.

A substantial part of the problem is that a key plank in the language of equal opportunity policies – "affirmative action" – is anathema to most white Americans. "In 1990," writes William Julius Wilson, "almost seven in ten white Americans opposed quotas to admit black students in colleges and universities, and more than eight in ten objected to the idea of preferential hiring and promotion of blacks" (1999: 109). Although some forms of affirmative action policy are quite popular among whites (ibid., pp. 109–10), the very words "quotas" and "preferences" are like red flags to those white Americans who have come to think of rights only in individual terms.

Much of the conflict is over language. As Carol Swain argues, "The majority of Americans . . . can agree on some affirmative action–related issues once we move beyond the racially inflammatory code words found all too often in existing surveys" (1998: 22). But affirmative action has afforded a rhetorical justification for racism, as research in the "symbolic racism" tradition has shown (Bobocel et al. 1998). Although many white Americans who oppose preferential policies justify their opposition because they violate traditional norms of meritocracy, the higher the level of prejudice in the individual, the more likely he or she is to oppose generic affirmative action programs. Wilson proposes flexible, merit-based language (such as "affirmative opportunity") to neutralize white opposition to generic "affirmative action" – language that would pass muster with the courts (1999: Ch. 4). At the policy level, his proposals have much to recommend them, but I am dubious about their making much of a difference.

Although much of this book has revealed the polysemic nature of language, it has also shown how deeply embedded in society linguistic signifiers can be. "Affirmative action," "quotas," "racial preferences": these became code words for unmerited black upward mobility in the 1980s. The resentment of the white firefighter who is passed over for a black competitor; of the white parent whose child is denied entrance to a top-flight college; of the white executive who is bitter because his firm wants to meet diversity quotas – these resentments will not easily be stilled by the construction of new language or new wrinkles in affirmative action policy. Symbolic racism is by now deeply embedded in white American culture.

So what remains? Wilson (1999) offers a possible answer, and it is a political one: coalitions that can bridge the racial divide. If we look back at the three major periods of transformative change in American history – the founding; the Civil War and Reconstruction; and the reformism of the 1960s – we see that all three were marked by formation of a broad coalition for change among diverse sectors of the population based on a common program of reform. Of course, the composition of none of these coalitions was homogeneous: the success of the American revolution was the result of a carefully constructed coalition between the North, the center, and the South, symbolized by the deft regional dosage on the committee that drafted the Declaration; the Republican Party that fought the Civil War was made up of northern abolitionists, western farmers, and not a few who wanted to keep blacks out of their states; and the coalition that fought for civil rights was a combination of southern blacks and northern white liberals, with the support of a politically opportunist administration. The end of the civil rights era was marked by the decomposition of that coalition, and the greatest failure of progressive politics in America today is the failure to replace it with a truly multiracial coalition that goes beyond electoral politics.

### The Missing Progressive Coalition

The structure of American electoral politics has always encouraged the formation of coalitions across class, ethnic, and even racial lines, but not all of these coalitions have been "coalitions for reform"; most have been "coalitions for patronage" (Shefter 1977). This is particularly clear at the local level, where urban machines traditionally formed cross-ethnic coalitions and still do so in many cities. But it is also true in national politics, where the 1932 election of Franklin D. Roosevelt brought a "New Deal coalition" of liberals, white ethnic groups, and white southerners to power. As white southerners began to flee the Democratic Party after World War II, that coalition was extended to blacks, who had traditionally supported the party of Lincoln (McAdam 1999 [1982]). From that time on, black Americans have been a reliable – perhaps the most reliable – component of the post–New Deal coalition.

But that coalition is largely limited to American electoral and legislative institutions.[30] When it comes to movement politics, it is as if a wall had been thrown up between progressive white social movements, black Americans, and other minorities. Neither in the environmental movement, the peace movement, the global justice movement, nor even in the recent Occupy movement have black Americans been well represented.[31] Nor do we find significant numbers of whites participating in the civil rights groups that were once so crucial in bringing the attention of the national media to the struggles of the 1960s.

There are many reasons for the gap between black Americans and white and Hispanic groups. One reason is the cultural conservatism of

[30] For example, the Leadership Conference on Civil and Human Rights strives to bring different minority groups together in policy coalitions. Go to http://www.civilrights.org/about/ for typical campaigns. I am grateful to Rogers Smith for pointing this out to me. Note the addition of the words "Human and" to what was previously known as the Leadership Conference on Civil Rights.

[31] A survey of activists in the various Occupy movements carried out in late 2011 showed that only 1.6 percent of the occupiers were black.

many black Americans, faced by the cultural values of the new liberal Left. For example, the same-sex marriage movement has had little appeal to the sexual values of religious blacks. Second, competition in the job and housing markets between black and Hispanic Americans has contributed to the absence of a "black-brown coalition" and, indeed, to widespread hostility between blacks and Hispanics (Wilson 1999: Ch. 5). A third reason has been that many black intellectuals have been more preoccupied with their own group identities than with fashioning a multiracial coalition that could bridge the gap between black and other minority groups.[32] The paradox is that the reconstruction of race examined earlier in this chapter may have made progressive black Americans more concerned with establishing their own boundaries than with forging ties with other, similarly situated groups in American society.

I should not exaggerate: groups like the Industrial Areas Foundation and community groups in places like St. Louis and San Jose have brought activists together across the racial divide (Swarts 2008; Wilson 1999: Ch. 3). In the trade unions, "social movement unionism" has attracted black, white, and Hispanic recruits (Turner, Katz, and Hurd 2001). And although the feminist movement began as a largely white middle-class effort, black feminists have been increasingly visible in that movement (Roth 2004). But there is no interracial progressive coalition on the American Left comparable to the strong coalition among Christian conservatives, economic neoconservatives, old-fashioned nationalists, and white supremacists who militate on the Right. And that is the major challenge for black Americans, who face opponents who no longer depend on the symbols of white racism but have turned the major weapon of the black American struggle – the language of rights – into a weapon that helps preserve racial inequality.

---

[32] Space precludes entering the complex debates among black intellectuals about the construction of race over the past two decades. For a brief but lucid summary, see Rodgers 2011: 137–9.

# 5

# Gender Words

On January 11, 2012, the BBC reported that a town council in the village of Cesson-Sévigné, in Brittany decided to ban the use of the term "Mademoiselle" from the town's official business.[1] The young mayor, Michael Bihan, was elected on the slogan "*La ville pour tous*" (the town for all) but then decided he had erred: "If I had it to do over again," he confided, "my slogan would have been '*La ville pour tous et pour toutes*'" (the town for all men and all women). As the BBC pointed out, its Anglo-Saxon tongue embedded deeply in its cheek, "From now on, teenagers, graying *grand-mères*, career girls there will all be known as 'Madame,' just as men of all ages become 'Monsieur' as soon as they grow out of shorts."

To Americans who have grown accustomed to the term "Ms." to designate women of whatever age or marital status, there is nothing surprising about such a shift – except that it took so long for the French to bring it about. Consider the Ngram comparison of the use of "Ms." and "Miss" in U.S. books from the 1960s on in Figure 5.1: in the 1970s and 1980s, "Ms." became widespread, before leveling off slightly behind "Miss" in the 1990s.[2]

[1] Stephanie Holmes, "The Beginning of the End for Mademoiselle?" at www.bbc.co.uk/news/magazine-16503341. Visited January 19, 2012.
[2] A similar move occurred in Germany with the virtual disappearance of the term *fräulein* and its substitution by the word *Frau*, which was once applied only to married women.

*Author's note*: This chapter has profited from the thoughtful comments of Cynthia Bowman, Sherry Colb, Mayo Fuster, Mary Fainsod Katzenstein, Catherine Le Magueresse, Catharine MacKinnon, Jane Mansbridge, Doug McAdam, Abigail Saguy, Kathrin Zippel, and Susan Zimmermann, and from the inspiration of Conny Roggeband's work on the diffusion of sexual harassment policy (2010).

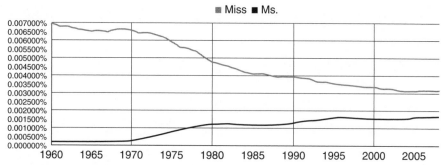

FIGURE 5.1. "Miss" and "Ms." in American Public Discourse, 1950–2008. *Source*: http://books.google.com/ngrams.

So why was this change in a small town in France worth an article in the internationally oriented BBC? First, a country that has a national academy that decides which words are French and which are not has always been conservative about its language. Second, the village of Cesson-Sévigné is in a traditionally Catholic region of France, where the *Vendée* counterrevolution broke out in the 1790s on behalf of refractory priests and unwilling conscripts: Catholic Bretons are not known for their revolutionary fervor. Third, rather than bubbling up from the grass roots, as was the diffusion of "Ms." in the United States, the change was an official act responding to an organized national movement using the tools of the Internet.[3]

The attack on *mademoiselle* came late, but it was not alone: in 1991, Parliament passed the first sexual harassment statute (Saguy 2004). But, even earlier, words had become touchstones for gender, both in ordinary speech and in movement discourse. It was in the 1920s that "birth control" became a flag of combat for some and a deeply contested term for others. This chapter traces the invention, struggle over, and decline of this contentious term in American public discourse. Then we turn to the 1960s and examine the brief life of the concept of "male chauvinism," which arose as a movement epithet in the 1970s before diffusing into common speech. Next, we turn to the concept of "sexual harassment," which entered law and public policy after its appearance in the mid-1970s. Finally, we turn to the diffusion of that term and explore how its

[3] Online sign-up forms were circulated by a group calling itself *Osez le feminisme!* (Dare to be feminist!) in 2011, inviting people to get rid of the term *madamoiselle*. Go to http://www.madameoumadame.fr/, visited August 31, 2012.

meanings evolved as lawyers and feminists struggled to implement sexual harassment policies in Europe and America (Saguy 2004: 614).

## The Rise and Decline of "Birth Control"

The feminist movement in the United States dates to the 1840s and grew up around the struggle for women's suffrage. Suffrage activists tiptoed around the practice of birth control – some opposing it and others employing the more genteel term "voluntary motherhood" (Gordon 1977: 233; 93–113). Americans remained deeply traditional about sexuality well into the next century. For example, the notorious Comstock Acts, passed in 1873 under the influence of Anthony Comstock and his Society for the Suppression of Vice, included information about contraception among its list of "obscene, lewd, or lascivious" language (Beisel 1997: Ch. 4).[4] Following passage by Congress, a large number of states passed "little Comstock acts," obliging local district attorneys and police forces to censor publications, speeches, and the sale of birth control information and materials. In 1880, Comstock reported the confiscation of more than sixty-four thousand "articles for immoral use" after the federal law's passage (ibid., p. 45).

Even as family structure and sexual mores began to shift in the 1920s, feminists, medical authorities, and civil libertarians failed to convince legislators to take the political risk of changing the laws on the diffusion of information about contraception (Kennedy 1970: Ch. 8). As late as the 1930s, the Postal Service was still actively pursuing purveyors of information about contraception. What this meant was that Americans' Puritan streak was still alive and well, but it also meant that significant numbers of Americans must have been finding ways to gain access to birth control information and contraceptive devices. It was on behalf of poor women who could not control their rates of natality that the first serious birth control movement began in America.

### Contentious Words

But there was a problem with the word "control" in "birth control": it could mean that *someone else* was controlling a woman's maternity – for example, the state – and that was precisely the intention of the eugenicists who favored the practice. Another was that it could mean women *themselves* would gain control of their bodies – a threatening idea to

---

4 Now 18 U.S.C. 1461, 18 U.S.C. 1462, and 19 U.S.C. 1305.

conservatives, whether male or female. And birth control was both a gender and a *class* issue, with undertones of racism. Judging from the size of the average family, in one form or another the practice was clearly being employed by the upper and middle classes, while the lower classes – many of immigrant Catholic background – continued to reproduce in large numbers.

One result of this imbalance was that, among some middle-class white intellectuals, a fear grew up of "race suicide" – that is, of the *white* race – giving way to the dominance of immigrant "stock." This imbalance fed into the nascent eugenics movement: "To eugenicists," writes Carole McCann, "differential fertility rates represented compelling evidence that Nordic-Teutonic America, in danger of committing race suicide, was being swamped by a 'rising tide of color'" (McCann 1994: 100). The differential birth rate among richer and poorer Americans was also visible to the Left. Noted radicals like Emma Goldman, Bill Hayward, and Eugene V. Debs supported birth control for the same reasons they supported full employment: the larger the lower-class population, they reasoned, the larger the work pool and the easier it would be to exploit the workers (ibid., Ch. 4).

Western Europeans did not appear to have the same aversion to the language of birth control as Americans (Gordon 1977: 208). In the Netherlands, under the term *geboorteperking*, Dr. Johannes Rutgers had opened a clinic to demonstrate birth control methods; in Germany, where the term used was the similar *geburtenkontrolle*, birth control methods were widely available from the 1880s on, and there was even support for legalized abortion (Woycke 1988; Bergmann 1992); in England, reformers like Havelock Ellis called for the control of natality as a necessary tool for society's evolution to a higher stage of civilization; in France, syndicalists like Victor Dave had been advocating the control of fertility since before the turn of the century, and, here and there, protests sprung up against the sexual blackmail of women workers by their foremen – the so-called *droit de cuissage* (Gordon 1977: 211–12; Louis 1994).

As in many cases when new and controversial practices emerge, the terms for birth control varied. France was typical of this unsettled linguistic repertoire. In that country, where at least thirty feminist journals were created between 1880 and 1914, in *La Fronde*, Marguerite Durand used the term "the right to voluntary maternity," similar to the American term "voluntary motherhood." Neo-Malthusians like Eugène Humbert and Paul Robin wrote of "regeneration" and "sexual education," but in this still largely Catholic country, neither writer dared employ a term that would imply interfering with the act of conception. In 1903, Humbert called for a *grève des ventres* (literally, a "strike of the wombs") in his journal *Régénération*.[5] The expression *contrôle des naissances* entered the French language only in the 1930s, apparently migrating from English and American usage.[6]

### Margaret Sanger and the Rise of "Birth Control"

In March 1914, under the influence of the anarchist and socialist ideas she had encountered in New York City, Margaret Sanger began to publish a review called *The Woman Rebel*. Under the banner "No Gods, No Masters," Sanger and a group of friends attacked capitalism and capitalists by name and also aimed their anger at philanthropists, social workers, and other lackeys of capitalism. Birth control seemed to Sanger an obvious way to help poor families stretch their meager incomes and release women from the burdens of constant motherhood. In the first issue of the journal, Sanger wrote an article "urging prevention of conception in order to frighten the 'capitalist class.'" In the June issue, she employed for the first time the term "birth control" (Kennedy 1970: 22, 23).

We do not really know how Sanger chose that particular term for the prevention of unwanted pregnancies, but its association with state control, together with its condemnation as "obscene" by the Comstock Acts, conspired to offend conservatives and church elders alike.[7] And although Sanger's articles provided no information about how to use contraceptive practices, the Postal Service found sufficient cause to declare *The Woman Rebel* illegal. On August 15, 1914, she was arraigned in the U.S. District Court for Southern New York for sending obscene materials through the mails.

After a delay, Sanger left the country, first for Canada and then for England and the continent. There she met notable feminists and advocates of birth control like Havelock Ellis, and practitioners like Dr. Rutgers, who convinced her that contraception needed to be prescribed by medical

---

[5] In 1913 there was a public debate around a similar concept – *gebarstreik* – in Germany, but that term too seems to have disappeared. I am grateful to Susan Zimmermann for this information.

[6] This paragraph draws on Albistur and Armogathe, *Histoire du féminisme français du Moyen Age à nos jours* (1977), and on the kind collaboration of Claire Andrieu and Catherine Le Magueresse.

[7] Sanger had not yet been to Europe, where similar terms were already being used. Apparently, in Germany, the parallel term *familienplanung* had already appeared, perhaps because it was more anodyne than "birth control." I am grateful to Susan Zimmermann for this information.

experts (Kennedy 1970: 26–35). Sanger's European stay convinced her that she was part of a worldwide movement, and she returned to the United States in 1915 full of ideas about and enthusiasm for birth control.

There were other reasons for Sanger's return. In her absence, her young daughter had died of pneumonia, and her husband, William, had been caught in a police trap for distributing her pamphlet and was in jail. Probably unwilling to try a grieving mother, the district attorney dropped his charges against her and the District Court dismissed them. Relieved of the threat of prosecution, Sanger opened the country's first birth control clinic in the Brownsville section of Brooklyn in October 1916. "There were two rooms, and three employees: Ethel Byrne, a nurse; Fania Mindell, a receptionist who was fluent in Yiddish," and Sanger herself (Lepore 2011: 48; also see Kennedy 1970: 83).

The response to the clinic by the poor Jewish and Italian women in the neighborhood was immediate, but so was that of the police: on October 26, police officers confiscated materials that Sanger was prescribing and recorded a lecture she had given to neighborhood mothers urging them to limit maternity. "No woman," intoned the judge who presided over the trial of Sanger and her colleagues, waving a cervical cap from the bench, had "the right to copulate with a feeling of security that there will be no resulting conception" (quoted in Lepore 2011: 49). The women were indicted under New York's "little Comstock act" for selling contraceptive devices and distributing "obscene" literature (ibid., p. 49; Kennedy 1970: 83). The charge against Mindell was eventually dropped, but Sanger and Byrne were convicted and sentenced to thirty days in jail, where the latter almost died in a hunger strike.

Sanger remained at the center of the movement for birth control. In 1921, she published a pamphlet, "What Every Girl Should Know." It frankly – for the time – discussed development, sexual desire, reproduction, and the costs of silence and ignorance. The pamphlet said little about birth control itself but argued that "there is some function of womanhood other than being a child-bearing machine" (p. 90). Sanger dedicated it to "the working girls of the world" and tried to set it in the framework of economic relations.

Sanger's radical roots, her abrasive personality, and her insistence on dominating the movement she had started were red flags to opponents and an irritant to other advocates, such as Mary Dennett of the Voluntary Parenthood League. For one thing, Sanger flirted with eugenics, appalling her old radical friends; for another, she needed to be the center of attention; third, her strategy was predominantly legislative and national, when evidence showed that the courts were the best hope for legitimating contraception (Kennedy 1970: 242–3). The key case was the bizarrely named *United States v. One Package of Japanese Pessaries* (86 F.2d 737 (2nd Cir. 1936)), in which the Federal District Court for the Southern District of New York held that the Comstock Acts could not be used to prevent the importation of diaphragms for legitimate medical use.

### The Decline of "Birth Control"

Over the next two decades, a wave of movement organizations was founded around the control of maternity. But when, after years of competing with each other, a joint commission of Dennett's American Birth Control League and Sanger's Clinical Research Bureau negotiated a merger, Sanger had made so many enemies that she was excluded from the leadership. And when, a few years later, the merged Birth Control Organization was formed, it dropped the incendiary "birth control," label, choosing the term "family planning" instead, and marginalized Sanger from the movement she had founded (Kennedy 1970: 256–7). From a contested truth around which a new movement was built, "birth control" – like Sanger herself – proved too controversial for the group's middle-class leaders and the doctors who had gained prominence within it. The new organization changed its name to Planned Parenthood Federation of America, which it remains today (Gordon 1977: Ch. 14).

Sanger and other activists had helped place the rights of women on the public agenda. But the Depression, World War II, and the cold war thrust class, economics, and foreign affairs ahead of women's issues on the public agenda, and the "old" women's movement fell into the "doldrums" (Rupp and Taylor 1987). It was only in the wake of the civil rights and antiwar movements that women began to mobilize again around issues that were primarily about gender (Evans 1980). But in the meantime, the class language of Sanger's youth was declining, and a new language of rights and difference entered the public arena (Rodgers 2011). The term birth *control* did not fit with the new rights-based discourse of the 1960s and 1970s. Figure 5.2 traces the gradual decline in the term's use from an Ngram search of Google Books in American English, and the growth of the corresponding rise of "family planning."

### Naming Men and Women

From the beginning, naming was a crucial issue for the new women's movement – beginning with the elemental question of what women

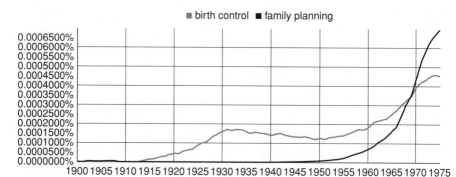

FIGURE 5.2. "Birth Control" and "Family Planning" in Books in English, 1900–1975. *Source*: http://bboks.google.com/ngrams.

themselves wished to be called (Riley 1988). In America, Adrienne Rich's *On Lies, Secrets and Silence* (1979), Carol Gilligan's *In a Different Voice* (1982), and Mary Daly's *Beyond God the Father* (1973) emphasized the dream of a common language among women. In France, Helène Cixious (1986) developed the theme of a distinct women's language. In England, Denise Riley (1988), along with feminists on both sides of the Atlantic, sought to deconstruct the very concept of women. "Feminists," writes Daniel Rodgers, "fought to make space for women's authentic voice, to release it from its external and internalized censors" (2011: 148).

But just as important as what to call women was how to name sexual relations and, particularly, what to call men, especially those who regarded women as inferior, or worse, as sexual objects. "Male chauvinism" expressed the first naming "project," and "sexual harassment" reflected the second. The first had a short life as a term of movement mobilization, whereas the second has had a long and extended career in law and public policy, both in the United States and in Western Europe.

### *"Male Chauvinism"*

The terms "male chauvinist" and its extension, "male chauvinist pig," appeared in the 1960s as part of the popularization of the new feminist movement. It evolved from an amalgam of two movement-related terms inherited from the past: "chauvinist," which came from the nineteenth-century French term *chauviniste*, was named after Nicolas Chauvin, an extreme nationalist in Napoleon's army; and "pig" was a term originally used to denigrate the police during the radical phase of the civil rights movement.

"Chauvinist" was adopted by the American Left when Stalin, in 1928, called attention to minority issues. In response to his use of the term, and to attract the support of lukewarm black workers, it was adapted from the language of nationalism by the American Communist Party to designate a racist (Mansbridge and Flaster 2007: 640–1). The term "pig" was extended by the New Left from the police to other figures of authority. Putting the two terms together produced a term of derision for men who considered that they were naturally superior to women. A similar French hybridization was *phallocrat*, a combination of the Greek term for a penis and the French term for an "aristocrat" – that is, someone who thinks the possession of a male sex organ gives him a title of nobility.

The American feminist movement soon turned to more institutional venues, where the provocative language of the 1960s would not have been welcome. As a result, both "male chauvinist" and "male chauvinist pig" begin to decline as terms of movement discourse, as Mansbridge and Flaster's data show (2007: Figure 2). The same was true in "high" culture in general: Figure 5.3 uses an Ngram search of Google Books to provide a rough idea of the appearance and decline of these two terms in American public discourse.

When it arose in the late 1960s and 1970s, the term "male chauvinist pig" had symbolic resonance for at least those feminists who were formed by the "new" American women's movement. But it lacked strategic modularity as a movement term, if only because it failed to connect to the kinds of issues that concerned women in general: equal access to jobs and salaries; breaking the glass ceiling in business and the professions; equal

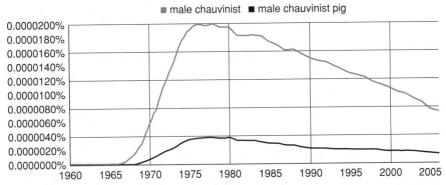

FIGURE 5.3. "Male Chauvinist" and "Male Chauvinist Pig" in American Public Culture, 1960–2008. *Source*: http://books.google.com/ngrams.

access to sports; and, increasingly, the right to abortion services.[8] The term "male chauvinist pig" was not easy to "theorize" across the spectrum of issues and groups in the women's movement (Strang and Meyer 1993).

Yet as the term disappeared from movement discourse, it diffused into ordinary speech. In a landmark article, Jane Mansbridge and Katherine Flaster reported on a conversation that Mansbridge had in Chicago in 1992 with Sonia Rice, a black woman on public assistance. Rice was describing a man of her acquaintance. "He's getting on my nerves," she said. "This one man is really touched, and I don't mean by God. He's gone. *He is a chauvinist pig. He is a chauvinist!*"

> Mansbridge: What does he do?
> Rice: He – he's a dipshit, is all.... and when I said he was a chauvinist pig, my girlfriend said, "You know it, you're right!" He really thinks he's the only rooster in the hen house. That's just what he's thinking, and he thinks when he clucks everybody's supposed to cringe. (Mansbridge and Flaster 2007: 648; italics added)

After her interview with Rice, Mansbridge asked almost everyone she interviewed, "Have you ever called anyone a 'male chauvinist'?" – a question that prompted many tales of "everyday activism" (Mansbridge and Flaster 2007: 649). She then placed a question on the 1992 and 1993 Chicago Area Survey, which showed that, in both years, 63 percent of the women interviewed reported having used the phrase. Not only that, "Although the phrase derives from the feminist movement, 58 percent of the women who did *not* describe themselves as 'feminist' in this sample said they had called someone a 'male chauvinist,'" and although the phrase is often associated with the Left, 56 percent of the women who used it called themselves "conservative" (ibid.: 649–50).[9] Even as it lost its edge as a movement term, "male chauvinist" was being normalized into everyday speech.

Sonia Rice could not have known that the word "chauvinist" was the product of the Napoleonic Empire or that, to curry favor with Stalin and his followers, American Communists adapted the term to designate

---

[8] The term may have offended liberal feminists for whom denigrating men did not seem the best way to advance the cause of women. It even risked painting feminists as "man-haters," a caricature that would carry water to the mill of the cultural Right.

[9] The data are reported in detail in the Northwestern University Survey Laboratory Chicago Area Survey (1992, 1993). The sample was representative of the English-speaking population of the Chicago area but was probably not representative of small town and rural America. I am grateful to Mansbridge for sharing these findings.

a racist. But those earlier appearances of the term helped give the symbol its resonance at the height of the women's movement, from where it migrated into ordinary speech. The same is true for many terms in the world of contentious politics: they begin as "voguewords" (Mansbridge and Flaster 2007: note 28) but are eventually normalized.[10] A term that both endured and diffused was "sexual harassment."

## Sexual Harassment

By the 1970s, the new women's movement was well established. Growing out of the consciousness-raising forums that were spawned by the New Left, it was also aimed at the indifference of male New Left leaders to women's issues (Evans 1980). Women were entering the workplace in large numbers, where they encountered strong cultural presumptions about the kind of work that was appropriate to them: secretaries, but not office managers; nurses, not doctors; teachers and social workers, not school administrators or engineers (Fuentes 1999). They also encountered the widespread assumption that women (or "girls," as they were often called) were in the office to satisfy the pleasures of their male supervisors.[11] But as the booming postwar economy and women's increasing educational achievement created new niches for women in the labor market, a number of issues – the glass ceiling, dual labor markets, and sexual harassment – were forced onto the public agenda.

Until the 1970s, women who experienced unwanted sexual advances "had few words with which to name their experience," writes Kathrin Zippel. "Women who left their jobs could not file for unemployment, because state agencies did not recognize sexual harassment as cause for quitting" (2006: 45, 46). Only in 1981 did a court rule that sexual harassment could result in eligibility for unemployment benefits (Mink 2000: 4). Even managers who believed that such complaints were valid often failed to take them seriously. Yet by 1980, well before any other advanced industrial democracy, the United States had created the Equal Employment Opportunity Commission (EEOC), which established guidelines banning unwelcome sexual advances, the creation of a hostile

---

[10] In a personal communication, Jane Mansbridge points out that "if you were to put 'groovy' next to 'male chauvinist,' it has almost the same trajectory: extremely rapid rise, peak, and gradual decline, remaining in the language but residually." I am grateful to Mansbridge for pointing out this subtle distinction.

[11] The popular TV series *Mad Men* reveals how much change there has been in overt office behavior since then.

environment, and quid pro quo sexual demands. Because it came in the wake of the Civil Rights Act of 1964, "sexual harassment" was framed as an issue of "discrimination" in the United States (Skretny 2002; Siegel 2004; Friedman and Whitman 2002–3). Abigail Saguy shows how this strategy emerged as a way of taking advantage of the existence of Title VII of the Civil Rights Act of 1964, which had banned employment discrimination on the basis of sex as well as other protected classes (Saguy 2000; 2004).

### From MacKinnon to Meritor

The term "sexual harassment," and its linkage to the discrimination frame, were widely diffused in America by the publication of Catharine MacKinnon's first book, *Sexual Harassment of Working Women*, published in 1979. "If ever words have been understood as acts," wrote MacKinnon, "it has been when they are sexual harassment" (1993: 45). The term was more widely diffused during the Clarence Thomas–Anita Hill controversy in 1991, but it was MacKinnon who gave it the definition that was eventually adopted by the EEOC, and which remains central today:

> Sexual harassment, most broadly defined, refers to the unwanted imposition of sexual requirements in the context of a relationship of unequal power. Central to the concept is the use of power derived from one social sphere to lever benefits or impose deprivations in another. (MacKinnon 1979: 1)

The 1986 Supreme Court case of *Meritor v. Vinson* (477 U.S. 57) established a broad reading of "sexual harassment," eventually leading government offices, private firms, and educational institutions to develop grievance procedures and substantive regulations to govern behavior in the workplace. As it evolved through court decisions and EEOC regulations, the term took on two meanings: what came to be called quid pro quo harassment, and the creation of a hostile work environment. If it could be proven, the claim of quid pro quo harassment depended on evidence that submitting to sexual demands was a condition of continued employment. More complicated was the question of how to give a consistent meaning to "creating a hostile environment," which could go well beyond the relations between an individual claimant and an individual defendant. For example, one of the first cases to reach the courts was filed in 1975 by Lois Jenson against vulgar and obscene behavior by coworkers, rather than against quid pro quo harassment

(*Jenson v. Eveleth Taconite Co.* 824 Sup. 847 (D. Minn. 1993)) (Zippel 2006: 45).

"Hostile environment" harassment opened the concept of sexual harassment to a wide variety of meanings and, among other things, provided a pretext for the issue to be branded as a product of "political correctness" and for defense attorneys to eventually develop a "First Amendment defense" of obscene or objectionable speech in the workplace.[12] The result was a series of court cases, of which the most influential was the case of Michelle Vinson, a black woman who was sexually abused for several years by her bank supervisor. The court held that employees have "the right to work in an environment free from discriminatory intimidation, ridicule, and insult."[13]

But the courts left unclear the mechanisms that employers would be required to use to combat these abuses until the late 1990s, when the Supreme Court decided two new cases: *Faragher v. Boca Raton* and *Burlington Industries Inc. v. Ellerth.*[14] In both cases, the legal responsibility of employers for employees' behavior was reinforced under some conditions, but the employer's responsibility was limited, in MacKinnon's phrase, to when "the quid completes the quo" – that is, until the environment is made severely or pervasively hostile (MacKinnon 2004: 685–6; also see Oppenheimer 2004). As a result, as we will see, the adjudication of sexual harassment moved away from the courts and into the private firm.

### Why in America?

Why was it the United States that pioneered in recognizing and challenging sexual harassment? One reason was the stronger tradition of sexual reserve in relations between men and women in the United States, compared with Europe's more liberal sexual environment, which European opponents often used as an excuse for not following in America's footsteps (Saguy 2004; Zippel 2006). Another was the availability of the discrimination frame, which had been legitimated in America by the civil rights movement (Mink 2000: 55–66; Zippel 50–3). A third reason was

---

[12] A good summary of the debate about the "free speech" defense against harassment claims can be found in Jack Balkin, "Free Speech and Hostile Environment" in Catharine A. MacKinnon and Reva B. Siegel, eds., *Directions in Sexual Harassment Law* (2004, Ch. 26).

[13] *Meritor Savings Bank v. Vinson*, 477 U.S. 57 (1986).

[14] 118 S.C. 1115 [1998] and 524 U.S. 742 [1998].

the strength of the American legal system in encouraging claimants to go to court, and the role of particular lawyers – like Sonia Fuentes – who went to work for the EEOC but was part of a wider network of activists (Fuentes 1999: 134). A fourth was the presence of a dynamic women's rights movement, which was evident as early as the mid-1970s, when groups like Working Women United arose out of a sexual discrimination case in Ithaca, New York, and forged links to feminists in Boston and New York (ibid., pp. 53–7). But once "sexual harassment" was named in America, there was a cascade of diffusion of both the term and efforts to regulate it in Western Europe and elsewhere.

### Diffusion and Normalization

In reflecting on the twenty-year history of sexual harassment law since the publication of *Sexual Harassment in the American Workplace*, Catharine MacKinnon writes that its recognition was "increasingly embraced and expanded, even taken as given, in the laws of nations around the world and in international forums" (2004: 677). MacKinnon is correct, as far as adoption of the *term* goes; but the diffusion of the term has not led to equivalent specification wherever it is found.

The early risers in receiving the concept of sexual harassment were the Anglo-American democracies of Canada, Australia, and the United Kingdom in the late 1970s; then Spain in 1989; Sweden in 1991; Austria, Belgium, and France in 1992; Germany in 1994, and Finland in 1995 (Zippel 2006: 17–28). With some national variations, the terms adopted overseas closely mirrored American usage, as Conny Roggeband points out (2010):

- In the Netherlands, "[i]nitially Dutch feminists decided to translate the issue as 'unwanted intimacies' (*ongewenste intimiteiten*), putting the emphasis on the right of women to define what behavior they perceived as unwanted." The concept was, however, often ridiculed in the press and on the workfloor ("what intimacies do you want?") and therefore was later replaced by the Dutch term for "sexual intimidation" (Roggeband 2010: 26).
- In France, "feminists . . . defined sexual harassment as a specific form of sexual violence in the workplace and labeled it as '*violences faites aux femmes au travail*.' The organization that took the lead in publicizing sexual harassment even included the term '*violences*' in its title (*Association Européenne Contre la Violence Faite aux Femmes aux*

*Travail* – AVFT); the French-Canadian translation '*harcélement sex-uel*' was eventually adopted."[15]

- "In Germany feminists chose the translation of '*sexuelle Belästigung*', which refers to bullying, but can also be used for physical attacks and intimidation by superiors" (Roggeband, ibid.).
- The Spanish term *acoso sexual* remained closely tied to the U.S. concept (ibid.), as did the Italian *molestie sessuale* and the Portuguese *asédio sexual*.[16]
- Even in China, the term adopted (性骚扰[*xing saorao*]) is literally "sex" (*xing*) and "harassment" (*saorao*).[17]

There were differences between the American and European meanings of the term, and they resulted from the different contexts in which it was accepted. Of these, Kathrin Zippel notes four in particular. First, the main impetus for European reform came largely from "state feminists" in gender equality offices at both the national and EU levels, compared to a stronger civil-society and lawyer-based movement in the United States; this led to a stronger administrative tradition of regulation and to a weaker influence of feminist groups and legal reasoning on the shape of eventual legislation (for example, see Saguy 2004: 605–6).

Second, given the stronger role of trade unions in Europe, the reforms relied on the implementation of workplace regulations through collective agreements between unions and employers. Although this was an advantage in some ways, in others it slowed progress, because unions were often reluctant to admit that their own members might be guilty of sexual harassment.

Third, in place of the U.S. discourse of "discrimination," which owed much to the precedent of civil rights, European advocates advanced a discourse of "dignity," which they argued was more "European" (Baer 2004; Friedman and Whitman 2002–3; MacKinnon 2004: 678).

Fourth, and most important, the "hostile environment" forms of sexual harassment, which proved so controversial in the United States, were far

---

[15] See AVFT, *20 Ans de lutte contre les violences sexuelles et sexistes au travail* (2006) for the history of this organization. Also go to http://www.AFVT.org for the flavor of its participatory-action approach.

[16] Under the Zapatero Socialist government (2004–11), a glaring case in which a mayor was accused of harassment of a local government official, a proliferation of new terms was proposed, including *violencia machista*. Thanks to Mayo Fuster for providing this information.

[17] I am grateful to Diana Fu for providing this reference and translation.

less present in European law and practice. In France, in particular, where harassment continued to be framed as a form of "violence," it was not easy to convince judges or employers that crude remarks or aggressive flirting in the workplace were a form of "violence."

### Mechanisms of Diffusion

How did the movement to sanction and regulate sexual harassment diffuse from the United States to Western Europe? Figure 5.4 lays out three processes of diffusion derived from the literature on social movements (see Givan, Roberts, and Soule 2010): *relational diffusion*, which depends on interpersonal ties between initiators and adopters of innovations; *nonrelational diffusion*, which relies on impersonal ties through the media or word of mouth; and *mediated diffusion*, which relies on the intermediation of third parties acting as translators or brokers among actors who might otherwise have no contact with one another or recognize their mutual interests (Tarrow 2005: Ch. 6).

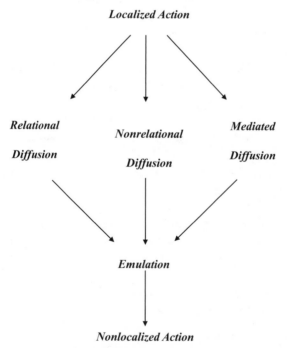

FIGURE 5.4. Alternative Pathways of Transnational Diffusion. *Source*: Sidney Tarrow, *The New Transnational Activism*, p. 105. Adapted with permission from Cambridge University Press.

All three processes were operating in the diffusion of "sexual harassment" to Western Europe:

*Relational diffusion:* as in the diffusion of the New Left from the United States to Europe in the 1960s and 1970s (McAdam and Rucht 1993), there were both formal and informal personal ties between feminists in the United States and Western Europe. "Women labor unionists, activists involved in anti-violence movements, (pro-) feminist labor experts, and academic women diffused the concept in international conferences throughout the 1980s" (Zippel 2006: 87). Activists in Europe also borrowed American strategies, such as consciousness raising, documenting harassment through surveys, and mobilizing protests around specific incidents (ibid., p. 88).

*Nonrelational diffusion:* Women in Europe and America were reading the same books on violence against women (Zippel 2006: 88). In a period in which the Internet had not yet come into its own, word of American reforms came mainly through the mainstream media. The problem was that many of these were either hostile to reform or were indifferent to sexual harassment.

*Mediated diffusion:* This pathway turns out to have been the most important in Western Europe. The lack of general receptivity to the discourse of sexual harassment in Europe left open a leading role for elite institutions – and particularly for the European Union – as brokers for the new language. Alongside its general neoliberal stance on market issues, the EU – and, in particular, the European Commission – took a progressively liberal stance on rights and, in particular, on gender equality (Alter and Vargas 2001; Caporaso and Jupille 2001; Cichowski 2001).[18] This involved a process of both upward and then downward diffusion as feminists first organized nationally, and then transnationally, before the EU passed its 2002 directive and nudged its national members to adjust to it.

Roggeband shows how two causal mechanisms – brokerage and scale shift – affected the reception and adaptation of sexual harassment in Europe. She writes,

---

[18] The commitment of members of the European Commission to sanctioning sexual harassment was no doubt through conviction but also because the commission "had been looking for issues that would consolidate its power and influence and help establish its profile as an active policy-maker" (Zippel 2006).

How sexual harassment became a central issue across Europe serves to demonstrate how diffusion is a political process in which actors at different levels adopt and adapt foreign examples to make national and transnational claims and change institutional legal settings, build alliances, and exert pressure. (2010: 22)

In particular, Roggeband points to the "brokerage" role of the EU in spurring feminists in the various European countries to push for regulatory changes that recognized sexual harassment as an offense in their respective countries (2010: 29–31), and to the shift of scale from Brussels to national governments that followed. It was the intervention of the powerful and unifying force of the EU that spurred feminists in these countries to adopt and adapt a term that many had at first considered foreign.

As it made its way from the United States to Western Europe, "sexual harassment" encountered different traditions of discourse, new institutional practices, varied political and economic interests, and different legal systems. For example, in France, sexual harassment was "legally categorized primarily as a defiant individual attack that is physically, psychologically, or morally harmful and violates the victim's free will, rather than as a form of discrimination" (Saguy 2004: 606). The result was to make verbal harassment of the kind covered in America by "hostile environment" rulings almost impossible to challenge in France (p. 604). The difficulty of getting successful prosecutions was increased after 2002, when Parliament substituted more-generic language for the more-precise 1992 statute. This led, in May 2012, to abrogation of the law by the Constitutional Court and to a new round of controversy.[19] Normalization of the concept of sexual harassment in Europe led to problems that American feminists did not encounter.

### Privatization in America
Even in the United States, the concept of sexual harassment has been normalized in ways that its original proponents may not have expected.[20] During the 1980s and into the 1990s, there was a steady increase in the appearance of the term in American public discourse. Figure 5.5 tracks

---

[19] Go to http://www.lexpress.fr/actualite/politique/harcelement-sexuel-la-loi-annulee-et-maintenant_1111247.html for an examination of this decision, which was vigorously opposed by the AVFT. The Socialist-led government promised to rewrite the law to specify behaviors that can lead to prosecution more precisely.

[20] This section is in debt to the work of Lauren Edelman and her collaborators, in particular, to Edelman, Erlanger, and Lande (1993) and Edelman, Uggen, and Erlanger (1999).

its upward progress in American books from the 1960s on. But the graph also shows a decline in its use after the mid-1990s, a decline that has continued into the new century. It is not entirely clear to what we can attribute this decline: possibly because the number of cases decided on the merits by the EEOC has declined;[21] possibly because the concept has been normalized; and possibly – following the window opened by the U.S. Supreme Court – because firms have established mechanisms for dispute resolution to meet these claims.

This last point merits further discussion. When the U.S. Supreme Court, in the *Meritor* case, decided that an employer could be sued for the harassing actions of a supervisor over his or her subordinate, it also described a grievance procedure that might hold the employer harmless (Edelman et al. 1999: 435).[22] This was the opening wedge in the creation of a private sphere of dispute regulation involving professional associations of human relations specialists. Even before *Meritor* was handed down, human relations personnel had begun to fashion grievance procedures that could insulate employers from liability for the actions of

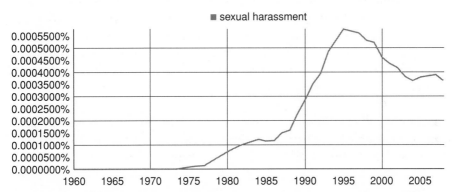

FIGURE 5.5. "Sexual Harassment" in Books in English, 1960–2008. *Source:* http://bboks.google.com/ngrams.

[21] Go to http://www.eeoc.gov/eeoc/statistics/enforcement/sexual_harassment-a.cfm. The number of submissions declined from 15,889 in 1997 to 11,717 in 2010. The proportion that led to "merit resolutions" increased in this period from 18.8% to 27.2%. The data were compiled by the Office of Research, Information and Planning from data compiled from EEOC's Charge Data System and, from FY 2004 forward, EEOC's Integrated Mission System.

[22] The Court wrote, "Petitioner's contention that respondent's failure should insulate it from liability might be substantially stronger if its procedures were better calculated to encourage victims of harassment to come forward" (*Meritor Savings Bank v. Vinson*, 72–3).

supervisors. *Faragher* and *Ellerth* gave "credence to the personnel profession's claim that employers may avoid liability where they have an internal grievance procedure in place and an employee fails to use it" (Edelman et al. 1999: 435–6). These two cases marked the definitive legal responsibility of employers for the actions of their supervisors in sexual harassment cases, but they also created the possibility of what came to be called the "Faragher-Ellerth defense" – creating internal grievance procedures that would avoid the cost and embarrassment of going to court.[23]

As the research of Laurel Edelman and her collaborators shows, grievance procedures could have problematic effects that were not envisioned when Title VII of the Civil Rights Act was passed (Edelman et al. 1993: 497). Privatizing the adjudication of sexual harassment claims increased the willingness of claimants to take action against harassment within the firm. But it also left in the hands of dispute negotiators the interpretation of the law. As Edelman's and her colleagues' work shows, employers are usually far more interested in repairing and improving relations between employees and their supervisors than in achieving redress or justice. Third, and most important, "employers' internal procedures lack some of the basic due process protections that arguably help to check bias on the part of decisionmakers and to compensate for power differences between the parties" (Edelman et al. 1993: 521).[24]

### Normalization in Europe

But what about Europe? As Gabrielle Friedman and James Whitman pithily put it, "European feminists who imagine that they are importing

---

[23] See, for example, Jathan W. Janove, "The Faragher/Ellerth decision tree: lower courts put new growth on five-year-old branches" (2003), outlining how the court's decisions affected the practice of internal grievance mechanisms five years after the Faragher and Ellerth decisions came down. Go to findarticles.com/p/articles/mi_m 3495/is_9_48/ai_108315194/?tag=content;col1 for this interesting account of how the lower courts have been interpreting these two decisions.

[24] The partial privatization of the law on sexual harassment in the workplace not only reduces the proportion of cases that go to court but also has had a reciprocal effect on the courts. As Edelman and her collaborators concluded from their statistical analysis of federal court cases from 1964 through 1997, "It would appear... that judicial recognition of grievance procedures did not motivate personnel professionals' claims and organizations' creation of grievance procedures but rather that *the courts were following institutionalized organizational practices*" (Edelman et al. 1999: 436, emphasis in original).

the American law of sexual harassment into their countries may discover that their import disturbs the local legal ecology in wholly unanticipated ways" (2002–3: 243).[25] For one thing, monetary damages – the heart of employer liability – gave way to penal penalties for convicted harassers in France (Saguy 2004: 613), where victims sometimes also receive small compensatory damages from the harasser. In addition, despite the brokerage role of the European Commission in diffusing the concept, it still had to be implemented through different national pathways in different countries (Friedman and Whitman 2002–3: 264). This meant that it was interpreted through different channels: mainly by "state feminists" in Scandinavia, legal theorists in Germany, and political parties in France, leading to different conceptual and legal normalization.

The most general conceptual shift was from the discourse of "discrimination" to that of "dignity." This was not simply because Europeans believe in "dignity" whereas Americans do not; America's 1960s history of racially oriented civil rights discrimination law was lacking in Europe. But more than this, in framing sexual harassment law, American legislators and jurists assumed a mobile labor market in which people could be fired or held back from promotion. This made the migration of "discrimination" language from race to sex appear natural. "So it is," note Friedman and Whitman, "that the Supreme Court, when it begins thinking about the nature of an 'abusive workplace,' quickly slips into discussion of 'remaining on the job, or . . . advancing in [one's career]'" (ibid., p. 267).

In contrast, in European economies, regulators could assume a stable labor market in which the concept of "discrimination" did not easily fit. Friedman and Whitman argue that Europeans talk less about "discrimination" than Americans do, in part because in the less mobile European labor market there is, traditionally, less hiring and termination. What Europeans turned to instead when they began to normalize "sexual harassment" was a focus on "dignity." "Dignity" may seem a more capacious concept than "discrimination," but it may be so capacious that it buries the distinctiveness of aggression by a woman's supervisor when she is at the lower end of a relationship of power.

Consider the case of Germany, where the concept of "mobbing" migrated from industrial psychology into the law as a general term to

---

[25] This section is in debt to the work of Gabrielle Friedman and James Whitman, "The European Transformation of Harassment Law" (2002–3).

designate abusive behavior.[26] This usage gave rise to advice clinics, popular publications, and even retreats to deal with its negative influences on the emotional health of employees, and it turned sexual harassment into a special expression for the protection of personality. Or consider the case of France, where a new penal code included a section on "offenses against the 'dignity' of the person" (Friedman and Whitman 2002–3: 267). In a wonderfully French combination of intellectual debate and political combat, it was the publication of a book, *Harcèlement moral: Démêler le vrai du faux* ("Moral Harassment: Separating Truth from Falsehood" [2001]), by a psychotherapist, Marie-France Hirigoyen, that set off a debate about the terms and conditions of employment. When the minority Communist partner in Lionel Jospin's center-Left coalition grabbed hold of the issue, Jospin's government was forced to introduce a new paragraph into the penal code criminalizing "moral harassment" (Friedman and Whitman 2002–3: 270). In French parlance, Friedman and Whitman note, "sexual harassment" is now coupled in the phrase "*moral* and sexual harassment" (ibid., p. 262). The problem for women is that talk of "moral harassment" obscures the specific nature of sexual harassment, which is exactly why the *Conseil Constitutionnel*, in 2012, abrogated the law of 2002.[27]

## Conclusions

This chapter has as its central theme the expressive role of words in the modern history of gender politics. "Birth control," "male chauvinism," "sexual harassment": these terms marked different phases and different aspects of the women's movement.

The first term arose alongside the more successful campaign for women's suffrage and endured until the less threatening term "family planning" began to displace it. By the 1980s the term "reproductive rights" began to displace that one, too.

---

[26] In their article, Friedman and Whitman describe the "anti-mobbing" movement in detail and provide copious citations. Note that the English term "mobbing" has been adopted into German from the industrial psychology literature.

[27] Friedman and Whitman see the two concepts as competitive, but other legal scholars, such as Anita Bernstein and Rosa Ehrenreich, disagree. They argue that injury suffered by women in the workplace really *is* an affront to their dignity and should be regarded as such. Others, such as Kathryn Abrams, think this way of framing the issue of harassment depoliticizes it. See Anita Bernstein, "Law, Culture and Harassment" (1994) and Rosa Ehrenreich, "Dignity and Discrimination" (1999); and, for a different view, Kathryn Abrams, "The New Jurisprudence of Sexual Harassment" (1998).

"Male chauvinism" and "male chauvinist pig" were typical products of the "new" women's movement in the 1960s, but neither one has remained prominent in feminist discourse, although both were normalized into everyday speech.

As for "sexual harassment," its rapid rise in the 1980s and early 1990s was the result of both its popularization by the new women's movement and its institutionalization through the EEOC or court decisions. Its success is shown by the decline in the number of cases dealt with on the merits by the EEOC, but that may also have been the effect of the ability of management to convince victims of sexual harassment to take their claims to grievance committees within firms.

Isn't a woman who suffers unwanted intimacies more likely to consult a friendly HR specialist down the hall than make the bold and time-consuming move to go to court or file a complaint with the EEOC? The answer is probably yes, but if words matter, to the extent that "sexual harassment" is dealt with through friendly "grievance procedures," then correcting it may come to be seen as routine negotiation of office civility. There is nothing wrong with civility; but it is not the same thing as rights. Of course, court decisions can also lead to backlash, as Americans saw with white southerners' responses to the Supreme Court's decision enforcing school integration (Andrews 2002). But the public words of a court – however wrapped in obscure legal language and hidden from the public eye – matter more for the construction of public discourse and private identity than the private words of a dispute resolution committee. The American penchant for dealing with public issues through the market has drawn part of the sting of legal opprobrium from sexual harassment.

# 6

## Citizens, Boundaries, and Nations

As the Soviet Union started to crumble in the 1980s, Yugoslavia, too, began to dissolve. Made up of a congeries of historically hostile ethnic and religious groups, the country had been held together by the will of its resistance hero, Marshall Josip Broz Tito, and by the loosely federated constitution he created (Bunce 1999; Gagnon 2004; Glenny 1992; Kaplan 1993). On Tito's death in the 1980s, central control loosened and reformist groups began to agitate within the League of Communists for political pluralism (Gagnon: Ch. 2). Conservative groups reacted against this, turning to the nationalist card as a wall against reformism. As a result of constitutional change and political polarization, the center, as Valerie Bunce recalls, "was reduced to little more than a battleground among warring republican elites" (Bunce 1999: 88, 111–12).

Some observers, such as Robert Kaplan, were quick to see the influence of the ghosts of "ancient hatreds" as the primary cause of Yugoslav disintegration (1993). Others saw the cause as the political opportunism of leaders like Slobodan Milosevic. But it was the country's federal institutions that gave Milosevic the opportunity to emphasize ethnic loyalties in Kosovo, loyalties that he then used to win allies in conservative circles and to delegitimize reformists (Bunce 1999). And it was the hope of liberal reforms triggered by the tumult in the rest of the region that gave reformers the hope of creating a liberal democracy. While the reformers put forward a message of *rebirth* along liberal lines, their claims gave Milosevic

*Author's note*: I would like to thank Shlomo Avineri, Marc Bernstein, Eitan Alimi, Mark Beissinger, Christine Leunberger, Aleksander Matovski, and Barak Mendelson for their comments on an earlier version of this chapter.

the threat he could use to develop a *redemptive nationalism* to defeat them and whip up support for a takeover of ancient Serbian-ruled territories, as well as to begin a war of expansion in Croatia and Bosnia. As the federation began to disintegrate, the military – the one surviving central institution in Yugoslavia – became the key player in a game that was ever more violent (Bunce 1999: 92–5; 117–20). We know the end of the story: civil war, irredentism, and – in the case of Bosnia-Herzegovina – genocide.

One Yugoslav republic that successfully avoided violence was Macedonia. On the southern slope of the Balkans, it was one of the most ethnically heterogeneous of Yugoslavia's republics, with a majority of Macedonian speakers and large minorities of Albanian, Turkish, Serbian, and other speakers.[1] Its territory had been historically contested from all directions, with Russian, Serbian, Bulgarian, and Turkish occupiers taking power during various stages of its history. Map 6.1 traces the rough outlines of the ancient kingdom of Macedonia, superimposed on the current boundaries of the Republic of Macedonia.

When the Macedonians declared a new state in the 1990s, calling it the Republic of Macedonia, a dispute broke out – not violent, but diplomatic – between Macedonia and neighboring Greece. The naming decision did not seem unreasonable to most people, even those who understood the checkered ethnic composition of the tiny republic. But this was not the view of the Greeks, whose northernmost region was called Macedonia, and two of whose most formidable historic heroes – Philip of Macedon and his son Alexander the Great – came from the region that was now being claimed as a name by a neighboring Slavic state.

The conflict was more than simply "verbal," because recent history raised the hackles of the Greeks. When the Greek civil war broke out after World War II, Tito had threatened to intervene on the side of the Greek Communists, hoping to gain control for Yugoslavia of both the Slavophone territory in northern Greece and Salonika on the Aegean.[2] In 1990, there was still a small Macedonian-speaking irredentist party in

---

[1] According to the 2002 census, 1,344,815 Macedonian citizens declared that they spoke Macedonian, 507,989 citizens spoke Albanian, 71,757 spoke Turkish, 38,528 spoke Romani, 6,884 spoke Aromanian, 24,773 spoke Serbian, 8,560 spoke Bosnian, and 19,241 spoke other languages. Go to http://en.wikipedia.org/wiki/Republic_of_Macedonia#Religion for these data and the original sources. Visited September 2012.

[2] Like everything in the Balkans, the civil war was complex. As Stathis Kalyvas writes, "[I]t was an exceedingly complex conflict blending ethnic and ideological conflict with such diverse participants as Slavophone Macedonians, Greek Macedonian Turkophone refugees from Asia Minor, Greek Macedonian refugees from Bulgaria and the Caucasus,

MAP 6.1. Ancient Macedonia, Contemporary Macedonia, and the Greek Macedonian Region. *Source*: http://en.wikipedia.org/wiki/Macedonia_naming_dispute.

Greek Macedonia, and a nationalist fringe within the new republic that insisted on gaining the region. The Greeks had strong memories of Tito's attempt to use the Greek civil war for his territorial ambitions.

Nothing resembling the bloodletting that was occurring in Croatia and Bosnia marked the Greek–Macedonian conflict. But even though outsiders tended to see it as a sort of comic opera, the naming controversy had real consequences, both external and internal. Externally, the Greeks worried not only about the slight to Greek civilization in the naming of a

and various groups of transient nomads – all speaking different dialects and languages."
Go to stathis.research.yale.edu/documents/kalyvascorr/spr99_000.pdf.

small Slavic country but also about the loyalty of the Slavic speakers who lived in the Greek region.[3] Internally, the dispute was inflamed by the remaining ethnic conflicts within Macedonia: with a one-third Albanian Muslim minority and two major Albanian-based parties to contend with, the leadership of the ruling Macedonian party, VMRO-DPMNE, affirmed its nationalist commitments by refusing to compromise with Greece in the naming controversy. When Prime Minister Gruevski erected a statue of Alexander the Great in the heart of Skopje, it was not only to claim him as an ethnic Macedonian hero but also to signal that he, Gruevski, was the representative of Macedonian identity. As Aleksander Matovski writes, "The more external pressure mounts against the Macedonian identity, the less willing the ethnic Macedonians will be to maintain the crucial inter-ethnic compromise with their Albanian compatriots" (Matovski 2008: 2).

The Macedonian–Greek naming controversy was about naming, but it was also about two more general features of nationalist conflict: the *redemption* of old identities, and the *rebirth* of nations:

- By "redemptive identities" I mean the development of orientations and strategies aimed at recovering rituals, practices, and territories associated with the history of a national group.[4]
- By "reborn" identities, I mean the attempt to construct new rituals and practices that break with inherited identities.

Both are strategies designed to transfer and construct systems of power; but they arise in different circumstances, take root in different subjects, and have different implications for nation building, violence, and conflict.

These two concepts guide us through the episodes of nationalism examined in this chapter. In France, between 1789 and Napoleon's seizure of power, you will see how citizen identities were mobilized, first to define a new state and then to redeem France's historical greatness. In Israel, you will see the shift in nationalist mobilization from rebirth to redemption, as an immigrant enclave became a powerful ethnic state under the banner of democracy. But before turning to these two cases, we need to clear away some underbrush about the concepts of "identities" and "boundaries."

---

[3] The Greeks say there are 10,000 of them; the Macedonians, 200,000. Both figures are improbable, but even guessing at an answer is impossible, because the Greek government does not include ethnicity in its census and recognizes only one ethnic minority – the Muslims of Thrace, who remained in Greece after the population exchanges of 1923.

[4] The term "redemption" has a broader meaning of reaching back and reinvigorating a tradition, as illustrated by constitutional lawyer Jack Balkin's *Constitutional Redemption* (2011).

## Boundary Formation and Actor Constitution

Since the pathbreaking work of Benedict Anderson, Alberto Melucci, Charles Tilly, and others, attention to identity politics has reinvigorated the study of social movements (Melucci 1988; Taylor 2009; Anderson 1991; Tilly 2002).[5] But political analysts and activists often described identities as if they were essential properties of the individuals possessing them. This use of "identity" had a primordialist tone, as if identities were labels stamped on individuals and groups from birth. There was little sense that identities might be multiple, could change throughout the life course, and could crystallize in relation to changes in the political and cultural context. Others criticized this essentialism, arguing that individual identities shift according to individuals' relationship to others, and that elites can manipulate, modify, and even invent identities to suit their purposes (Laitin 1988).

But if identity is everywhere, it might be nowhere (Brubaker and Cooper 2000). Both essentialists and nominalists missed an important part of the structuring of identities: individuals do not adopt a new identity as simply as they put on a new suit of clothes; it is the political context of resources and threats, competition, and external shock, that brings about the constitution of new actors. In particular, the identities of contentious actors are activated and changed through interaction between actors that are crystallized during "troubled times" – episodes of contention or critical junctures (Swidler 1995; Collier and Collier 1991). As one expert has written of the former Yugoslavia,

> The ethnic conflicts in the former Yugoslavia were an attempt to force a reconceptualization of ethnicity itself for political ends. The violence achieved this end by constructing ethnicity as a hard category, and ethnic groups as clearly bounded, monolithic, unambiguous units whose members are linked through ineffable bonds of blood and history and who thus have a single, objective common interest, which is identified with the status quo elites. (Gagnon 2004: 8)

Identities have largely been studied in relation to ethnic conflict, but not all identity change takes place in the context of ethnicity. All processes of nation building – and the construction of political systems in general – produce efforts by elites to subsume formally fluid and complex identities

---

[5] This discussion draws on the thinking, and on some of the language, from Charles Tilly and Sidney Tarrow, *Contentious Politics* (2007: Ch. 4), which in turn drew on Tilly's *Identities, Boundaries and Social Ties* (2005a: Ch. 9), both published by Paradigm Publishers, to which I am grateful for permission to quote from these sources.

into "a hard category." That category has both internal and external facets: external, in aiming to create a boundary between the nation and others; internal, as a tool for fashioning, mobilizing and demobilizing those inside that boundary.

Boundaries commonly take shape outside contentious politics, as a result of a complex, consequential process we can call "boundary formation" (Tilly and Tarrow 2007: Ch. 4; Tilly 2005a: Ch. 9). Once identities are formed, however, political actors regularly use them as part of contentious politics, attempting to reduce fluid and overlapping identity relations. In Macedonia, the insistence on the use of the contested term "Macedonia" was a tool both to assert the new state's place in the international system and to establish the hegemony of its political class internally; it threatened the Greeks because it claimed a prior identity for Macedonian-speaking Greek citizens.

In contentious politics, identities center on boundaries separating "us" from "them." On either side of the boundary, people maintain relations with each other: relations within X and relations within Y. They also carry on relations across the boundary: relations linking X to Y. Finally, they create collective understandings about the boundary, about relations within X and Y, and about the relations between X and Y. Those understandings usually differ from one side of the boundary to another, and often influence each other.

Boundaries between social classes, ethnic groups, religious faiths, neighborhoods, and other categories organize some of routine social life. But elites attempting to construct new collectivities typically work to activate one of these boundaries while deactivating others that could have been relevant (Laitin 1988). Once that happens, conflicts between groups are almost sure to follow.

This chapter begins with the first deliberate attempt to construct a new identity: the French Revolution's construction of the concept of the "citizen," in contrast to its opposite, the "aristocrat." I then turn to the creation of the state of Israel in 1948, and to the peculiar problems Israeli leaders faced in constructing a territorialized identity in the face of both a hostile indigenous population and their virtual absence from the land for most of the preceding two millennia. What unites these two very different episodes is that both the French Republicans and the Israeli Zionists were constructing new states around a concept – citizenship – that had both inclusive and exclusive meanings. I conclude with a reflection on the implications of the two major routes to national identity: redemption and rebirth.

## Citizenship and Nation Building in France

The concept of citizenship is an old one, going back to the Greek republics and designating the primordial unit of political association: the city (Calise and Lowi 2010: 66). But during its development, the meaning of citizenship shifted from a collective attribute, one that could not be exercised as an individual right, to an individual one (Biener 1995: 261). Medieval thinkers had no problem defining citizenship as collective, and the estate system that endured until well into the eighteenth century reflected this. As Calise and Lowi put it, "[C]itizenship respected the status and class orders of the late feudal systems. Nobility, clergy, merchants, country gentry, and perhaps others would each be accommodated with their own representation" (ibid., p. 67).

The most important result of the revolutions of the late eighteenth century was "the virtual abolition of legally recognized corporate groups and the coupling, or recoupling, of citizenship on a voluntary basis" (Calise and Lowi 2010: 68; also see Palmer 1959: 28–9). But the French Republicans were ambivalent about the meaning of citizenship: although they outlined a long list of the rights of citizens in the *Declaration des Droits de l'Homme et du Citoyen* (Rials 1982), they also retained the idea of corporate rights and duties, expressed most dramatically in the language of labor (Sewell 1980) and in the increasingly draconian restrictions on free expression that eventually overtook the emphasis on rights in the declaration. Citizenship was bound up from the beginning with the idea of collective national will.

### Shaping National Identity

Revolutionary France was probably the first place in which the language of speech, costume, and festivities was deliberately shaped to form a new national identity (Agulhon 1982; Hunt 1984; Ozouf 1988). The Parisian *sans-culottes*, so named for the ordinary trousers they wore in contrast to the fancy pants of the upper classes, more than once attacked "aristocrats" in the name of ordinary citizens. Without official sanction, republicans took matters into their own hands: "You could tell a good republican by how he dressed," notes Lynn Hunt. "The costume of a true republican was predictable, whereas the 'sell-outs' (*les achetés*) never had their own look... and the 'fat cats' (*les enrichés*) wore whatever pleased them as long as it was glittering and luxurious." "Dress," she concludes, "was not so much the measure as the maker of the man" (1984: 81, 83).

The refashioning of identities went well beyond outward signs of dress. As they responded to the contingencies of foreign invasion and domestic strife, republican elites fashioned a new concept: the citizen. In Chapter 2, you saw how the word "patriot" became part of contentious politics in Holland and America, and eventually returned to France in 1789. The term *citoyen* was not unknown under the Old Regime; it had appeared in Rousseau's *Confessions*, where he referred to himself as a "citizen of Geneva." It appeared again in the religious debates during the years running up to 1789, especially those involving the Jansenists (Plongeron 1973). It reappeared in republican guise in a controversial pamphlet of 1775 called *Le Catéchisme du citoyen*, which "emphasized the need for a citizen body fully conscious of its rights and obligations" (Baker 1990: 123). In its revolutionary incarnation, the term came to be associated with natural rights, that is, "the exercise of political rights as the expression of liberty in society" (Vovelle 2004: 20).

In defining themselves as "citizens," republicans not only set themselves off from "the aristocrats" but also tried to fashion a new man: virtuous and dedicated to the goals of the revolution; simple in dress and austere in habit; the Frenchman reborn. It is sometimes forgotten that the document we remember as the "Rights of Man" was headed "Les Droits de l'Homme *et du Citoyen*" and that when the document was renamed by the successors of the Jacobins, it was called "The Rights *and Duties* of the Citizens."[6] From a document intended to declare the rights of Frenchmen (women were another matter), the convention attempted to crystallize both the rights and the duties of a good French citizen. But the term came not only from above: in the popular societies and sectional assemblies following 1789, *citoyen* was seen as a substitute for *monsieur* and was a symbolic mark of austerity, simplicity, republican virtue, and disdain for the aristocracy (Hunt 1984). "Citizen" became a slogan for mobilization. When France, in 1792, was attacked by a coalition of hostile monarchies, it responded by building the first "citizen army."

### The Citizen Army

From Renaissance Florence onward, theorists had seen the enlistment of active citizens in the defense of their native land as a source of virtue. For example, Leonardo Bruni thought that virtue required "the fullest participation in the life of the city" and this included participating directly

---

[6] The texts of the various versions of the declaration can be found in Stephane Rials, ed., *Textes Constitutionnels français* (1982).

in its defense (Pocock 1975: 86–8). In the same tradition, Machiavelli had urged on the rulers of Florence the development of a civil militia.[7]

Teachers of French history were once fond of declaring that revolutionary soldiers invaded foreign countries with copies of the *Declaration of the Rights of Man* on their bayonets. That may not have been quite true, but the trope captures the combination of assertive nationalism and citizen mobilization that explains much of the success of the French military. For the republicans, military mobilization was valuable not only as a way to defend the state but also as a way to create republican citizens (Rousseau 1978: 101–20). Rousseau might have been counseling the future revolutionaries on how to respond to the threats on their borders when he wrote,

> As soon as public service ceases to be the main business of the citizens and they prefer to serve with their pocketbooks rather than with their persons, the State is already close to its ruin. Is it necessary to march to battle? They pay the troops and stay home. (1972)

But the use of the term "citizen" went well beyond the republican tradition to the constitution of a new actor (Gough 2010: 37). New recruits brought a revolutionary enthusiasm to the front that was lacking in the Old Regime army. But their enthusiasm could not make up for their lack of experience and discipline. Not only resistance to conscription but also defection and malingering were rife. Nor were class cleavages absent from this "citizen" army, any more than they were from French society. The citizen army, writes Isser Woloch, embodied both modern citizenship and its inequalities (1994: 316, 317).

The citizen army was a mechanism that tied (male) citizens to the state and to each other through improved education, geographic and social mobility, the integration of new immigrants, and, more than anything, the inculcation of a sense of belonging to a common community (Lynn 1983: Ch. 6). The obligation for adult males to serve in the military was the counterpart, in the military realm, of the public school and the expansion of the suffrage in the civilian one. You will see that it can also serve as an instrument for the socialization of immigrants.

### Mobilization and Demobilization

Ultimately, "citizen" was a term of division as well as one of inclusion: the mark of a boundary between republicans and "aristocrats," men and

---

[7] The classic statement is in *The Prince* (1977: 35–42, 59–63).

women, Paris and the provinces. "Citizen" was at first a symbol for the mobilization of the *sans-culottes* against the Girondins in the National Assembly; of good republicans against bad "aristocrats"; of the Parisian republic against the Vendée counterrevolution (Martin 1998); and, ultimately, of the citizen army against the invader. Propaganda spread among the troops attempted to school them in the duties of citizens as well as in the rewards – conquest, liberation, solidarity – of fighting for the *patrie* (Kestnbaum 2002).

But "citizenship" was also a concept that could be employed to demobilize potentially or actually troublesome population groups. The Abbé Sieyès, that paragon of Third Estate rights, argued that "all the inhabitants of a country must exercise the rights of a passive citizen . . . but not all of them have the right to take part actively in the choice of public policy: *not everyone is an active citizen*" (Vovelle 2004: 20, italics added). The first revolutionary constitution gave the vote only to property holders and, of course, only to males. And while the Convention of 1792 was chosen by universal manhood suffrage, the Constitution of the Year III returned to the limited suffrage of the first one.

The revolution triggered an explosion of new newspapers and clubs, among them clubs attempting to represent the rights of women. At first, such widespread participation was welcomed, but allowing women to participate in public was too much for the republicans, who suppressed women's clubs. They were willing to call women *citoyenne* but wouldn't hear of giving them the vote. As Joan Landes writes,

> Having revolted against the older patriarchy of the Father-King, fraternal men imposed on women a legally secured definition of politics – this time, the patriarchy of brothers and honorable husband-fathers. The contradiction between political democracy and private virtue was resolved in favor of a mediated existence for women in the reformed Republic. (Landes 1988: 148)

Not only did the republicans strive to demobilize women after the first flush of the revolution, but they also struggled to quiet the provincial forces that the revolution had triggered. In the west, recalcitrant priests and devout peasants revolted against the Civil Constitution of the Clergy and conscription; in the southeast and southwest, whole regions rose in federalist revolts; cities like Lyons and Marseille tried to establish their own republics. But it was mainly war that led to the practice of declaring that certain citizens were "outside the law" (*hors de la loi*) so that summary justice could be applied to them (de Mari 1991). From then on, it was a short step to the creation of a system of military justice that would operate outside – and largely subvert – the rights created with such fanfare in 1789.

What applied to individuals would eventually be applied to entire cities and *départements*. In 1791, a new law did away with the powers of military officials in "places of war" and limited these places to a carefully demarcated list of fortresses and fortified towns (Le Gal 2011). But after war was declared and the provinces began to rise in revolt, military officers increasingly used the instrument of the "state of siege" to quell dissent. In the west, the Morbihan was declared under a state of siege forty-one times, the Ille and Vilaine thirty-four times, the Deux Sèvres twenty-two times, and the Finistère seventeen times. In the south, the Hérault was placed in a state of siege twenty-nine times, the Bouches du Rhône twenty-five times, the Vaucluse twenty-five times, and the Ardêche sixteen times. Figure 6.1 traces the state of siege from Sebastian Le Gal's original work to show how the liberties of the citizen were at first gradually, and then geometrically, eroded until Napoleon came to power and turned the entire country into an armed camp.[8]

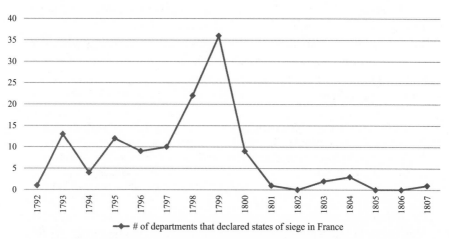

—◆— # of departments that declared states of siege in France

FIGURE 6.1. Departments That Were Declared in a State of Siege in France, 1792–1807. *Source*: Analyzed by the author from Sebastien Le Gal, "*Les origines de L'état de siège en France; Ancien Régime – Révolution*," Appendix. University of Lyons PhD Thesis, 2011.

[8] I am grateful to Le Gal for sharing his original work with me. The source of the data in Figure 6.1 is his PhD thesis (2011). The most accessible sources of his work are Le Gal 2005 and 2012.

The new era of citizenship lasted less than a decade. Under Napoleon and even more during the Restoration, the rights so theatrically created in the early 1790s were eroded and reversed. But the concept of citizenship left a heritage for nation builders that would endure until the present century. The interaction between the construction of internal and external boundaries; the mixture of the rights and duties of citizens; degrees of citizenship within the same national boundaries; and the role of the citizen army: these were a heritage of the French Revolution that would be found throughout Europe and as far away as Japan and the Middle East.

### What Has Happened to Citizenship?

In their innovative dictionary of political terms, Mauro Calise and Theodore Lowi point out that, paradoxically, once formed, the concept of citizenship began to shift back toward its earlier collective meaning. Leaving aside the collective citizenship of Soviet-type and fascist systems, in the liberal states of the West, first civil, then political, and finally social rights were established (Marshall 1964). Although the nineteenth century was a period of individualizing rights and their attachment to individuals as citizens (Calise and Lowi 2010: 69), social rights marked the beginning to a return "to a collectivist concept of citizenship and rights and to citizenship composed of several categories, applying differently to different classes of citizens – minors, women, minorities, immigrants, foreigners" (pp. 70–1). Complicating matters still further are the elements of citizenship that adhere to resident foreigners (for example, the right to vote in local elections) that have been advanced by the trend toward transnational cooperation and political union (Soysal 1994).

As a result of these trends, the term "citizen," which once seemed univocal, may be losing its clarity and its importance. The trend, if it is a trend, seems most advanced in the United States. When the concept of the citizen army gives way to a largely professionalized army backed by platoons of mercenary troops; when U.S. citizens suspected of terrorism are denied some of the fundamental rights of citizenship; when a pro-business lobbying group that seeks to legalize anonymous campaign contributions calls itself "Citizens United," then the term "citizen" may be losing its meaning. Consider one more example: in the past few years, controversies about taxation and what pundits call "entitlements" have soared in American politics. But almost never during these debates have we heard politicians talk about the rights of citizens. Looking more broadly at the language of books in American English, the Ngram analysis in Figure 6.2 shows a decline in the appearance of the term "citizen,"

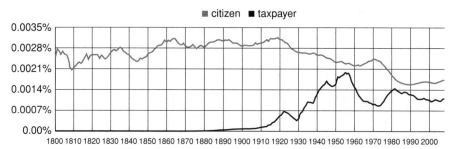

FIGURE 6.2. "Citizen" and "Taxpayer" in an Ngram Analysis of Books in American English, 1800–2008. *Source*: http://bboks.google.com/ngrams.

just as the term "taxpayer" has been increasing in usage. Nothing can symbolize more dramatically the decline of the concept of the citizen that was shaped amid great fanfare in the age of the democratic revolution than its tendency to give way to "taxpayer" in American public speech.

### Nation Building in Israel

If revolutionary France gave birth to the modern concept of the citizen, what of the "new nations" that were created on the ruins of colonialism in the twentieth century? With new elites coming to power, recently enfranchised electorates, and projects of national renewal, they would seem to be ideal sites for the construction of identities of rebirth. And indeed, when we retrace the rhetoric of the new nations formed in the post–World War II period, we encounter endless metaphors of rebirth. David Apter's *Gold Coast in Transition* – which traced the transition of the British colony into today's state of Ghana – reflected exactly this trope (1954).

But not all the "new nations" were very "new." India's history as a state goes back as far as that of its colonial master; in Africa, long regarded as empty territory by its European occupiers, new states were often superimposed on the framework of traditional kingdoms, such as the Baganda Kingdom of Uganda (Apter 1961); as for the territories composing the Ottoman Empire, many – such as Egypt – had longer histories than that of their colonial master. Many of these new states were composites of old territorial units and new ones, some more artificial than others.

Of all the states to emerge from the post–World War II period, the Jewish state that was constructed in 1947–9 between the Jordan River and the Mediterranean was the most composite (Tilly and Tarrow 2007:

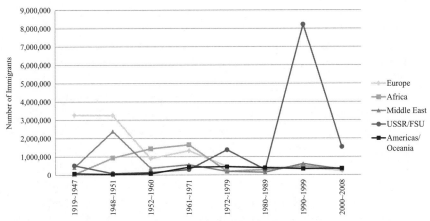

FIGURE 6.3. Immigrants to Israel, by Period of Immigration and Country of Birth or Last Immigration, 1919–2008. *Source*: http://en.wikipedia.org/wiki/Aliyah.

Ch. 8). For not only did the new state contain a significant minority of Muslim and Christian Arabs, but also most of the world's Jewish people lived in *galut* (exile) and few were Zionists before the declaration of the new state. The vast in-migration of the 1950s brought hundreds of thousands of Sephardic North African and Middle Eastern Jews to the new state, and the 1990s brought a wave of Russian Jews. Figure 6.3 traces the numbers of Jewish immigrants to Israel from 1919 to 2008, when the most recent census was taken.

The founding of the new state was unusual in several ways.

First, most of the families who took up citizenship in 1949 had been in the country for less than half a century. The first *aliyah* ("ascent") of Jewish settlement was a tiny wave that arrived between 1882 and 1903, consisting mainly of families who settled in the cities but also those who founded the first farming villages, the *moshavot*. The second *aliyah*, from 1904 to 1914, was made up mainly of individuals inspired by the Zionist movement, including many from Eastern Europe who were influenced by socialist ideas and founded the *kibbutzim*, collective agricultural settlements. The third *aliyah*, between 1919 and 1923, brought an increasing number of Labor Zionists, who settled mainly in the cities. The fourth and fifth *aliyot*, between 1925 and the postwar years, were products of the rise of Polish anti-Semitism, and then of Nazism. This was a composite population that was destined to become even more composite as waves of Jewish immigrants from the Maghreb, the Middle East, and the Soviet Union began to arrive.

Second, although the Labor Zionists from the second and third *aliyot* gained cultural superiority within the *Yishuv*, their political hegemony was never uncontested. Zionism grew out of the nationalist wave of the late nineteenth century (Avineri 1971; Lustick 1999; Sternhell 1998).[9] Alongside the Labor Zionists – who themselves divided into a "soft" and a "hard" faction – were two contesting currents: religious Zionists, who sought to redeem the entire land of Israel; and the revisionists. The latter, who eventually came to power with the Likud Party in 1977, embraced free market ideas, promoted a militaristic strategy, and contested the statism that the Labor Zionists were inclined to embrace.[10]

What was most distinct about Zionism was the fact that it arose thousands of miles away from its chosen territory, and among a dispersed and diverse population that was soon in competition with the indigenous Arab residents. Despite the claims that there was no such thing as a Palestinian nation to displace, Zionism helped create a Palestinian nationalism (Avineri 1971; Ben-Eliezer 1998: 5–6). Both Israeli and Palestinian identities were constructed on both sides of the "who I am" and "who you are" boundaries.

Before the founding of the state, the Jews in Palestine were never more than a minority of the population. For that reason – but also because of their dream of return to the Promised Land – rapid and massive immigration was seen as a primary policy priority. It was also an existential necessity after the tragedy of the Holocaust and in the face of the continued hostility of the Arab states of the Middle East and of the Palestinians; as Ben-Gurion told the Knesset, "Security is not possible without immigration" (quoted in Ben-Eliezer 1998: 207).

The military success of the Israelis in the 1948 war was due in part to support from abroad, and in part to the incompetence of the Arab armies, but it was mainly the result of the fact that the Zionist movement had been building the core of a state, an armed force, and a militaristic culture since the Arab revolt of the mid-1930s (Ben-Eliezer 1998: Ch. 2). The representative institutions created by the Zionist movement in the

---

[9] Zeev Sternhell's thesis that the Labor Zionists were at heart only nationalists caused great consternation among scholars of Zionism in Israel, some of whom – like Anita Shapira (1992, 2005) had provided a synthesis of the two strands of theory. What is certainly true is that Labor Zionism drew from both of these traditions – socialism and nationalism – as could be seen in the symbolism and the rituals of the Zionist youth movement.

[10] There were also two non-Zionist groups: the Palestinian Communist Party and the right-wing non-Zionist religious Jews, who did not believe a state could be legitimately created until the coming of the Messiah.

1930s were ready to become those of the new state, and paramilitary organizations that had been formed to protect the settlements from their Arab neighbors became the core of the future Israeli Defense Force (IDF). Youth groups, many of them with socialist orientations, offered young people military training and discipline, and a military doctrine of "strike fast and disproportionately" grew out of the methods used to defend agricultural settlements against hostile Arab neighbors.

The most unusual feature of the new state was its peculiar combination of universalism and particularism. While embracing the universalist institutions and practices of parliamentary democracy and enthusiastically joining international organizations that fought for human rights, the founders of the new state passed no written constitution, had nothing resembling a Bill of Rights, and made no bones of the fact that they intended to create a Jewish state, in a country in which Muslims and Christians constituted a substantial proportion of the population. "Citizenship" in Israel has as many lacunae and contradictions as it did in the first French republic.

## Creating the "New Jew"

The transformation of Jewish identity from a mainly religious to an ethnic–national one had already begun in Europe in the late nineteenth century. Part of the reason was the Jewish reaction to the rise of Eastern European nationalisms; part of it was the influence of the Jewish enlightenment (*Haskala*), with its secular bent, which strove to redefine Jewish identity in ethnic, cultural, and linguistic terms; and part was the rise of a new, racist form of anti-Semitism in east-central Europe and in Russia.

There was a general rise of political anti-Semitism around the turn of the century, even in the more "evolved" nations of Europe – for example, the notorious framing of Colonel Alfred Dreyfus in France and the election of Karl Lueger, a virulently anti-Semitic mayor of "civilized" Vienna. There was also a rise in cultural anti-Semitism: as Anita Shapira writes, "Newspapers and popular literature cultivated the stereotype of the sly and cunning Jew, devious, cowardly, overly ambitious, ugly" (Shapira 1992: 3).

The Zionists who settled Palestine in the first half of the twentieth century were loath to take the Jewish image from Europe with them. Many were socialists who shared the anti-Semites' view of the Eastern European Jew as parasitic, urban, money-grubbing. In contrast, Hebrew existence in the homeland in biblical times was seen as a golden age. Many preferred to call themselves "Hebrew" rather than "Jewish." "Sabra," a term that referred to the prickly pear – tough on the outside and sweet on the inside – began to be used to refer to the native-born rural settlers.[11] These locutions were fashioned to denote the growing distinction between the Jew of the Diaspora and the new native Jew of Palestine: rural, direct, militant, and masculine (Almog 2000: 4; Shapira 1992: 8). Ironically, the indigenous Arab population was increasingly constructed much as European anti-Semites had constructed the Jew: wily, devious, "sinister, menacing weavers of insidious plots" (Ben-Eliezer 1998: 203–6).

Integrating new Jewish citizens from diverse cultural backgrounds – including those from the Arab states of North Africa and the Middle East – lent an inevitable component of rebirth to Israeli nationalism. If Israel was not to be submerged into what many European-bred Zionists regarded as "the Levant," a new identity would need to transform the survivors of European Jewry and the expected waves of immigrants from North Africa and the Middle East. Not only were the future Israelis "new" in the sense that they were newly arrived, but also their identity would need to be shaped in a new land by a new state and its new institutions, primarily the school system and the military, and by the language that most of them had never spoken, except in prayer.

At the heart of most of the currents of thought that fed into the image of the New Jew was an admixture of the concept of the frontier and the idea of work on the land. Zionist theorist A. D. Gordon's concept of "the religion of labor" was a translation of Russian populism. But in the background of these secular ideas was the ancient dream of return to the Promised Land. This was reflected in the term chosen for immigration – *aliyah* – which had been employed as a semantic trope since biblical times: Shapira writes,

> The image of ascent to the summit of the mountain was a very natural motif to choose.... The term *aliyah* is laden with deep emotions and bestows upon the act of immigration to Eretz Israel [i.e., the land of Israel] a supernatural meaning, far beyond the limits of the prosaic equivalent *immigration*. (1992: 32)

The integration of the new immigrants was the predominant concern not only of Israel's leaders but also of its educational system and cultural

---

[11] The parallel is ironic, because the prickly pear, like the Jewish migrants themselves, was imported to Palestine and was used by Arab farmers to delineate the borders of their property. See C. Bardenstein, "Threads of Memory in Discourses of Rootedness: Of Trees, Oranges and Prickly-Pear Cactus in Palestine/Israel," *Edebiyat* (1998).

production. In the schools, children of new immigrants were relent-lessly hammered with the assumption that the land was Jewish, had only become non-Jewish through the vicissitudes of history, and would need to be settled with Jews to hold off hostile neighbors. School textbooks propagated an image of the Jews as unwilling conquerors and reluc-tant occupiers of land that the Palestinians had sacrificed through their unwillingness to accept the compromises offered by the UN and the Israeli government.

The burgeoning new cultural industry was also engaged in the identity-building project. For example, as Marc Bernstein writes of the film indus-try founded after 1948,

> The dominant mode of filmmaking which began in this period but contin-ued after the founding of the state maintained a conservative adherence to a master narrative that sought to impose a single, cohesive identity, one that was beholden to the melting pot myth that blithely expunged the eth-nic and cultural backgrounds of immigrants and marginalized individual experience. (Bernstein 2012)[12]

But at the heart of the construction of the New Jew was the central socializing institution in the country: the military.

### The Citizen Army

You saw earlier that the French revolution produced a citizen army that became an instrument for state building and nationalism. But France in 1789 already had a national identity, a national language, and a national territory that stretched back for centuries. For the Zionist elites who created the Israeli state, the task was far more difficult. As with France in 1792, they faced enemies both external and internal and felt the need to move quickly to defend themselves. But unlike the French republicans, they had to build a state at the same time as they created a nation; and their population was diverse and was destined to become more so, as waves of European, Middle Eastern, and North African immigrants arrived. "Since everything depends on the people as a whole and on all the people," Ben-Gurion declared, "we must ask ourselves a question that no other people asks: Are we a nation?" (quoted in Ben-Eliezer 1998: 199–200)

---

[12] Typical in this regard were the Bourekas films, those highly popular comedies and melodramas that employed Middle Eastern and Eastern European folk traditions to resolve interethnic and interclass conflicts through the "happy ending" of assimilation to the normative "Israeli" identity, often emblematized through the "intermarriage" of characters from different Jewish ethnic groups.

His answer in the late 1940s was no.

The solution that Ben-Gurion hit upon was to turn the army into the major socializing instrument of the new state. Ben-Eliezer summarizes:

> [H]is major purpose was to familiarize the immigrants with the army project and to rebuild the immigrant as a new being, as an Israeli of a new species.... The new Jew was sanctified to be part of the new strong army, which is ready to battle Israel's enemies.... Conscription was universal; even youths fourteen to eighteen years old were placed within a security framework.... Compulsory service for males was two years. (1998: 201)

The army was responsible for running the transit camps (*ma'abarot*) for newly arrived immigrants; it looked after accommodations, transportation, food supplies, children's care, and medical aid; and most important, it taught many of them Hebrew – a Hebrew that was constructed around the nation and state-building goals of the elite. Ben-Gurion at one point forced IDF officers to adopt Hebrew names. The army, concludes Ben-Eliezer, was not depicted as the instrument of organized violence "but was overlaid with a civil image, as an intimate, friendly force" (1998: 200). It remains the most popular institution in a country whose political elites have lost legitimacy over the decades since 1948.

### Redeeming the Promised Land

The "New Jew" might be leaving behind an unregretted Diaspora and building a new identity, but he (and the image of the New Jew was almost always masculine) was also redeeming an imagined past. For some, the part of that past that was to be recovered included a vague idea of possession of what they called the "Whole Land of Israel"; for others, it was the presence of Jews in their ancestral homeland that was important; for a third group, the construction of the state was the first requisite. These differences would remain in the Israeli imaginary and, more important, in the conflicts among the various strands of Zionism after the state was established.

The partition plan of the 1947 UN declaration reflected the interests of the Great Powers but also the pragmatic decision of Labor Zionists like Ben-Gurion to take what they could get and build a state on it. Biblical Palestine was roughly remembered to have occupied both banks of the Jordan River. When the British mandate was declared after World War I, the east bank and the vast desert territory behind it was separated from the west bank of the Jordan River and administered by the British as

"Trans-Jordan." The UN not only accepted this division, but also, in its partition plan of 1947, assigned much of the west bank to an unnamed and nonexistent "Arab state," leaving Israel with a fraction of the land its leaders had historically claimed (Galnoor 1995: 284). The UN armistice following the 1948 war left Israel with somewhat more territory and assigned the remainder to Jordan, rather than engage in the questionable enterprise of creating an Arab state (ibid., p. 294). Map 6.2 compares the territory of Mandate Palestine with the map of the new state of Israel as delineated by the 1949 armistice.

The willingness of the Labor Zionists to accept the UN partition plan was largely explained by the movement's international dependency but also by the waiting strategy of its leaders. Ben-Gurion, scarcely a moderate when it came to nationalism (Sternhell 1998), brought his party around to accepting the territorial compromise but left the door open to territorial changes in the future. "Every schoolchild knows," he lectured his colleagues, "that history makes no final arrangements – not in regime and not in borders and not in international arrangements" (quoted in Galnoor 1995: 286). There were negative reactions to the territorial compromise from both the revisionist and the religious Zionist camps. The revisionists wanted to claim much more territory, "including present-day Israel, the West Bank, Gaza Strip, Jordan, and southern Lebanon" (Shelef 2010: 5). As for the religious Zionists, their rhetoric claimed everything from "the River of Egypt to... the River Euphrates – including present-day Israel, the West Bank, Gaza Strip, Jordan, Lebanon, Syria, and parts of Iraq and Turkey" (ibid.), but their practice was far more moderate.

Maps are never neutral or objective descriptions of reality (Pickles 1991). From the beginning, the new Israeli elite used mapping – and the words on the maps – to put forward their visions of the land (Leunberger and Schnell 2010). The practice began even before the new state was established, with the little blue boxes that American Jewish kids, including the author, carried around to their friends and family to collect nickels and dimes for Israel.[13] The Jewish National Fund (*Keren Kayemmet*) placed the Jordan River in the center of the map drawn on the side of the box, with the West Bank on one side and an unnamed Jordan on the other (ibid., p. 809).

Maps contain not only visual images but also verbal signals of control and hegemony. Not long after Israel was established, Prime Minister

---

[13] Go to http://secure6.austiger.com/jnf/index.cfm?Action=bluebox.

MAP 6.2. Mandate Palestine, 1922, and the Borders of the State of Israel, 1949–1967. *Sources*: http://www.mythsandfacts.org/conflict/mandate_for_palestine/mandate_for_palestine.htm and http://www.bible-history.com/maps/israel_1949.html.

Ben-Gurion appointed an official Governmental Names Commission to examine place names throughout the territory of the new state. Their orders were to "Hebraicize" the place names of Israeli territory that could be connected to past Hebrew settlements. A map that resulted from the commission's work "was placed in schools all over the country in order to 'influence the schools, their teachers and pupils, to take upon themselves the task to uproot the foreign names and to root the Hebrew names'" (Leunberger and Schnell 2010: 810). "The Israeli map and its concurrent cultural landscape thereby obliterated the Palestinian and Bedouin landscape and cultural topographies" (ibid., p. 812; also see Azaryahu and Golan 2001; Khalidi 1992).

Maps were also used to make more-deliberate political statements. In the 1950s, to remind Israelis of the vulnerability of the new state, the Labor government produced a poster in which Israel, which is "carved out and elevated from the rest of the territory, appears like a sliver surrounded by Arab territory.... The 'Arab threat' is embodied in a demonized and stereotyped faceless Arab, who from his superior territorial position threatens to destroy the constructive Jewish project" (Leunberger and Schnell 2010: 813). Israel's diminutive size, its vulnerability, and the looming presence of larger Arab lands were relentlessly portrayed to maintain the alertness of the population to danger, underscore the importance of increasing the population through immigration, and maintain the support of the foreign – mainly American – Jews defending the "little David" Israel against the looming "Goliath" of the Arab states.

Given the high level of politicization in Israeli society, it was inevitable that different political parties would use mapping images to press their claims to power. In 1981, the Likud Party, the major political representative of revisionist Zionism, published a poster that drew circles from within the West Bank – now under Israeli occupation – to the coastal cities, with artillery pieces drawn at the center of each circle to show how vulnerable the Jewish population would be from attack if these territories were returned to Palestinian control (ibid., pp. 825–6). But the most effective mapping strategy was one of naming. The Zionist movement had always rejected the old Roman-derived name "Palestine" – preferring its own term, "Eretz Israel"; it has never adopted the more neutral term "West Bank" for the territories occupied in 1967. Soon after the Six Day War, but especially after Likud took power in 1977, the Israeli government drew on biblical lore to call the area south of Jerusalem "Judea" and the area north of it "Samaria." A website designed for foreign Jewish consumption went under the label "Can Israel Be Safe without Judea and Samaria?"[14]

### Rebirth and Redemption

From the beginning, the motifs of rebirth and redemption struggled for dominance in the Israeli imagination. The Labor Zionists came with a vision of rebirth, and their imagery – the "New Jew" – reflected this vision; but gradually, symbols of rebirth gave way to symbols of redemption. Not only were Israeli maps redolent of biblical imagery but so were Israel's wars. The Israeli army began quite soon to invent scriptural references for its military operations. According to the Israeli scholar Dalia Gavirely-Nuri, 38 percent of names given to Israeli military operations and weaponry allude to the Bible. For example, Operation Yoav was intended to remind IDF recruits of the heroism of King David's military commander; Pillar of Cloud, the name given to Israel's 2009 attack on Gaza, was adopted from the book of Exodus.[15] Consider the various names used for the 1948 war. Descriptively, that war is sometimes called, simply, *Milḥemet Tashaḥ* ("the 48 war"). But the more common term is *Milḥemet ha-'Atsma'ut* ("the war of independence") or *Milḥemet ha-Shiḥrur* ("The war of liberation").

These are typical images of rebirth in nation-building nationalism, even if the British were fleeing and there was no one to be liberated from. But there was also a somewhat archaic term adopted for the 1948 war, *Milḥemet Ha-Komemiyut*, derived from the biblical root meaning "to rise or stand" or "cause to rise or stand." The word *Komemiyut* comes from the phrase "I am the Lord your God, who brought you forth out of the land of Egypt, from your being slaves to them, and I broke the bars of

---

[14] Go to http://israelmatzav.blogspot.com/2009/12/can-israel-be-safe-without-judea-and .html. This "divide and fragment" strategy was a classic tactic of colonial control; not only the Israeli Right, but also the dovish Left, used maps and naming strategies to advance its political project. The small but significant Peace Now movement produced a series of carefully drawn maps to demonstrate the Likud government's strategy of turning the Arab West Bank into a series of semiisolated enclaves, many of them surrounded by Israeli settlements – some of them illegal (Leunberger and Schnell 2010: 827–30). "Maps of the region," these authors conclude, "have become one of the many battlefields in which political conflicts over land claims are being waged" (ibid., p. 833).

[15] Sigal Samuel, "A War By Any Other Name," in www.thedailybeast.com/articles/2012/ 11/14/a-war-by-any-other-name.html.

your yoke, and made you *walk upright.*"[16] Seldom has there been a more redemptive expression in the language of a nationalist movement.

Redemption was central to the religious Zionists' vision of Israel. For example, when Ben-Gurion and the Labor Zionist leadership advanced a partition plan for Palestine in 1946, Rabbi Berlin responded in the name of the religious Mizrahi Party,

> Instead of continuing the struggle and being prepared for suffering and distress until such time as the Lord will favor his people and his estate, they [the Labor Zionists] wrote and signed a deed of sale which relinquishes the largest portion of Eretz Israel... all for the name of a state and a flag of sovereignty.... Is it permissible for the representatives of the people... to transfer the land of our forefathers, to violate a heavenly command, and to *hand over willingly* to another people that which is not theirs, but ours? (quoted in Galnoor 1995: 281)

The most potent outcome of the rise of religious Zionism was practical: its capacity to obstruct the so-called two-state solution for Israel and Palestine after 1967. Its settlement arm, Gush Emunim, became the most aggressive sector of the settlement movement (Sprinzak 1981, 1991; Hirsch-Hoefler 2008). In 2005, activists associated with the group violently resisted the evacuation of the Jewish settlements of the Gaza Strip by the government of Ariel Sharon (Alimi 2010). Their redemptive attitude toward the boundaries of the land was captured in a blog post, referring to the biblical commandment, "You Shall Possess the Land and You Shall Dwell on It!" (Numbers 33:53). The posting quotes the revered twelfth-century rabbi, the Ramban, who "states irrefutably that the conquest of Eretz Yisrael is a *mitzvah* (i.e., a blessing with the sense of a command) for Israel in every generation and that *we are forbidden from allowing any part of our country to fall into – or remain under – gentile control*" [italics added].[17]

Labor Zionism – at least after 1948 – took a more pragmatic approach to the boundaries of the land of Israel. Ben-Gurion's acceptance of partition was based on the reasoning that having a state was more important

---

[16] I am grateful to Eitan Alimi and Marc Bernstein for providing me with this information about the various namings of the 1948 war.

[17] Go to http://israelseen.com/2012/07/21/you-shall-possess-the-land-and-you-shall-dwell-in-it-parshat-masei/, visited on July 28, 2012. The site describes itself as "a labor of love that is a portal to the other side of Israel. We provide content from a wonderful array of innovative, interesting, and dynamic Israelis. Our content is rich in vision, compassion, education and understanding of the human condition."

to the Jews than possessing all the land of historic Israel. The expansion from the UN partition plan to the armistice lines of 1949 was the result of a war Israelis did not want to fight but that – once they triumphed – left them in a better strategic position than under the 1947 plan. The planting of a small number of Jewish settlements on the West Bank after 1967 was justified by strategic criteria as well. But once in place, and especially after Likud government took power in 1977, the settlement project was sustained by a redemptive ideology and with a tenacity that had little or nothing to do with security.

Redemption became the metaphoric engine of Israeli nationalism. This had its most symbolic expression when broad sectors of the Israeli public complained that President Obama, in his 2009 Cairo speech, referred to the Jewish settlement of Israel as a result of the Holocaust. "Around the world," he said, seeking Arab understanding of the tragic history of the Jews, "the Jewish people were persecuted for centuries, and anti-Semitism in Europe culminated in an unprecedented Holocaust." Israelis of Left and Right protested that the president had forgotten the three-thousand-year connection between Jews and the Land of Israel. Four years later, during his March 2013 visit to Israel, Obama tried to undo the damage of his Cairo speech by proclaiming, "I know that in stepping foot on this land, I walk with you on the historic homeland of the Jewish people. More than 3,000 years ago, the Jewish people lived here, tended the land here, prayed to God here."[18]

## Conclusions

Israel was not alone: although revolutionary France used the concept of the citizen in a progressive and universalistic mode, that concept was used to mobilize a citizen army. Not only that, the successful French military example was soon copied by Prussia, which developed a citizen army of its own and used it to inculcate the values of hierarchy, autocracy, and traditionalism in its peasant soldiers. The Prussian elite developed youth groups, student associations, societies for the navy, the church, and associations of veterans, and revived Hegel's idea that war had a cleansing effect on society. "Comprehensive mobilization enabled the state to give the conscripts, who came from every part of the country and

---

[18] Go to http://www.nytimes.com/2009/06/04/us/politics/04obama.text.html?pagewanted =all&_r=0 for Obama's speech. For Obama's back-pedaling during his 2013 visit, go to http://www.israelhayom.com/site/newsletter_article.php?id=8135.

were suspected of religious, ethnic, regional, and certainly class pluralism, a nationalist-militarist indoctrination" (Ben-Eliezer 1998: 196). In turn, the Prussian military model was adopted in Meiji Japan in the name of even more traditional military values and became a bulwark of Emperor worship and militaristic samurai values (ibid.). The trope of the "new man" also appeared in both Lenin's and Stalin's Soviet Union, where that image was used to mobilize millions of citizens to transform the economy (Bauer 1952), and in Italy after Mussolini's March on Rome in 1922, when the Italian Fascists attempted to "create a fascist self" through a deliberate cultural project (Berezin 1997).

All of these experiences showed how easily "rebirth" can give rise to "redemption": France used the images of the Roman republic to inculcate nationalism in the French people; Israel turned to biblical images to reinforce its initially secular project; Mussolini strove to re-create the image – if not the reality – of the Roman Empire; and Stalin turned to imagery drawn straight from the Tsarist autocracy to mobilize his citizens against the German invader.

Nor has redemptive nationalism been absent from America's history, and, in fact, it was revived repeatedly as new movements emerged, recalling an imagined past before Irish, Catholics, the Chinese and Japanese, Jews, blacks, illegal immigrants, and so on, appeared on the scene. For example, the 9/11 massacres resulted in "the creation of a newly insistent and imperious 'we'" that "simultaneously constructed others as outsiders" (Rodgers 2011: 260). Once again, as in the era of the Know-Nothings and the Liberty League, the "American creed" was reborn as a redemptive faith in which civic religion brushed aside civil liberties and almost destroyed the element of rule of law (Margulies 2013).

The tea party activists who showed up in revolutionary garb at town hall meetings in America in 2009–10 were also attempting to redeem a past they saw as besmirched by the Obama administration. Here is how one tea party group described itself:

> Tea Party Nation is a user-driven group of like-minded people who desire our God-given individual freedoms written out by the Founding Fathers. We believe in Limited Government, Free Speech, the 2nd Amendment, our Military, Secure Borders and our Country.[19]

There is nothing overtly racist or even nationalist in this self-description, but when Theda Skocpol and Vanessa Williamson (2011)

---

[19] http://www.teapartynation.com/.

interviewed a sample of grassroots tea party activists, they found that the sentiment that was most common among them was hatred for the United States' first black president. And this takes us to the final chapter in our exploration of the language of contention: the language of love and hatred.

# 7

## Love and Hatred

On December 2, 2012, more than ten thousand Hungarians filled Budapest's Kossuth Square to protest against resurgent anti-Semitism in that country. Marton Gyongyosi, a parliamentarian of the radical nationalist party, Jobbik, had called for Jewish citizens to be put on a registry because they were possibly a national security risk. Later, he said he had only meant to warn of the danger posed by those Hungarian Jews who served "Zionist Israel."[1] The demonstration was called not only to protest Gyongyosi's outrageous statement but also the growing threat to Hungary's fragile democracy from a rise of nationalism, racism, and anti-Europeanism. As elsewhere in Europe, extreme love of country brought risks of renascent hatred.

Jobbik had appeared in the early 2000s with a viciously anti-Roma, anti-Semitic, and generally fascistic program and a violent, skinhead fringe. In this sense, it was not much different from other far-right parties that arose in Eastern and Central Europe over the past two decades (Mudde 2007). But the association of the term "register" with the lists of Jewish citizens that the Nazis had used in liquidating more than 500,000 Hungarian Jews in 1943 sent shivers across Hungary. The despair deepened when polls showed that 8 percent of the electorate supported Jobbik, a number that likely accounted for the reluctance of the country's ruling Fidesz Party to immediately condemn Gyongyosi's

---

[1] The story was covered extensively in the European press. Go to Bloomberg.com/news/2012–12–04/Hungary's depressingly-familiar-anti-semitism.html.

statement.[2] In the past few years, trying to ward off the extremist threat to its right, the governing Fidesz Party had remained silent about the growing cult of Miklos Horthy, Hungary's wartime leader, who stood by as the Nazis deported his compatriots. Fidesz also pushed through a number of antidemocratic laws and a new constitution that elevated the Crown of St. Stephen to the status of a mythical religio-nationalist symbol (Scheppele 2000). As is traditional in this part of the world, rising nationalism brought anti-Semitism in its wake: the *Economist* reported that Orthodox Jews on the streets of Budapest now expect to hear racist remarks "almost as a matter of course as they go about their business" (December 8, 2012, p. 56).

Fear, love of country, outrage, and hatred – but also jockeying for political advantage – combined in this squalid incident. Historical memories of discrimination (Hungary was the first European state to enforce limits on Jewish participation in certain professions after World War I), extreme nationalism, class divisions, and antiforeigner sentiment were all exposed by Gyongyosi's attack. But so was antifascism and grudging resistance, as the country's president, Victor Orban, eventually condemned the suggestion of registering Hungary's Jews and met with the head of the Jewish community.

The story reminds us that strong emotions are a fundamental part of contentious politics and that these emotions intersect with and trigger other emotions. I argue that contentious language not only expresses mobilization but also stimulates emotions and drives episodes of contention. In this chapter, I introduce the themes of love and hate through a "thin" analysis of public culture regarding social movements from books in English. Then we turn to the mechanisms that mobilize atrocities and to an episode of "hate speech" in the United States. After shifting to the language of love in two American movements – civil rights and the movement for marriage equality – the chapter closes with some reflections on the interaction of love and hate in episodes of contentious politics.

## Love and Hate in Social Movement Scholarship

"There are two major passions that can unify individuals or groups for a common goal. Commonly, people are bound together by a uniform hate

---

[2] The three major political parties eventually coalesced in condemning the statement. Go to www.Economist.com/news/Europe/21567961-politicians-all-stripes-rally-protest-againstmerton-gyongyosi-speech-united-against-jobbik, visited December 10, 2012.

towards someone, something, a group, or an idea. Conversely, love for someone, something, a group, or an idea can be a similar bond.... More often than not, the bonds of hate are broken with the disappearance of the object of the hatred which makes room for the injustice to manifest again. Love, however, can be a permanent solution to any injustice provided that this love is genuine and towards the community at large."[3]

It would be comforting to think that love is a more enduring emotion than hatred in contentious politics, and we find some superficial evidence for this in public culture. When Google.com was queried for the combination of the words "love" and "social movements," there were some 1,600,000 responses, while the combination of "hate" and "social movements" produced only one-quarter as many. Google Scholar registered 59,000 hits for the combination of "love" and "social movements," against 29,800 for the opposite combination of words. Even allowing for the false positives that such crude searches are bound to produce, it does seem as if writers and scholars attach the emotion of "love" to social movements more often than "hate."[4] This, of course, may be the result of the kinds of movements we study.[5] When a range of movement sectors were searched in Google Scholar together with "love" and "hate," it turned out that "love" appeared more often than "hate" in *all* the movements analyzed – and not only in the "good" movements. Table 7.1 summarizes these results for eleven movement sectors, with "good movements" listed in the top half of the table, and "bad" ones in the bottom half.

Of course, these findings may tell us more about the preferences of scholars than about the emotional tenor of the movements they study. The urge to "bring emotions back in" has led to more research about

[3] Quoted from a blog post by Bryant Muldrew in *Education Week's Blogs*, November 20, 2012, available at http://blogs.edweek.org/edweek/democracy_and_education/2012/06/love_and_hate_in_social_movements.html.
[4] Examples of false positives are *"first* love" and "social movements" or "I hate social movements."
[5] Since the 1960s, scholars have focused more often on "good" movements, such as the peace, environmental, and women's movements, than on "bad" ones (but see Koopmans 1996; Bob 2011). Rosabeth Moss Kanter's study of deliberate communities in the nineteenth century showed how important affective commitments were in the communes that endured (1972). Verta Taylor (1995) and Verta Taylor and Leila Rupp (2002) observed the role of love in the American and international women's movement. Silke Roth studied the role of affection in a women's labor organization (2005). Deborah Gould examined a wide range of emotions in the lesbian, gay, bisexual, transgender (LGBT) community's response to HIV/AIDS (2009).

TABLE 7.1. *Mentions of "Love," "Hate," and "Love/Hate" in Various Social Movement Sectors from Google Scholar*

| Sector | (1) "love" | (2) "hate" | (3) "love/hate" | Total Hits | % of "love" | % of "hate" | % of "love/hate" |
|---|---|---|---|---|---|---|---|
| Civil rights | 50,900 | 26,700 | 21,100 | 178,000 | 28.6% | 15.0% | 11.9% |
| Feminist | 29,300 | 9,610 | 8,160 | 68,300 | 42.9% | 14.1% | 11.9% |
| Labor | 21,900 | 7,880 | 5,660 | 146,000 | 15.0% | 5.4% | 3.9% |
| Revolutionary | 17,600 | 6,170 | 4,900 | 40,000 | 44.0% | 15.4% | 12.3% |
| Environmental | 14,800 | 3,450 | 2,670 | 59,000 | 25.1% | 5.8% | 4.5% |
| Peace | 12,600 | 5,280 | 4,170 | 31,800 | 39.6% | 16.6% | 13.1% |
| Student | 10,800 | 3,790 | 2,980 | 28,000 | 38.6% | 13.5% | 10.6% |
| Nazi | 3,450 | 2,030 | 1,480 | 7,330 | 47.1% | 27.7% | 20.2% |
| Islamist | 1,580 | 921 | 520 | 6,030 | 26.2% | 15.3% | 8.6% |
| Guerilla | 567 | 235 | 161 | 1,910 | 29.7% | 12.3% | 8.4% |
| Skinhead | 210 | 274 | 156 | 475 | 44.2% | 57.7% | 32.8% |
| Total Hits | 163,707 | 66,340 | 51,957 | 566,845 | 28.9% | 11.7% | 9.2% |

*Note:* The data were calculated for each term found with the noun "movement" from Google Scholar on November 21, 2012. No account is taken in this table for false positives (e.g., "love canal," "hate crimes"). The correlation between "love" and "hate" is .578[†], between "love" and "love/hate" is .705*, and between "hate" and "love/hate" is .980*** (***p<.001; **p<.01; *p<.05; †p<.1).

positive emotions like "love" than to negative ones like hate. It is only in studies of extremist movements, such as German and Italian terrorism, that we find sustained attention to hate (see della Porta 1995).[6] To find more evidence about hatred, we need to turn to the literature on atrocities and genocide.

## The Language of Atrocity

As Helena Flam notes, "[H]ate is sadly as widespread as it is under-analyzed in the literature" (2005: 24). One reason is that "hate" and "hatred" are composed of a number of different emotions. "The common association of hatred with anger brings immediately the question of whether hatred means anything more than strong anger" (Chirot and McCauley 2006: 72). Psychologists have found several components in hate, including contempt, disgust, and a mixture of anger and fear (Sternberg 2003). "If hatred is steady and enduring," conclude Dan Chirot and Clark McCauley, "it cannot be simply an emotion or combination of emotions but must be something more like an appraisal or attitude, that is, a stable evaluative reaction to some individual or group" (ibid., p. 74).

These complexities make it especially difficult to define and recognize the language of hate among ordinary people, as we will see when we turn to the debates over "hate speech." But it should not be difficult to detect hatred among elites when they – as they frequently do in cases of violent movements – attempt to tap into and energize the feelings of ordinary people against those they want to destroy. Of course, they use organization, coercion, and political opportunities, too, but what is most striking is how often the same language mechanisms communicate hatred from violence-bent elites to their followers.

### *Mechanisms of Atrocity*

In their chillingly eloquent study, *Why Not Kill Them All?* Chirot and McCauley point out that populations that produce mass murder almost always feel a combination of disgust, fear, anger, and hate for their

---

[6] This is a striking shift from the period following World War II, when the experiences of fascism and Stalinism led scholars working in the "collective behavior" tradition to focus on the racial and class hatreds that underlay these interwar movements (Goodwin and Jasper 2006: 612–14).

victims, together with a sense of shame and humiliation, as well as that of pride and love for their own in-group (2006: Ch. 2; also see Scheff 1994).[7] We might expect these varied emotions to give rise to languages of atrocity that are just as different, but this is in fact not the case: over and over, observers have found remarkably similar linguistic tropes in the language of elites spurring on their followers to engage in atrocities. Writing of genocide, Chirot and McCauley single out "essentialization" and the "narcissism of small differences" as recurring mechanisms of appeals to genocide (pp. 81–94), but more recent scholarship has identified a somewhat broader syndrome of mechanisms, consisting of dehumanization, guilt attribution, threat construction of the enemy, and a corresponding representation of the killers as "deagentified," virtuous, and future oriented (Leader Maynard 2014).

### Dehumanization

"A wide range of theorists have observed the consistent manner in which proponents of mass violence engage in discursive, material and symbolic efforts to dehumanize their victims," notes Jonathan Maynard.[8] Part of this discourse is essentialization – "the capacity to see millions of diverse individuals as a single object" (Chirot and McCauley 2006: 82) – but another part is, more literally, representing the enemy as not human. The appearance of this linguistic trope is too common across time and space to be an accident. Communists, Jews, Ibos, Tutsis, and urban Cambodians were portrayed by American, German, northern Nigerian, Hutu, and Khmer Rouge elites, respectively, as animals, diseased, filthy, foul-smelling, vermin, lice, criminals, money grubbers, subhumans, cockroaches, malignant diseases, microbes, pests buried within, or traitors boring in (ibid., pp. 80–1).

Leader Maynard (2014) points to three routes through which dehumanization promotes atrocity: first is the basic revulsion it can cause among listeners; second, it excludes targeted groups from a society's "normal domain of moral consideration"; third, it "opens the door to an important reservoir of euphemism – once dehumanized, killing can be referred to as 'pest-control,' 'cleansing,' or 'surgery.'" Thus, Lenin

---

[7] This section is in debt to the work of a young British scholar, Jonathan Leader Maynard, who has allowed me to quote from his unpublished essay, "Rethinking the Role of Ideology in Mass Atrocities" (2014). Also see his PhD thesis, "Ideologies and Mass Violence," Oxford University, in preparation.

[8] The bibliography on this question is vast. For brief introductions, see Adam Jones (2010), Jacques Semelin (2007), and Peter Weitz (2003).

referred to the execution of whites as "cleansing"; the Nazis referred to the destruction of the Jews as "delousing"; and the Serbs regarded the liquidation of their Bosnian neighbors as "ethnic cleansing." All three tactics were used by leading authorities, who employed the media, speeches, and visual symbols to reinforce the dehumanization of their victims (ibid., p. 12).

### Guilt Attribution

The victims of atrocities are not simply portrayed as nonhuman; they are seen as outside the universe of obligation. Accusations of heinous crimes not deserving of morally restrained treatment are based on rumors, unsubstantiated assertions, and repetition of anecdotal cases and are "often sufficient to create a confident social perception of victim guilt" (Leader Maynard 2014).

Accusations of guilt can be generic (e.g., "the Jews" were responsible for the Versailles treaty) but can have specific origins: the worst massacre of black Americans in the twentieth century took place in Tulsa in 1921, based on the rumor that a black man had assaulted a white woman in an elevator. Guilt was assigned to the entire black community, and in the end about thirty-five blocks of Tulsa were burned down and more than three hundred people were killed, many in their burning homes. "It was the claim of rape, whipped up by local newspapers, that set off the incident as angry crowds of whites demanded revenge" (Chirot and McCauley 2006: 69–70).

### Threat Construction

"He who is about to commit murder presents himself as the victim. What could be more logical?" (Semelin 2007: 48) No claim is more common in justification for atrocities than the idea that the victims are bent on the destruction of their tormentors. In the Soviet Union, the campaign against the Kulaks was justified by the claim that these peasants were "undermining the foundations of the Soviet state"; in Germany, Jews were portrayed as "instigators of this war"; in Rwanda, government authorities "propagated an 'awareness' of Tutsis as threatening"; in Cambodia, Pol Pot claimed that "enemies attack and torment us" (Leader Maynard 2014). In Italy in the post–World War I period, fascist punishment squads justified their attacks on Socialist and labor union headquarters with the claim that there were brigades of Red Guards threatening the state (Lyttelton 2004). As Semelin points out, "[W]ar turns neighbors into enemies"; the Croat neighbor who goes to the police station for protection is seen as doing so to get arms with which to threaten his Serb neighbors (Semelin 2007: 143).

Threat construction usually has nothing to do with the intentions or capacities of the victims. The Italian Leftists who wanted to do "like they did in Russia" hadn't the slightest idea of how to make a revolution, but their vitriolic language so frightened the Italian bourgeoisie that it allowed the country to fall into the hands of an adventurer and a band of thugs. There was just enough evidence in the rhetoric of the Socialists to justify the construction of a threat by their fascist tormentors. The same was true in Indonesia, when hundreds of thousands of Communist youth were slaughtered in the 1965–6 coup, after Suharto and the generals blamed the PKI for the coup (Anderson and McVey 1971).

Such threat constructions are often sincerely believed. Leader Maynard points out that in the USSR, "classified senior figures in the Stalinist state really did believe that their victims and prisoners were dangerous enemies" (2014). It is striking, write Chirot and McCauley, that negative emotions and sentiments about the enemy are often stronger in the leaders than in those who actually carry out the atrocities:

> Mao talking about capitalist roaders, Stalin talking about kulaks, Hitler talking about Jews, Hutu leaders talking about Tutsis, Pol Pot talking about Cambodians with Vietnamese minds – here in the discourse of elites is where one finds the strongest evidence of anger, fear, humiliation, and disgust directed at the enemy. (2006: 91)

Like many mechanisms of contention, these three sets of mechanisms, and the routes they open up to atrocity, concatenate and reinforce one another (McAdam et al. 2001: Ch. 1). If you are ready to believe that a young black man on an elevator abused a white woman, then you are just as likely to sense a threat to white womanhood in general, and equally likely to see all black Americans as essentially nonhuman. We see far less evidence today of such biological racism in America (see Chapter 4); but we do find a great deal of abusive speech on the Internet about black Americans, Jews, Hispanics, and Muslims (Blee 2002: 78).

## Hate Speech

The Hungarian story with which I opened this chapter was atypical for the directness with which Gyongyosi was willing to publicly threaten Hungarian Jews and his willingness to recall one of the worst episodes in Hungarian history. But it is not unique; racists in democratic societies frequently make explicit reference to the Nazis to publicize their extremist views in the media and to outrage ordinary citizens. Even without the intention or the capacity to bring about the crimes they associate with, they tend to use similar mobilizing language to the dehumanization, guilt attribution, and threat construction you saw in the preceding section. A clamorous case of hate speech in the United States illustrates this similarity.

In 1977, Frank Collin – an American born, apparently, of one Jewish parent – and a few dozen followers chose to proclaim their support for Nazism in Skokie, Illinois, the home of thousands of Jews, among them a large number of Holocaust survivors. Collin wanted to organize a meeting of his "National Socialist Party of America" in Chicago wearing Nazi uniforms and insignia and carrying a large flag bearing the swastika (Strum 1999: Ch. 1). When the city demanded a large indemnity as insurance, Collin canvassed a number of suburban governments announcing his intentions, and Skokie's government, in a monument of miscalculation, agreed. When a local court denied his right to assemble there, Collin went to the Chicago chapter of the American Civil Liberties Union, which agreed to protect his right to free speech.

And what kind of speech! Collin had distributed warning leaflets carrying a headline reading "WE ARE COMING!" and bearing a swastika that was "reaching out to throttle a stereotyped Eastern European ghetto Jew." The leaflet read, in part, "Where one finds the most Jews, there one will find the most Jew haters." "I hope they're terrified," he added,

> I hope they're shocked. Because we're coming to get them again. I don't care if someone's mother or father or brother died in the gas chambers. The unfortunate thing is not that there were six million Jews who died. The unfortunate thing is that there were so many Jewish survivors. (quoted in Strum 1999: 15)

The Skokie march was never held. After the courts provided mixed signals, the City of Chicago eventually agreed to allow Collin to hold a march there, one that never took place. The only long-term effect was that a large museum and education center on the Holocaust was built in the village of Skokie.[9] But before it was over, the conflict led to a crisis in the ACLU, to a national press campaign against allowing free speech for racists and anti-Semites, to a powerful movement of local survivors whose rage at the prospect of a Nazi presence in their city led to an

---

[9] Go to http://www.ilholocaustmuseum.org/.

outpouring of grief and hatred, and to the insertion into the controversy of Meir Kahane's proto-fascist Jewish Defense League (JDL). It also led to an eruption of hateful language on the part of the survivors and their supporters: "May God strike you and your family dead," read one letter to the ACLU lawyer who had agreed to take the case (quoted in Strum 1999: 67). "If I see a Nazi marching, I will break his head," warned Kahane (ibid., p. 73); another JDL activist asked opponents of the march, "What do we want?" "Nazis dead!" responded the crowd (ibid., p. 75). The irony was that Collin, who had not yet been permitted to say a word in public, and was stopped at the exit from the freeway by a group of police, triggered an outpouring of hatred from ordinary citizens. Hate, not to put too fine a point on it, is contagious.

In spite of its notoriety, the Skokie case was only one in a series of conflicts in the United States over hate speech – a series too long and too complex to summarize here.[10] The United States is almost alone, among parliamentary democracies, for the willingness of its courts, under the First Amendment, to allow hate speech to be publicly aired almost without limitation. This contrasts with Germany, which, because of its history, has strong limitations on speech and the publication of materials with even a hint of sympathy for its National Socialist past. American jurists' grudging, but ultimately firm, support for free speech is one of the jewels in the crown of American rule of law. In the long run, as Justice Holmes argued, in a noted dissent from an opinion restricting free speech, "When men have realized that time has upset many fighting faiths they may come to believe...that the best test of truth is the power of the thought to get itself accepted in the competition of the market."[11] But in the thrust and parry of political debate, as the Skokie story illustrates, hate speech – or even its threat – can trigger hateful counterspeech. But then, so does the language of love, when it threatens existing hierarchies, customs, and inequalities.

---

[10] I am grateful to my colleague Steve Schiffrin of the Cornell Law School for his help in preparing this section. For an introduction to this complicated topic, see Schiffrin's "Racist Speech, Outsider Jurisprudence, and the Meaning of America" (1994), Lee Bollinger (1986), Ivan Hare and James Weinstein, eds. (2009), and Anthony Lewis (2007).

[11] *Abrams v. United States*, 250 U.S. (1919). Also see Richard Polenberg, *Fighting Faiths: The Abrams Case, the Supreme Court, and Free Speech* (1999). For a view of the Skokie story that applauds the courts' "free speech absolutism," see Geoffrey Stone's speech at the Skokie Holocaust Museum at http://www.huffingtonpost.com/geoffrey-r-stone/remembering-the-nazis-in_b_188739.html?utm_hp_ref=email_share. For a more reserved analysis of the Supreme Court's speech doctrines, see Schiffrin (1994).

## The Language of Love

> It's easy; All you need is love
> All you need is love.
> All you need is love, love
> Love is all you need.[12]

Students of social movements have been less optimistic than the Beatles about the redemptive qualities of love; indeed, they have recognized that love is less an emotion in a direct, reflexive sense than a complex of emotions, including joy, elevation, and pride, and ranging from romantic love to love of family and friends to love of nation, ethnic group, and religion (Chirot and McCauley 2006: 74). They have also recognized that love rises and falls within contentious communities, and it too easily gives way to rage when the messengers of love are greeted with the police dogs of hatred, as it did in the Gandhian–Christian wing of the civil rights movement. But there has been less attention paid to how the language of love can help transform the political status of marginalized groups, as you will see in the section that follows on the cause of same-sex marriage.

### Unrequited Love: The Gandhian Repertoire in the United States

> We affirm the philosophical or religious ideal of nonviolence as the foundation of our purpose, the presupposition of our faith, and the manner of our action. Nonviolence as it grows from Judaic-Christian traditions seeks a social order of justice permeated by love. Integration of human endeavor represents the crucial first step towards such a society. (James Lawson at the Raleigh Conference of SNCC, April 1960, quoted by Carson 1981: 23)

James Lawson was the most determined Gandhian in the civil rights movement. A conscientious objector during the Korean War, he had spent part of his sentence in Napbur, India, where he taught for Hislop College and had contacts with leaders of the most important Gandhian organization at the time (Chabot 2012: 140). Returning to the United States soon after the Montgomery bus boycott, Lawson determined to help build a Gandhian movement in the United States. In Nashville, he became a leader of the Christian Leadership Council, which was affiliated with Martin Luther King Jr.'s Southern Christian Leadership Conference (SCLC). There, Lawson organized a series of workshops on nonviolent direct action. "Early on," writes Sean Chabot, "the workshops focused on critically examining the idea of nonviolence, especially the Christian love

---

[12] From "All You Need is Love" by the Beatles (Lennon-McCartney, 1967).

ethic and Gandhi's philosophy" (ibid., p. 141). Lawson was convinced that "[w]hen you don't retaliate with a personal insult, but instead offer a friendly, generous gesture, that's what Jesus meant when he said 'turn the other cheek'" (quoted in Chabot, ibid., p. 141).

The Gandhian vision of love, combined with Lawson's Christian faith, was the idea that he used as he encouraged Nashville students to take part in the wave of sit-ins that were organized throughout the South over the next few months. By 1960, with the Southern sit-in movement at its peak, SCLC's Ella Baker organized a conference in Raleigh, North Carolina, to establish an autonomous youth wing of the movement. This was the conference that led to the creation of the Student Nonviolent Coordinating Committee (SNCC). Although it was King who drew the most public attention, "it was Lawson who really captured the student activists' imagination" with his concept of "the beloved community" (Chabot 2012: 145; Carson 1981: 21). The final document expressed Gandhi's philosophy in familiar Christian language, declaring that

> Love is the central motif of nonviolence.... Such love goes to the extreme; it remains loving and forgiving even in the midst of hostility. It matches the capacity of evil to inflict suffering with an even more enduring capacity to absorb evil, all the while persisting in love. (quoted in Chabot, p. 145; also see Carson 1981: 23–4)

Lawson was not alone in the attempt to "translate" Gandhian nonviolence into American conditions: from the 1930s, a series of movement missionaries, some of them clergy and others secular activists, transposed the Gandhian repertoire into American terms, blending it with Christian humanist ideas and adapting it to the peculiar conditions of the American South.[13] This was the amalgam that guided the emergence of two of the key civil rights organizations: SCLC and SNCC (Carson 1981). Lawson, who drafted SNCC's statement of purpose in 1960, emphasized again that "the moral force of sit-in campaigns enhanced their political power" (Chabot 2012: 154).

Lawson was never representative of the civil rights movement as a whole, and the moral power of love, so important in the early stages of the movement, did not endure through the tough, violence-plagued

---

[13] Chabot (2012: Ch. 4) tells this story of "translation" in detail. The key "translators" appear to have been Richard Gregg (pp. 68–72), theologians Mordechai Johnson, Howard Thurman, and Benjamin Mays (pp. 74–6), and Indian nationalists Haridas Muzumdar (pp. 72–3) and Krishnalal Shridharani (pp. 88–93).

1960s. First, as the movement shifted its focus from public accommodations to the vote, more-pragmatic tactics – such as one-on-one canvassing of black voters – took the place of the sit-ins, in which the ethic of mass passive resistance was a powerful publicly aired weapon (McAdam 1988). Second, the violent reaction of white crowds and the repressive tactics of southern police forces made it difficult for pacifists like Lawson to continue to guide the movement to maintain the ethic of nonviolence. By 1964, "the number of SNCC members who saw Gandhian nonviolence as merely a tactic grew" (Chabot 2012: 174), and a more aggressively combative attitude began to gain adherents in the movement. Even King, who had become the most articulate spokesman for the civil rights movement, retreated in part from the message of love: "I want to tell you this evening that it is not enough for us to talk about love.... Not only are we using the tools of persuasion but we've come to see that we've got to use the tools of coercion."[14] Following the bloody repression in Selma in 1965 and the rise of black power, the language of nonviolence and love largely gave way to the rhetoric of conflict and self-defense (Carson 1981: Ch. 14; Chabot 2012: Ch. 8). By the time of the ghetto riots of the late 1960s, the concept of the "beloved community" had retreated to the fringes of the movement. In a more recent movement, the language of love appears to have had greater success.

### Love Requited: Moving to Marriage Equality

Between 1993 and 2013, a movement centered on conjugal love among couples of the same sex took root in the United States, one that may eventually change the meaning of the institution of marriage. It began in far-off Hawaii, shifted to Washington D.C., and then diffused to a number of other states. As of March 2013, it ended up in the U.S. Supreme Court. Here are the main high points of its history:[15]

- In 1993, in the case of *Baehr v. Lewin*, 74 Haw. 530, 852 P.2d 44 (1993), the Hawaii Supreme Court declared that the state's refusal to grant a marriage license to a gay couple was discriminatory.
- In 1996, responding to *Baehr* and to what it saw as a threat to traditional marriage, Congress passed the Defense of Marriage Act

---

[14] Quoted in Chabot (2012: 132); also see Stewart Burns (1997: 10).

[15] A more detailed chronology will be found in the Introduction to Mary Bernstein and Verta Taylor, eds. (2013), in George Chauncey (2004), and in Michael Klarman (2012). Also see Verta Taylor et al., "Culture and Mobilization: Tactical Repertoires, Same-Sex Weddings, and Their Impact on Gay Activism" (2009).

(DOMA; HR 3396); it passed by a vote of 342–67 in the House on July 12, 1996, and by a vote of 85–14 in the Senate on September 10, 1996. The law was signed by President Clinton on September 21, 1996. It read, in part, "In determining the meaning of any Act of Congress, or of any ruling, regulation, or interpretation of the various administrative bureaus and agencies of the United States, the word 'marriage' means only a legal union between one man and one woman as husband and wife, and the word 'spouse' refers only to a person of the opposite sex who is a husband or a wife."

- A number of states followed DOMA, defending traditional marriage through either constitutional amendment, referendum, or legislative enactment.
- In 2003, two key court decisions laid the groundwork for the eventual success of the marriage equality decisions of 2012: first the U.S. Supreme Court struck down remaining state laws against sodomy (*Lawrence v. Texas*, 539 U.S. 558, June 26 2003); then, in an epochal decision, the Supreme Judicial Court of Massachusetts held, "We construe civil marriage to mean the voluntary union of two persons as spouses, to the exclusion of all others" (*Goodridge v. Department of Public Health*, 440 Mass. 309; March 4, 2003–November 18, 2003).
- Other state courts followed, legalizing same-sex marriage under their constitutions: California and Connecticut in 2008; Iowa in 2009. Meanwhile, same-sex marriage was made legal by legislation in three other states – Maine, Vermont, and New Hampshire – and the District of Columbia in 2009–10; and in New York in 2011, but it was declared illegal in a number of others. As of the end of 2011, there were eight states that in one form or another either had made gay marriage legal or were in the process of doing so, and six more, plus the District of Columbia, that recognized civil unions or domestic partnerships.
- In March 2013, the Supreme Court considered two important cases: a decision of the Ninth Circuit Court of Appeals, which had overturned a referendum denying the right of same-sex marriage in California (*Hollingsworth v. Perry* 2012); and a case challenging DOMA's denial of spousal inheritance rights to a widow of a same-sex marriage in New York State (*United States v. Windsor* 2012). As of this writing, these two epochal cases, which promise to have the same importance for sexual minorities as the Brown case did for black Americans, had not yet been handed down. Map 7.1 lays out the distribution by state

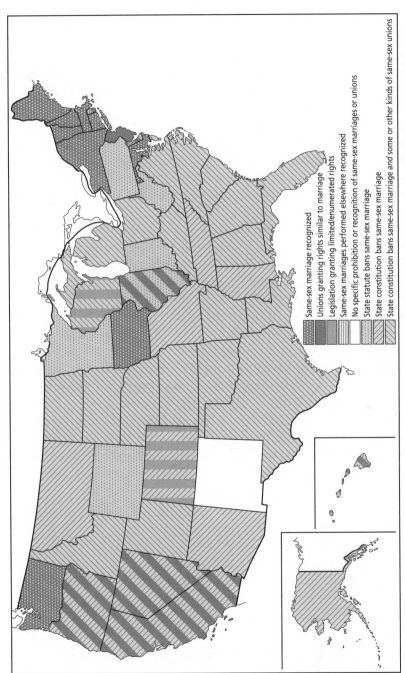

MAP 7.1. The Status of Same-Sex Marriage in the United States as of November 2012. *Source:* http://en.wikipedia.org/wiki/ Same-sex_marriage_in_the_United_States, visited November 15, 2012.

Same-sex marriage recognized
Unions granting rights similar to marriage
Legislation granting limited/enumerated rights
Same-sex marriages performed elsewhere recognized
No specific prohibition or recognition of same-sex marriages or unions
State statute bans same-sex marriage
State constitution bans same-sex marriage
State constitution bans same-sex marriage *and* some or other kinds of same-sex unions

of the progress of the marriage equality movement as of the election of 2012.[16]

Movement politics and institutional politics combined in the same-sex marriage campaign. Hawaii's decision was the fruit of an isolated effort of a gay couple and one court to legitimate their relationship; DOMA was the response of a Republican majority in Congress to restrain what its leaders saw as the "threat" of gay marriage; the Massachusetts decision was the result of an organized campaign by GLAD (Gay and Lesbian Advocates and Defenders), a movement of LGBT activists responding to the offensive of the Republican Right; and the 2012 decisions were made by electorates in four states, backed by the campaign contributions of gay rights organizations and individuals.[17]

What had changed between 1993 and 2012? First, a dramatic shift had occurred in public opinion: either because the controversy brought same-sex marriage to the attention of the public for the first time, or because society was changing in fundamental ways, attitudes toward marriage evolved dramatically in favor of an acceptance of same-sex marriage during the same period. Figure 7.1, reproducing the findings of the Pew Center for Religion and Public Life, shows the dramatic changes in the attitudes of Americans polled between 2001 and 2012 on the gay marriage issue. Young people's attitudes evolved most rapidly, but this was not simply a matter of generational change, for there was an increase in support for gay marriage among every generation of Americans polled between 2001 and 2011, from the youngest "millennial" generation to the oldest of the "silent" generation.[18]

It was not the dynamics of public opinion that brought these changes about but the actions of a dedicated set of advocacy groups, working

---

[16] Go to www.en.wikipedia.org/wiki/Same-sex_marriage_status_in_the_United_States_by_state, visited August 27, 2012.

[17] This capsule summary is drawn from Michael Dorf and Sidney Tarrow, "Strange Bedfellows, Unlikely Issues: How Same-Sex Marriage Entered the Public Arena and Who Did It," unpublished paper, Cornell Law School, N.D., itself a radical simplification of a long and complex story of movement–countermovement interaction around the issue of marriage equality.

[18] So sharp was the move from opposition to acceptance of gay marriage in public opinion that a number of major companies – including Google, Microsoft, and Amazon – contributed to the campaign for marriage equality. By July 2012, the chainstore Target's ad for its wedding registry featured two grooms nuzzling over the label "Be Yourself, Together." Go to http://abcnews.go.com/blogs/politics/2012/07/target-and-amazon-are-the-opposites-of-chick-fil-a-on-gay-marriage/, visited July 28, 2012.

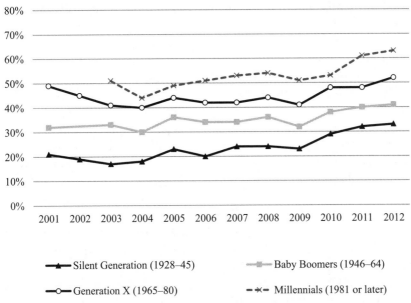

Silent Generation (1928–45)

Baby Boomers (1946–64)

Generation X (1965–80)

Millennials (1981 or later)

FIGURE 7.1. Generational Change in Attitudes to Same-Sex Marriage, 2001–12. *Note*: The graph indicates the percentages who favor same-sex marriage. *Source*: The figure is reproduced from a *Pew Research Center's Forum on Religion and Public Life* slideshow at http://features.pewforum.org/same-sex-marriage-attitudes/images/Samesexmarriage-download-slide-02.png.

through the courts, the referendum process, the legislatures, and the party system. Part of the reason for the turn to marriage may have been an increase in the appeal of monogamy for some gay men, after the HIV/AIDS epidemic created havoc in the LGBT community (Crimp 2002: 290); another was the growing empathy in the straight community, as the ravages of the disease became evident and the pain of gay couples was exposed to the public (Gould 2009).

But marriage was not always a popular cause in the organizations of the LGBT movement: during the 1970s and 1980s, in fact, most of these organizations focused much more on economic issues such as discrimination against gays in the workplace than on "cultural" issues such as marriage equality; well into the new century, a debate raged among LGBT activists about the risks of "normalization" (Duggan 2002; Warner 2000). Both because of opposition to marriage within the movement, and because of what was seen by many as the impossibility of the goal (Bernstein and Taylor 2013: 4), it was not until the 1990s that movement leaders seriously faced the issue of marriage equality.

What had happened between 1993 and 2012 to change this cautious approach within the LGBT movement? The first, and most dramatic, source of change was the Hawaii case, which produced enormous excitement at the apparent political opportunity it suggested; the second was the passage of DOMA by Congress, reflecting an anticipatory countermovement by the Christian Right (Fetner 2008; Dorf and Tarrow 2013). It was in response to this combination of threat and opportunity that organizations like GLAD, the Human Rights Campaign, and Freedom to Marry took the field to disseminate the idea of the legitimacy of gay marriage under the "equal protection" clause of the U.S. Constitution.

But the "movement–countermovement" dynamic between LGBT organizations and the Christian Right was not only a conflict among elites: when Michael Dorf and the author undertook a series of interviews with LGBT advocates in 2012, we found evidence that DOMA had triggered a grassroots surge of interest among gay and lesbian couples (Dorf and Tarrow 2013). These were people, for the most part, who had been living quietly among their neighbors and had not previously been active in the movement. After DOMA, we found, many of these couples began to put pressure on the LGBT organizations to take up the cause of marriage equality, and some began to make major donations to support the cause. This increased activism of ordinary people could be seen in the "strolling wedding parties" in California on Valentine's Day in 2004 and after the defeat of same-sex marriage in the Proposition 8 referendum in 2008 (Taylor et al. 2009: 869–73).

The increased activism of LGBT couples and organizations also produced a number of court cases that forced the judiciary as well as politicians to take more nuanced positions on marriage equality. Until the 1990s, according to Cheshire Calhoun, judges had accepted flimsy, and frequently homophobic, legal arguments against homosexual marriage (1999). Like much of the public, they assumed that gays and lesbians were incapable of romantic love. Supreme Court Justice Byron White, in the case of *Bowers v. Hardwick*, had seen "no connection between family, marriage, or procreation on the one hand and homosexual activity on the other" (478 U.S. 186, 1985). And when the Defense of Marriage Act was debated in the House of Representatives in the mid-1990s, Representative Bob Barr relieved himself of the opinion that "[t]he flames of hedonism, the flames of narcissism, the flames of self-centered morality are licking at the very foundation of our society: the family unit."[19]

---

[19] Quoted at http://abcnews.go.com/Politics/congress-evolves-doma-sex-marriage/story? id=17888075#.UMKZ2qyH_Tp, visited December 7, 2012.

The first major breakthrough came with the Supreme Court's decision to strike down a Colorado proposition that denied LGBT Coloradans protection against discrimination – protection that their municipalities had offered them (*Romer v. Evans* 517 U.S. 620 1996). *Romer* was not about marriage, but in his opinion for the majority, Justice Kennedy argued that the state legislature, by reversing municipal antidiscrimination decisions, had shown "animus" toward gay and lesbian Coloradans (ibid., p. 632). The case was important for the future of same-sex marriage, because it reflected what has become "a cross-ideological consensus that some government actions, words, and symbols are constitutionally impermissible by virtue of the meaning they convey" (Dorf 2011: 1267).

"Animus" was the major rationale of Judge Reinhardt in the *Perry* case against Proposition 8 in California. Dodging the general issue of whether denying same-sex marriage rights is unconstitutional, Reinhardt held that California's decision to offer marriage to gay couples, and then to retract the offer after a popular vote, was so arbitrary that no court could uphold it. The Second Circuit Court's decision on DOMA in New York State used similar reasoning.

### Love and Marriage

What was most striking about the campaign for same-sex marriage was that not only LGBT activists, but also politicians eager to court public opinion, increasingly came to use the language of love to describe it. The central position of lawyers in the movement had given it a rights-based foundation, both within and outside the court system. But ordinary Americans were not easily impressed with the language of rights when it was applied to gay marriage. This became clear in the failure of the gay rights coalition to beat back the campaign in California known as the "Prop 8 campaign"; there, a well-financed coalition of Christian conservatives with significant outside funding defeated same-sex marriage in a referendum after cities like San Francisco and the state legislature supported it and thousands had flocked to the City by the Bay to get married.

In the run-up to the referendum, supporters of gay marriage turned to the language of civil rights. Senator Dianne Feinstein, who had been a supporter of gay marriage since the 1978 murder of Harvey Milk, used the language of discrimination to oppose Prop 8; celebrity and actor Samuel Jackson compared the ban on gay marriage to the internment of Japanese Americans in World War II. But to the majority of Californians, marriage didn't seem to be the same as either discrimination or internment, and Prop 8 passed with a majority of 52–48 percent of the electorate.[20]

Why had the campaign for gay marriage failed in so liberal a venue as California? The easy answer was "outside money," and indeed it was a shrewd national campaign consultant, Frank Schubert, who managed the successful campaign on behalf of a coalition of churches and right-wing groups.[21] The defeat was followed by an enormous amount of polling and focus groups around the country. The major finding was that the movement was not connecting to the way most Americans thought about marriage – not in terms of rights but in terms of love and commitment. As Molly Ball summarizes,

> In survey after survey, researchers would ask people what marriage meant to them – not gay marriage, but the concept of marriage itself. And the answers were always the same: Marriage meant love and commitment. Even people who'd been divorced three times would say the same thing. Then the researchers would ask, "Why do you think gay people want to get married?" and the answers would change: They want rights and benefits. They're trying to make a political point. They don't understand what marriage is really about. Most commonly, respondents said they simply didn't know.[22]

The movement's research showed that the campaigns had erred in presenting gay marriage as something distinct from love and commitment; in the words of a Freedom to Marry research memo in the wake of the Prop 8 debacle, the most effective message was "committed, long-term gay couples doing the same thing that married couples do."[23]

Freedom to Marry began field-testing a new campaign model in Oregon, in which gay couples were shown alongside straight couples, talking about how long they had been together and how they did the laundry, shared the chores, and faced the same problems as other middle-class

---

[20] This account draws on Molly Ball, "The Marriage Plot: Inside This Year's Epic Campaign for Gay Equality," *Atlantic*, December 11, 2012, accessed at http://www.theatlantic.com/politics/archive/2012/12/the-marriage-plot-inside-this-years-epic-campaign-for-gay-equality/265865/2/.

[21] For Schubert's description of the campaign, go to http://www.campaignsandelections.com/print/176127/passing-prop-8.thtml.

[22] Ibid.

[23] "Moving Marriage Forward: Building Majority Support for Marriage." A report from Freedom to Marry, November 2011, accessed at http://freemarry.3cdn.net/cc86bd386cbe909dcd_z8m6bupow.pdf, December 13, 2012. Note the absence of the words "gay" and "same-sex" from the title of the report. In our interviews, too, advocates pointed repeatedly to gay couples living quietly in the suburbs, "hosting barbecues in their backyards." See Dorf and Tarrow (2013).

Americans did. The statewide referenda campaigns in Maine, Washington, Maryland, and Minnesota in 2012 were all animated by this new and more homespun framing (and sustained by an enormous inflow of campaign contributions). In response to these findings, the language of love began to displace the language of rights in the movements' campaigns.

But the real proof of the success of the "love and commitment" line was the "conversion" of Barack Obama. Obama's "evolution" is instructive. In 2004, he said that for him, marriage was a union "between a man and a woman"; in the 2008 campaign, his position had moved to support for civil unions; in 2011, his attorney general, Eric Holder, announced that the Justice Department would no longer defend DOMA; and in the 2012 presidential campaign – with some nudging from Vice President Joe Biden – Obama came out in behalf of the right of gay and lesbian Americans to marry. The first clear expression of support came at a campaign stop in Seattle in May, where Obama included "the freedom to love" within the American creed:

> We came together because we believed that in America, your success shouldn't be determined by the circumstances of your birth. If you're willing to work hard, you should be able to find a good job. If you're meeting your responsibilities, you should be able to own a home, maybe start a business. You should be able to give your kids the chance to do even better than you – no matter who you are, no matter where you come from, no matter what you look like, no matter what your last name, no matter who you love.[24]

Just as interesting was Obama's effort to link his decision to support same-sex marriage to his Christian faith, to his popular wife, Michelle, and to his children. "But, you know," he told NBC News,

> when we think about our faith, the thing at root that we think about is, not only Christ sacrificing himself on our behalf, but it's also the Golden Rule, you know, treat others the way you would want to be treated. And I think that's what we try to impart to our kids and that's what motivates me as President and I figure the most consistent I can be in being true to those precepts, the better I'll be as a dad and a husband and hopefully the better I'll be as president.[25]

---

[24] Go to http://projects.washingtonpost.com/obama-speeches/speech/1056/, visited December 10, 2012.
[25] http://www.huffingtonpost.com/2012/05/09/obama-gay-marriage-religion-faith_n_1504158.html.

Obama also sought to normalize same-sex marriage by making reference to soldiers or airmen or marines or sailors "who are out there fighting on my behalf and yet feel constrained because they *are not able to commit themselves in a marriage*" [italics added].[26] And in sharp contrast to the proverbial wisdom that held that homosexuals are not capable of romantic love (Calhoun 1999), Obama assimilated the right to marry the person you love to equality of opportunity. As he closed his election victory speech on November 6, 2012, he said,

> America, I believe we can build on the progress we've made and continue to fight for new jobs and new opportunity and new security for the middle class. I believe we can keep the promise of our founders, the idea that if you're willing to work hard, it doesn't matter who you are or where you come from or what you look like *or where you love*. [italics added]

## Love–Hate

In their pathbreaking survey of the role of emotions in social movements, Ron Aminzade and Doug McAdam pointed to the importance of understanding the interaction among emotions in contentious politics (2001: 15–16). Like others, they focused on the *dynamics* of emotions over time (Aminzade and McAdam 2001; Gould 2009; Summers Effler 2010) but retreated before the difficulty of doing so. Jeff Goodwin and James Jasper also recognized the importance of the interaction of emotions in movements, but their stimulating review did not suggest how to accomplish this task (2006). Perhaps the reason for this lacuna is that most scholars working in the social movement canon focused on single movements as their object of analysis, rather than on interactive episodes of contention in general (McAdam et al. 2001; McAdam and Boudet 2012).

The rapid survey of the role of "love" and "hate" in this chapter cannot hope to fill this lacuna, but by focusing on broad episodes of contention, rather than on single movements, it has turned up some evidence of how emotions intersect. First, and most superficially, our "thin" survey found a significant number of connections between these two emotions and social movements in the scholarship on movements. Look back at Table 7.1: column (3) of the table lists the number of articles about movements that include mentions of both "love" and "hate." "Love" and

---

[26] http://www.ivillage.com/obama-endorses-gay-marriage-cites-malia-sasha-catalysts/8-a-453772.

"hate" are two opposing emotional complexes that frequently co-occur in the scholarship on social movements.

Second, I've shown how hatred is routinely mobilized in different episodes of genocide, in particular, and of atrocity in general, and how often the same language appears over a wide range of time and space. Most of these mechanisms – such as dehumanization, guilt attribution, and perception of threat – construct negative images of the victims; but scholars have also found evidence of the mobilization of love of collectivity, community, and nation in episodes of genocidal atrocity. "Identification," write Chirot and McCauley, "means that our emotions are positively...linked to the welfare or reputation of the group identified with.... [A]t the bottom of conflict and violence there is love – love for friends, family, village, clan, tribe, class, nation, or religion" (2006: 75, 76). "The result of this double essentializing is a battle of good and evil," conclude Chirot and McCauley, "of two incompatible essences in which love of the good means necessarily hate for the threatening out-group" (2006: 86).

Third, although the "beloved community" was an important trope in part of the civil rights movement in the South, it did not survive long after the early days of sit-ins and freedom rides. Faced by leering, spitting, insult- and rock-throwing crowds of white youth, Klan bombings, and police repression, activists began to consider nonviolence simply one tactic among others, and it ceased to motivate the movement; on the contrary, as the movement moved north, antiwhite and anti-Semitic sentiments began to appear among new waves of activists, who saw the need to defend their community from white racism. The message of love that had animated the movement's early evolution in the South began to disappear before this more militant language.

We have not studied the evidence of hate in the story of same-sex marriage, although it is likely that homophobic reactions are the result of a mixture of moral disapproval and visceral disgust. However, during the past decade, when social acceptance of homosexuality appears to be accelerating dramatically, we have also seen a dramatic increase in the number of gay and lesbian teens bullied and harassed; according to recent statistics, nine out of ten gay and lesbian teenagers report being bullied, and an astonishing 30 percent of teen suicides are related to sexual identity.[27] Despite a general decline of homophobia, it is difficult

---

[27] These statistics come from http://www.bullyingstatistics.org/content/gay-bullying-statistics.html, visited December 13, 2012.

to avoid the conclusion that hate is at the base of this surge in gay and lesbian bullying and suicide.

Research on other types of movements also shows a reciprocal relationship between love and hatred. In her work on Italian and German left-wing terrorism, Donatella della Porta found not only profound hate for the regimes but also sentiments of deep affection and trust for others in the movement, many of whom came from among family or friendship groups (della Porta 1995: 158–61; 177–9). Her respondents recalled the time spent with comrades as "a very happy one," of "affective generosity," "solidarity even in the small things," of the group as "a family," of "warmth," "care," and "love" to describe relations with other members (p. 177). The bonds of love seem to have expanded during life in clandestinity and from the thrill of participating together in dangerous activities. At the same time, there was a process of "depersonalization" of the victims of their campaign that was strikingly similar to the dehumanization mechanism described by students of genocide. As one German respondent said, "Even today, I do not feel any general scruple concerning a murder, because *I cannot see some creatures – such as, for example, Richard Nixon – as human beings*" (quoted in della Porta, ibid., p. 173, italics in original). In terrorist movements, love was the reciprocal of hate.

I cannot claim to have carried out a systematic analysis of the relations between love and hate in social movements – let alone of the vast range of emotional language in movements. Clearly, the interactions I have examined are far from typical. What I think this chapter does show is that we can best understand the role of emotion-charged language by placing both emotion and the language that expresses it in the context of relational, concrete, and dynamic episodes of contention: of "loosely-coupled ensembles" of conflict disseminated beyond the confines of the daily world of experience (Steinberg 1999b: 5). But how loosely coupled can these ensembles of conflict be and still be considered part of the same episode of contention? And how tight must the interpersonal bonds of activists be for us to consider them part of the same movement? These issues were less important in the past, when most movements were scaled-up aggregates of local conflicts, producing coherent movements through concrete organizations with known routines of contention and coherent ideologies. But when boundaries are becoming porous and Internet communication is bringing activists together across broad swaths of territory, can we still speak of "loosely-coupled ensembles" of conflict? Evidence is accumulating that transnational movements and digitally powered networks are gaining an established place in the repertoire of contention. What has been the effect of such "distant movements" and of the influence of the Internet on the language of contention? We turn to this issue in the final chapter after reviewing the major findings of the study.

# Conclusions

Thomas Paine had been in Philadelphia for less than two years when he wrote the following lines:

> These are the times that try men's souls. The summer soldier and the sunshine patriot will, in this crisis, shrink from the service of their country; but he that stands it now, deserves the love and thanks of man and woman. Tyranny, like hell, is not easily conquered; yet we have this consolation with us, that the harder the conflict, the more glorious the triumph.[1]

We cannot know how much Paine's words actually stirred the hearts of the American colonists or whether he was simply registering in more eloquent terms what they were already feeling. We do know that, in the three months after the publication of *Common Sense*, an estimated 100,000 copies were sold in a population of less than two million nonslave inhabitants. Historian Gordon Wood describes it as "the most incendiary and popular pamphlet of the entire revolutionary era" (Wood 1991). We still hear the echoes of Paine's words in political rhetoric today: how freedom, banished from the Old World, found a home in the new; how Americans should join hands across the ties of party and faction; how the "good citizen" should be a resolute friend, a supporter of the rights of man and of the free and independent states of America.

Paine's words endured from the critical juncture in which he wrote to suffuse American political culture. Now shift the focus to the Philippines on January 16, 2001. A protest had broken out against the president of the

---

[1] From "The American Crisis, No. 1," in Michael Foot and Isaac Kramnick, eds. (1987: 116). Or go to http://www.ushistory.org/paine/crisis/c-01.htm. I am grateful to Isaac Kramnick for insisting on the relevance of this eloquent quotation.

former American colony. "Towards midnight," write Charles Tilly and Lesley Ann Wood, "text-messaging mobile phones . . . began transmitting this message":

### Go 2EDSA, Wear Blck

In the condensed language typical of today's social media, "Go 2" meant "go to"; the acronym "EDSA" stood for Epifaneo de los Santos Avenue, which had symbolic importance to Filipinos for its association with the democratic revolution of 1986; and "wear blck" asked people to come in black to mark their solidarity and escape the attacks of the police.[2] Those words lacked Paine's eloquence, but they spread instantly, and over the next two days, hundreds of thousands of Manilans heeded the call of the cell phone mobilization, assembled, marched, and formed a human chain ten kilometers long. Rock groups and high school bands performed. The language was flat and foreshortened, but the words helped bring down a president (Tilly and Wood 2009: 96).

What a change in the language of contention since Paine wrote his immortal lines! The rapid transnational diffusion of protest; the shift in scale from the local to the national and international levels; the rise of personalized digital media, which have, to some extent, edged out more traditional ways of mobilizing people (Bennett and Segerberg 2013). Some of these changes, revolving around conflicts over Islam and the West, are discussed later in this chapter. I try to go beyond the findings of the study to reflect on changes in contentious language. But first, let us review what you have learned from the episodes in this book: how episodes of contention give rise to contentious language; how symbolic resonance and strategic modularity make this language endure; how contentious language spreads; and how it affects future episodes of contention.

### The Origins of Contentious Language

I began this book with a story about the Occupy Wall Street movement, which led me, in Chapter 1, to make a preliminary claim about the origins of contentious language. I argued that words empowering contention can emerge from a variety of sources, including ordinary speech, popular folktales or music, commercial media or huckstering, previous experiences of war or conflict, or authoritative statements of law and

---

[2] Quoted in Charles Tilly and Lesley Ann Wood (2009: 95).

policy. In the following chapters, you encountered many examples of this diversity:

- The term "revolution" came from the revolution of the planets, and was also used for natural disasters, before it came to mean assaults meant to overturn a political system.
- The term "boycott" came from shunning a man whose name happened to be Boycott.
- The term "harassment" had the prosaic meaning of being annoyed with something or someone before it came to be employed to mean unwanted sexual advances.
- As for "black," it was at first a descriptive term for the skin color of African slaves before it was adopted as a term of denigration, and was later adopted as their preferred term for themselves by black Americans in the late twentieth century.

The diverse sources of these terms should not deceive us that their construction is random: contentious language emerges through interactions among challengers, opponents, and those who record their interactions. Some of these interactions – such as the original use of "boycott" – were relatively insignificant; but many emerged from critical junctures like those examined by David Collier and Ruth Collier in Latin America (1991), by Charles Tilly in 1820s England (1995a and b), by Mark Traugott in 1848 in France (2010), and by this author in the 1960s in Italy (Tarrow 1989). In these moments, conflict intensifies, common consciousness grows, new actors are constituted, and clashes between challengers and their opponents crystallize new languages of contention.

Think of the birth of Zionism in the late nineteenth and early twentieth centuries: the movement was born as a variant of the nationalist movements that developed in Eastern and Central Europe, using similar language and rituals and experiencing similar internal struggles. But it also grew in reaction to the anti-Semitism of many of those movements, drew strength from non-Zionist ideologies among Eastern European Jews, and was refined in the diplomatic game their leaders were playing with the Western powers. After significant numbers of Jewish settlers sought a foothold in Palestine, the movement and its language were reshaped by the settlers' relationship to the indigenous Arab population and to the land they sought to possess, as you saw in Chapter 6.

The Zionists' language was shaped by these interactions and then by the wars that the settlers fought. At first, the emphasis on youth, rurality, and purity (i.e., "the New Jew") was remarkably similar to the language of other European nationalisms; but its strident secularism developed in reaction to the dominant religious identity of Jews in Eastern Europe. Its obsessive emphasis on the land and its productivity was a motif of both redemption and the struggle of a people to be reborn (Avineri 1971). The series of wars that followed the establishment of their state in 1948 gave their language a harder edge and a more bellicose tone: wars and place names were named for the Bible; people took the names of biblical heroes; and military leaders were popularly greeted as *melech Yisroael* (king of Israel).

Each of the movements we have studied developed its characteristic language out of a crucible of contentious interaction but then was shaped by subsequent developments:

- French republicanism long retained the centralization, the secularism, and the statism of the First French Republic.
- English workers retained a corporate sense of themselves as "the working class," a sense that was gained in the struggle for the reform act as they came to the realization that middle-class reformists were unreliable allies.
- Black Americans experimented with different forms of self-appellation, finally settling on the term "blacks," in favor of "Negroes," "colored people," and the awkward "African Americans."
- The Greeks who protested the choice of their Macedonian neighbors to call their country the Republic of Macedonia were animated not only by national pride but also by their memory of Tito's attempt to stir up Slavophone nationalism during the Greek Civil War.

The struggles that produce the language of contention sear themselves into the memories of those who lived through those struggles, but also in the collective memories of their descendants and those who identify with them. Two key mechanisms – symbolic resonance and strategic modularity – help distinguish the words that survive as terms of combat from those that fade into obscurity or become part of ordinary language.

### Symbolic Resonance and Strategic Modularity

Not all words for contention endure beyond their origins. In Chapter 1, I argue that a term's *symbolic resonance* and its *strategic modularity* are the key mechanisms responsible for the durability of some terms and the disappearance or normalization of others. By "symbolic resonance" I mean the degree to which a particular term resonates with culturally familiar concepts in a particular culture. By "strategic modularity" I mean the degree to which terms that emerge in one strategic context can be transferred to others without loss of the strategic advantages they originally possessed. The most enduring terms combine symbolic resonance and strategic modularity.

### Symbolic Resonance

In the course of this book, a number of symbolically resonant terms were described and analyzed.

- "The Terror," which you first met in Chapter 2, was invented by the French revolutionaries precisely to terrorize recalcitrant citizens. It diffused, in the form of "terrorism," for much the same purpose.
- "Nigger," a term of denigration under slavery, was normalized in the postbellum South to reinforce the subjugation of blacks. While it has largely disappeared from public speech among whites, black Americans now often use it as a term of humor or affection.
- "Male chauvinism" was adapted from earlier uses of the term "chauvinism" by the radical wing of the American women's movement in the 1960s and normalized into ordinary speech by the 1970s.
- *Sabras*, originally an imported desert cactus, was adapted to distinguish native-born Israelis – supposedly hard on the outside with a soft interior – from their immigrant compatriots.
- "Marriage" has great symbolic resonance in most societies, and that made it a contentious term in America as gays and lesbians sought its benefits and its symbolism over the past two decades.

What gives a term symbolic resonance? It is hard to isolate one single factor, but the central reason a term "takes" in a particular setting is its association with a wider social discourse. Think of rights: "The rights of Englishmen," in whose name American colonists began their struggle against the Crown, were understood at first to be traditional, inherited, and attached to particular social groups. When the American founders inscribed the idea that there was such a thing as "natural rights," it seemed to observers such as Jeremy Bentham both ridiculous and dangerous to expand the term to everyone (Rodgers 1987: 45–6). But in the course of the revolution and its subsequent constitutional interpretation, Americans expanded the narrower English notion of rights into a universal category, ignoring the fact that a sizable portion of women and blacks had none.

## Strategic Modularity

Resonance with existing discourses is not enough to explain the durability of terms of contention; if it were, there would be little change over time in the language of contention. The second key mechanism that accounts for the durability of contentious language is its "strategic modularity" – the adaptability of contentious language to new settings and other actors. In the course of this book you have encountered a number of terms that endured locally and diffused nationally and transnationally because they were strategically adaptable to a number of settings.

- The "convention," which you met in Chapter 2, was adapted from British practice for use against the British by the American colonists, who broadened its reach and meaning. It then recrossed the Atlantic to France, where it was the name given to the governing institution of the republic.
- "Citizen" was an ancient word deriving from the Greek *polis* that was revived in the French Revolution to distinguish good republicans from the so-called aristocrats, who were accused of undermining the republic.
- The "boycott" spread because it was strategically adaptable to a wide variety of targets and settings – from the boycott of Jewish businesses in interwar Poland to the boycott of grapes in California in the 1960s.
- The "New Negro," for a period before the invention of "black power," reflected black Americans' urge for a new identity, much as the term "New Jew" became a symbol for the Zionist movement's desire to transcend the image of the Jew in Europe (see Chapter 6).

## When Symbolism and Modularity Combine

Some of these terms – such as "New Negro" – never gained much traction, but others earned a permanent place in the lexicon of contentious politics. The most enduring combined symbolic resonance with strategic modularity. Words like "strike," whose origin was the nautical term to "strike" a sail, gained strategic modularity from its adaptability. The strike could stop production and paralyze industry. It then spread to confrontations involving the ordinary routines of social life – e.g., "rent strikes," "bus strikes." The strike gained symbolic resonance not only from the drama and excitement of the term but also from its association with the great successes and clamorous defeats of the working class in the past.

Similarly, the "demonstration" combined symbolic resonance with strategic modularity: originally only an adjectival modifier (e.g., "a demonstration of support"), it came to mean any assembly of people called together to demonstrate a claim in public space. The term gained resonance from its origin in religious processions but earned its modularity from its ease of organization and its capacity to concentrate numbers of supporters in one place and to communicate both mood and determination (Tartakowsky 1997). The demonstration was remarkably flexible: it could be serious (e.g., funeral marches for martyrs killed in combat), martial (workers banging pots and pans as they marched), or ludic (feminists demonstrating in the costumes of witches to parody the images of their opponents), or it could impress by its numbers, like the Million Man March in America in 1995 or by turning up in unexpected places, like courtrooms. By the 1960s, the demonstration had become the most modular and most symbolic term in the dictionary of contentious politics.

Over time, language that arises in moments of heated contention – what Aristide Zolberg called "moments of madness" (Zolberg 1972) – can become institutionalized, stale, and irrelevant. The "turnout" – which originally brought community members into the street in support of strikers – disappeared as strikes became national and strike activity was taken over by professional organizers. In Italy in the 1970s, assembling all the workers to plan a strike gave way to *assemblearismo*, a wearying routine of meetings that left the workers in the hands of minorities. Language that arises in "moments of madness" can become ritualized, shorn of its original connotations, and, over time, impoverished.

But some words not only endure but also diffuse to other social groups and cross borders to become part of a universal language of contention. Symbolic resonance and strategic modularity intersect in the dynamics of contention. But this does not explain how terms that arise in one discursive context are adapted in other settings; for this we need to examine the mechanisms of diffusion.

## Mechanisms of Diffusion

Linguistic and cultural differences are an impediment to the diffusion of words for contention, and yet great commonalities in language and usage have developed across borders. Recall the uniformity we found in the terms used in different languages for "terrorism," "boycott," "sexual harassment," and the "strike" and the "*grève*." One of the most striking findings of this study is the degree to which words for contentious politics *do* diffuse – sometimes amazingly rapidly – even to places where languages, organizations, and ways of treating public contention differ widely.

Think of the diffusion of the Arabic phrase *ash-sha'b yurid isqat an-nizam* (the people want the overthrow of the regime), which spread across Cairo in the first days of the 2011 rebellion against the Mubarak regime and then, in one version or another, diffused across the Middle East. Or the language of the *indignados* movement, which arose as an antiausterity protest in Spain in May 2011 and spread across Europe in the following months. The Internet and social media helped these terms to spread, but even in the pre-electronic past, forms like the barricade appeared across Europe during critical junctures, like the 1848 Revolution.

The traditional image of diffusion is one of "contagion" or "wild-fire," something that gives the impression of a spontaneous spread, like that of a disease or a conflagration. But diffusion does not take place automatically; it requires agents, making contact with other agents, or learning about their actions, for a term and a practice of contention to diffuse. Some scholars (Merry 2006; Chabot 2012) have employed the term "translation" to indicate how this occurs, but I prefer the broader term "brokerage" to indicate the process through which a third party creates a connection between two other actors who would otherwise remain unconnected (McAdam et al. 2001). You saw brokerage taking place through a variety of submechanisms.

*Agencies of communication*: in Chapter 3, you saw how the British and American press diffused the word "boycott" from Ireland, first to London and then to Chicago in the late nineteenth century.

*Halfway houses*: These are organizations or institutions whose purpose is not protest, which diffuse information to other countries; think of the role of the European Commission in diffusing information about sexual harassment in Europe (Roggeband 2010) or of the Catholic priests who diffused the language of "Christian base communities" to poor peasants in Latin America. They were not themselves responsible for movements like the Chiapas rebellion, but their message was translated into collective action in many of the villages where they had preached their doctrine of the People of God (Trejo 2012).

*Movement missionaries*: These activists, either deliberately or as a product of migration, bring contentious language from one country to another, as you saw in the transmission of the Gandhian repertoire from India to the United States in Chapter 7 (Chabot 2012).

*Transnational organization of protest*: These activities transmit the language of contention simultaneously to a number of countries through participation in the same events. You will see such a case in the so-called Danish cartoon controversy later in this chapter.

### Common Terms, Evolving Meanings

As contentious language diffuses, its meanings often change – sometimes by degrees but often with major transformations. You saw in Chapter 2 how "the Terror" – originally used to mean a state's repression of its enemies – was transformed into "terrorism," to mean attacks on the state by those who use violent methods. The two meanings of the term still remain in the lexicon of violence. In Chapter 4 you saw how "male chauvinist pig" changed its meaning as it percolated from the radical wing of the feminist movement to ordinary Chicagoans (Mansbridge and Flaster 2007). The term "Holocaust," originally a biblical term for burnt offerings, was shifted after World War II to refer to the destruction of European Jewry but was then expanded to refer to atrocities of all kinds.

Such changes are seldom random: they are the responses of concrete actors to the symbolic cultures and strategic settings around them. As Bakhtin taught, it is the context of words and their relation to other words that determine their meanings (Bakhtin 1981). New actors facing new opponents take the cloth of contention – language – and turn it into costumes that match different conflicts and different opponents.

Think of how the concept of "rights" evolved from the specific rights of particular social groups in the estate societies of the late Middle Ages to the generalized term we know today. The new meaning of the term was both subversive and elastic: it could be used to defend the rights of property holders, the rights of taxpayers, the rights of workers, and, ultimately, the right of slaves to be considered human beings. After its expansion in the French and American revolutions, the term "rights" gave rise to specialized versions: "civil rights" for the rights of freed slaves after the Civil War; "women's rights" in the 1960s and 1970s; the right of gays and lesbians to marry in the new century. Yet at the same time, the term was expanded to a broader discourse of "human rights" after World War II, not because the world had become more humane – far from it – but because it was a useful umbrella term that could cover a variety of cultural and political settings (Moyn 2010). As it diffused through UN agencies and democracy advocates in transitioning autocracies, "rights" became contested terrain: did they, as in the original Western connotation, refer only to individual rights, or did they extend to collective or social rights?

This takes us to two questions that go beyond the evidence presented in this book. How have recent international changes since September 11, 2001, affected the language of contention? And how is the rise of digital communication transforming contentious politics? I argue that, since 9/11, a new religiously inflected language has infiltrated both domestic and transnational politics, and also that the new forms of communication present a risk of bringing about a decline in the quality of political language.

### Critical Junctures and Changing Repertoires

Throughout this book, I have identified critical junctures of contention as the crucibles from which changes in language emerge (Tarrow 1995). I identify several such junctures: the period of suffrage reform in England in the 1820s and 1830s; the civil rights, antiwar, and feminist movements of the 1960s; and the ongoing extension of equal rights to gay and lesbian people today. These junctures occurred mainly within national settings, but our world has become much more global, and communication more rapid, more personalized, and more transnational. How has this affected the language of contention? If there was a critical transnational juncture in our lifetime, it probably began with the bombings of the World Trade Center and the Pentagon on September 11, 2001, and the global religio-political conflict that followed. Say "9/11" to any American, and it still calls up a tangled web of emotions: rage, mourning, desire for revenge, the determination to protect what is unique about their country, and increasing suspicion of the religion of Islam. This is not to say that all conflict since the turn of the century has revolved around a religious axis, but only that, since 9/11, many more areas of social life have become inflected with religion than before. We can see evidence for these changes both in the Middle East and in the United States.

### *When Words Can Kill*

On September 30, 2005, a Danish newspaper, *Jyllands-Posten*, published a series of twelve satirical cartoons showing the prophet Muhammad in comical, threatening, and even insulting poses.[3] Most offensive was a cartoon showing Muhammad standing on a cloud, calling out to a group of

---

[3] This brief sketch relies on the partly complementary reports of Hervik (2006), Lindkilde (2008), and Olesen (2007). I hasten to add that I do not read either Arabic or Danish and cannot check original sources on these events.

dead suicide bombers, "Stop, stop; we have run out of virgins!" referring
to the widespread belief that *jihadis* are encouraged by the hope that they
will be welcomed by beautiful virgins in heaven.[4] Like many European
countries, secular Denmark had experienced a large inflow of immigrants
over the previous few decades, leading to discomfort among parts of the
Danish population and to a rise of anti-immigrant xenophobia (Hervik
2006). This was the setting in which *Jyllands-Posten* published the cartoons, an action that led to a wave of protests and violence throughout
the Muslim world.

Of course, the newspaper maintained that the purpose of publishing
the cartoons was to oppose what its editors saw as the unwillingness of
Danish authorities and journalists to criticize Muslims (Hervik 2006). But
that was not the view of Danish Muslims nor of the international Muslim
community. Soon, an organization called the Islamic Faith Community
(Det Islamiske Trossamfund) protested the publication of the cartoons,
and ambassadors from Muslim countries urged the Danish government
"to take all those responsible to task under the law of the land in the interest of interfaith harmony, better integration and Denmark's overall relations with the Muslim world." Prime Minister Anders Foch-Rasmussen
refused to meet with them and lectured them on the importance of freedom of expression and maintaining a clear line between government and
the press (Olesen 2007: 43).

Freedom of expression was the major frame within which Denmark's
media and most Western governments responded to the protests, although
some of them did not have an unblemished record of representing Muslims. During the 2001 elections, an MP from the right-wing Progress
Party had warned, "Muslims are just waiting for the right moment to kill
us"; a candidate from the Liberal Venstre had warned, "Certain people
pose a security risk solely because of their religion, which means that they
have to be placed in internment camps"; and even a Social Democratic
MP warned, referring to Muslim organizations, that "it is a historical
rule that rats always find new holes, if you cover up the old ones." Nor
had the press much of a record of religious tolerance vis-à-vis Muslims;
in 1997, a newspaper had condemned three Pakistani immigrants who
had "infiltrated" Danish political parties.[5]

---

[4] Any number of websites reproduced the cartoons, some of them in too small a format to
easily grasp. An accessible one with English translations is http://www.outsidethebeltway.
com/danish_muslim_cartoons/, visited December 16, 2012.

[5] I rely for these examples on the article by Peter Hervik (2006: 226–7), whose translations
from the Danish I have adopted.

Det Islamiske Trossamfund's protests led nowhere in Denmark, but by early 2006, the controversy had escalated to the transnational level. First, a delegation of Islamic organizations, dissatisfied with the reaction of the government and *Jyllands-Posten*, created an umbrella organization called the European Committee for Prophet Honouring and toured the Middle East.[6] Some of its representations of the cartoons were less than accurate, but the important point is that it acted as a broker, giving the controversy a transnational resonance.

Toward the first of the year, Middle Eastern governments, the Organization of Islamic Cooperation, and the Arab League took their protest to the European Union and the UN High Commissioner for Human Rights (Olesen 2007: 43–5). The Egyptian government, perhaps spurred by the rising power of the Muslim Brotherhood, "seemed especially bent on keeping the issue alive, and served as a prominent broker in attempting to create awareness and mobilization against *Jyllands-Posten* and the Danish government" (ibid., p. 43).

As these communications crossed the globe, transnational media sources – especially the new outlets *Al-Jazeera* and *al-Arabiya* – gave the issue front-page attention. On January 27, the cartoons were a major theme in Friday prayers in Egypt, Saudi Arabia, and Iraq. On February 1, the Egyptian state-owned newspaper, *Al-Jumhuriya*, called for a boycott of Danish goods and called the cartoons "a crime against the Muslim world." A number of other newspapers in the Arab and Muslim world followed Egypt's example (ibid., p. 42). But neither institutional pressure nor transnational press coverage moved the Danish government from framing the episode as an issue of freedom of expression.[7]

With tension growing both at the institutional level and in the media, it was probably inevitable that street protests would explode in the Middle East, and when they did, many turned violent. In early February the Danish embassies in Damascus and Beirut were set on fire, and two hundred people were reported dead across the Arab world. Free speech may have triumphed, but so did Western insensitivity to Muslim religious feeling and an early sign of the deep resentment of the "Arab street."

---

[6] The actions of this delegation have been carefully traced on Wikipedia at http://en.wikipedia.org/wiki/Jyllands-Posten_Muhammad_cartoons_controversy#Danish_Imams_tour_the_Middle_East, visited December 17, 2012.

[7] Hervik (2006: 229–30) casts some doubt on the sincerity of the Danish government's commitment to freedom of the press and sees it as an argument that works well in diverting attention from racism, Islamophobia, and xenophobia. I am not in a position to judge the accuracy of this claim.

While the Western media saw the conflict in terms of freedom of the press, Arab opinion almost unanimously read the publication of the cartoons as the expression of Western racism and disdain for the Muslim religion.

### A New Linguistic Paradigm?

What do these tangled relations between Copenhagen and the Arab world over a sordid set of cartoons tell us about changes in the language of transnational contention in the new century? First, such incidents of Muslim rage and Western incomprehension have multiplied. Second, the evidence for these enormities is not imaginary. The U.S.-led attack on Iraq, based on false evidence of weapons of mass destruction, the torture scandal at the Abu Ghraib prison in 2004, the threatened burning of a Quran by Terry Jones, an American pastor, the desecrations of the Quran by American troops, and the explosive documentary film that fed the riots of the summer of 2012 in Benghazi – the post 9/11 world has provided ample evidence to Muslims that "the West" harbors insensitivity, arrogance, and hatred of Islam.

Third, we can see a causal link between what happened in New York and Washington in September 2001 and the rise of Islamist parties throughout the Middle East and North Africa after the "Arab spring," passing through episodes such as the Muhammad cartoons in the middle of the decade. As Thomas Olesen, one Danish observer, states, "[T]he events of September 11 have significantly shaped the opportunity structures in which the cartoons conflict took place.... Politics in this context consequently gravitate around the appeasement and/or violent oppression of Muslim protest and claims." Olesen adds, "The cartoons conflict became a chance to vent the anger of groups and individuals motivated by an Islamic worldview" (Olesen 2007: 45–6).

What evidence do we have of such a paradigm shift? This is not the place to attempt an analysis of whether, as some have argued, "everything changed after September 11."[8] But clearly, many things *have* changed, and the language of politics is one of them. Contentious language has become more transnational, more heated, and more simplified, while at the same time its sources have become more diversified and more personalized as more and more people gain access to public space through

---

[8] The most thorough and original treatment of what has and has not changed in post–9/11 America is Joseph Margulies (2013). For full disclosure, I confess that this book is, in part, dedicated to this author.

digital media (Bennett and Segerberg 2013). Yet politics still takes place not in cyberspace, but on the ground. A venue for many of the most important trends in contentious language since 9/11 can be seen in the United States.

### A Bruised Behemoth

By the end of the Reagan presidency, the language and syntax of the Cold War had begun to recede from American political discourse. Studying Ronald Reagan's speeches, historian Daniel Rodgers found that "by the end of the 1980s the language and style of the Cold War presidency were clearly in eclipse." The theme that emerged in their place was "an ultimate state of boundless possibilities" – "dreaming," in Rodgers's words (2011: 28–9). And with "dreaming" of a "city on a hill" came an inflation of American self-confidence, especially after the Soviet Empire imploded and the world appeared to be approaching the "end of history" (Fukayama 1989). As the turn of the millennium approached, there was much self-congratulatory talk of "the American century," of a "Pax Americana," and a "widespread sense of the naturalness of markets" (Rodgers 2011: 254).

This colossal self-confidence was one reason – though not the only one – that 9/11 hit the American psyche with such drama and pathos. America was not only a country in mourning; it was the most powerful, the best, the most successful country in the world, and it had been deeply bruised by nineteen pitiful Muslim fanatics who successfully infiltrated American defenses to murder three thousand people. Yet interestingly enough, as Margulies shows, hatred of Muslims was at first muted, and Americans were insistently reminded that the "American creed" did not include hatred of those who are different from ourselves and that American Muslims should not be blamed for the outrages of a few foreign fanatics (Margulies 2013: Ch. 7). But in the course of the decade that followed, new and more acidic wine was poured into the vessel of the American creed, as Margulies's analysis vividly shows (ibid., Chs. 6, 8).

Americans have always described their country as the "greatest country on earth"; but after 9/11, excesses of self-congratulation, now with an undercurrent of tragedy, began to mark public speech. Almost immediately after 9/11, there was an outpouring of nationalist signs and symbols, flags and bumper stickers (Rodgers 2011: 258). Alongside the American flags and yellow ribbons, there was also a rapid rise in patriotic language. Surveys on national pride show a surge in "extremely proud" Americans

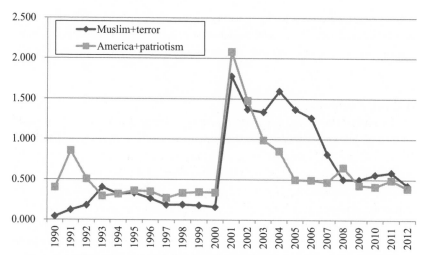

FIGURE 8.1. "America + Patriotism" and "Muslim + terror" in American News Articles, 1990–2012. *Note*: The chart records the number of mentions of these combinations of words per 1,000 newspaper articles, 1990–2012. *Source*: News-Bank (http://nl.newsbank.com/).

from 59 percent in January 2001 to 65 percent in June 2002, peaking at 70 percent in January 2003, before falling to 48 percent in 2009.[9]

It was not only in the polls that love of country surged after 9/11: the press, too, recorded a spike in patriotic sentiments. Figure 8.1 shows how often the words "America" plus "patriotism" appeared in the NewsBank database.[10] The sharp peak of this patriotic trope immediately after 9/11 is unmistakable, although it also continued after the beginning of the Iraq War, when Americans could feel pride that their troops were on the ground in the Middle East. Alongside heightened love of country, the Iraq and Afghanistan wars brought a glorification of military valor: soldiers who went off to the front in World War I had been "doughboys"; in World War II, they were memorialized in the lovable "G.I. Joe"; but as soldiers began to return from the deserts of Iraq and the mountains of Afghanistan, they were more likely to be referred to as "heroes" or "warriors."

The wars in Iraq and Afghanistan brought about another change in public speech: an increase in the combination of the words "Muslim" plus "terror," which peaked in the press in close correlation with the

---

[9] These data come from a Pew Research Center for the People & the Press longitudinal table at http://www.pewresearch.org/2010/07/01/proud-patriots-and-harsh-critics-of-government/.

[10] http://nl.newsbank.com/.

increase in extreme pride in America in the polls. Figure 8.1 also records the trend line, alongside the trend line of "America" and "patriotism" from 1990 to 2012. It is important not to overinterpret these findings. For example, if we query NewsBank for the words "Islam" + "peace" for the same period, we find a similar increase in frequency after 9/11, and the results include articles with an opposite valence, such as "Islam is Peace" (*Fort Worth Examiner*, 2010) and "Islam is not a religion of peace" (*Portland Examiner*, 2010). What we were seeing in public speech in the months after 9/11 was an increased salience of patriotism and religion rather than a uniform condemnation of Islam. In fact, Margulies's research on American public culture shows that, immediately after 9/11, a near majority of Americans expressed a favorable opinion of Islam (47 percent), compared to 39 percent whose attitudes toward Muslims were negative (Margulies 2013: Ch. 7). He writes of 9/11, "At the moment of greatest perceived threat, when fear of another attack was at its peak, favorable attitudes towards Muslims and Islam were at a record high through all segments of the population" (ibid., pp. x–xi).

But negative changes were soon evident on the American street: "Students who could be singled out by a Muslim-sounding name reported receiving batches of hate e-mails in the weeks after 9/11. The creation of a newly insistent and imperious 'we' simultaneously constructed others as outsiders" (Rodgers 2011: 259–60). These incidents were vigorously condemned by the Bush administration, which called on the American creed to restrain resentment. From the tolerant beginnings after 9/11, favorable attitudes about Muslims declined steadily, and unfavorable attitudes rose to 49 percent among the general population, and 67 percent among Republicans (Margulies 2013: 140). By the beginning of the second decade of the new century, writes Margulies, "tens of millions of Americans denounce Islam in the most incendiary terms, and counter-terrorism policies that President Bush apparently never dreamed of have been codified into law" (2013: xi).

At the same time, attitudes toward torture shifted dramatically. At the start of the Iraq War, writes Margulies, most Americans, along with the overwhelming majority of elites, recoiled from the idea of torture as government policy. Torture was a symbol that distinguished "us" from "them," and the determination to resist its temptations was a treasured mark of American exceptionalism (ibid., pp. 11, 209–10). But as the decade advanced, there was a gradual shift in public language, and beneath it a change in attitudes as well. Americans no longer talked of "torture," a practice that continued to be condemned by public opinion and elites alike, but of "enhanced interrogation techniques." Continuing to use the language of a now-transformed American creed, Margulies reports, by the end of the decade, Americans supported the use of the "enhanced techniques" by substantial margins, including 70 percent of Republicans and 58 percent of Democrats (ibid., p. 227).

The inflation of patriotic rhetoric and the growing suspicion of Muslims soon were conflated with tropes from the "culture wars" of the 1990s, especially on right-wing talk radio. The nation's defenses had been weakened by a decline in absolute moral standards; the murderous attacks of 9/11 were the result of the same "nihilism" found on the post-modern Left; an angry God, "impatient with a nation tainted by abortion, paganism, feminism, and homosexuality, had withdrawn his veil of pro-tection over the United States," said televangelist Jerry Falwell (Rodgers 2011: 260). Racism – never far from some sectors of American political culture – merged with anti-Muslim sentiment: people with dark skin – even Sikhs, whose religion has no connection with Islam – were targeted by racial attacks.

The conflation of these trends came to the surface in 2008, with the presidential election campaign of Barack Obama. In addition to the sense among some sectors of opinion that no black American could lead this country, there was an extraordinary diffusion of the rumor that Obama was a Muslim. "Despite repeated news stories, fact-checking Web sites, and Obama's self-professed [C]hristian affiliation," some 12 percent of American adults during the campaign continued to identify him as Mus-lim (Hollander 2010). After carrying out a careful panel study of Ameri-cans' opinions, Barry Hollander found that "political and religious con-servative beliefs predicted a belief in Obama as Muslim, [and] exposure to the news media did little to moderate this effect" (2010: 55). These changes in political language tracked closely the growing polarization of opinion in general. Anti-Muslim feeling, outraged patriotism, and cul-tural conservatism came to a head in the election of 2010, with the electoral triumph of the tea party. It is obvious that something deeper than information about Obama was motivating these voters.

I do not want to claim that the protests against the Muhammad car-toons in the Middle East and the growing American hostility to Muslims were no more than two sides of the same coin. But it is hard to ignore the confluence and expansion of religious language in these different parts of the world, each of which contributed to greater insularity, mutual mis-understanding, and conflict. Even in countries such as France, detached from both the Iraq War and the cartoon controversy, Middle Eastern immigrants – who used to be referred to by their country of origin or as "*arabe*," are now more frequently referred to in the press as "*musulman*," while white French people are characterized as "French at the root" (*les français de souche*). The language of religion has become conflated with the language of race, nationalism, and social conflict.

### Contradictions in Connective Language

At the same time, many of the contentious events of the past decade have been driven by the growth of Internet-based communications. The "Battle of Seattle" in 1999 was partly organized through the new mechanism of websites (Lichbach and DeVries 2007); the anti-Estrada protest in Manila was based on mobilization through text messaging (Tilly and Wood 2009); the global anti–Iraq War protest of February 2003 was the result of an organized e-mail campaign (Walgrave and Rucht 2011); and social media played a critical – though partial – role in the Arab spring protests of 2011 (Hassanpour in press). As for Occupy Wall Street, it got its start from an online magazine, *Adbusters*, in Vancouver, Canada, and spread rapidly from New York across the continent via the Internet (Vasi and Suh 2013).

Occupy Wall Street was organized at two different levels: at the local level, people interacted through horizontal networks; and at the national level, they met through what Lance Bennett and Alexandra Segerberg call personalized and digitalized "connective action" (2013). The campouts and general assemblies in New York and elsewhere created intense interpersonal solidarity as long as they lasted, while connective action across space gave the movement an almost immediate national and international resonance.

But there was a tension between these two "moments" of political communication almost from the start, as Bennett and his collaborators discovered when they tried to help former occupiers use digital media to create a permanent discussion platform online (ibid., Ch. 6). The tension was in part about the kind of discourse – intensely personal versus digitally organized – favored by activists in a movement that had grown up through intense interpersonal interaction (Graeber 2011). Digital communication, though it admits a great deal of variation and debate, uses a patterned, condensed, and stereotyped language.

Remember the contrast at the beginning of this chapter between the quotation from Tom Paine's *The American Crisis* and the foreshortened language of the Manila protest campaign? "These are the times that try men's souls" cannot be evoked without recalling Americans' emotion at the thought of the ill-clad Continental army shivering through the winter at Valley Forge. Now think of the text message that mobilized students against President Estrada in the Philippines: it was curt, standardized, and telegraphic.

These two fragments, coming from very different critical junctures in two different countries two centuries apart, are in many ways symbolic of the changes in the language of contention. Paine's call to arms was sonorous and abstract, and it drew on the language of classical republicanism and the Bible; the Manila protesters' text message reflected the urgency of the moment and the abrupt syntax of social media.[11] Imagine if Paine had been able to communicate the message of *Common Sense* to the colonists through an SMS. Instead of writing, "These are the times that try men's souls," he might have said,

**Oppose Geo 3; Supt Geo W!**

I put forward this imaginary message tongue-in-cheek, but the comparison reveals a tension in the newly discovered power of personal media: the Internet, Facebook, and Twitter encourage what Bennett and Segerberg call "personalization in contentious political action" (2013). The term "personalization" evokes associated autonomy, creativity, and diversity, and one of the virtues of the new forms of communication is that they allow even relatively isolated individuals and groups to contribute to contentious conversations by virtue of their access to a smartphone, a computer, or a server. That is a real alternative to the more conventional, and more hierarchical, forms of collective action social movements inherit from the past.[12] From this point of view, personalized, digital communication ought to produce more creative, more individualized communication within networks of activists. As Bennett and Segerberg persuasively argue,

> personalization processes pose challenges to modern conventions for organizing political action, such as promoting memberships and branded

---

[11] See Jane O'Brien, "Learn English online: How the internet is changing language" at http://www.bbc.co.uk/news/magazine-20332763 for evidence of how English is being condensed and adapted as a transnational Internet language.

[12] This is the central insight of the work of Lance Bennett and his collaborators over the past decade, and of the Center for Communication and Civic Engagement that Bennett directs. For more information and for access to the reports and publications of the center, go to http://ccce.com.washington.edu/index.html.

identification with formal organizations and their causes.... Personal action frames allow people to specify their own connection to an issue as opposed to having to adopt more demanding molds. (2013: Ch. 6, in press).

But I am not so sure that messages can scale upward without losing a considerable degree of effectiveness. For example, examination of the mission statements of a large number of Occupy sites in American cities in 2011 revealed three main properties.

First, these forms of communication moved *fast*. The news of the southern civil rights movement sit-ins diffused across the South in a matter of days (Andrews and Biggs 2006), and the news that the Berlin Wall had fallen reached citizens of Leipzig in hours (Lohmann 1994). The text message about the Manila protest of 2001 spread across the city in minutes (Tilly and Wood 2009: Ch. 5), but the news of the pepper-spraying of University of California students in Davis "went viral" in seconds.

Second, the new language of contention spreads *far*. The slogans of the Occupy movement reached across the continent in a matter of days (see Figure 1.1). Not only did "Occupy" spread across the United States and Canada, but also the Occupy activists were in close touch with militants in Europe who were simultaneously occupying the squares of Milan, Athens, and Barcelona.

But, third, electronic communication is *condensed*. "Go 2EDSA, Wear blck!" did not tell intended recipients what kind of protest was being planned, what goals were held by the organizers, or what they were planning for after the Estrada government fell. Neither does the slogan "We represent the 99 percent!" Communicating a protest on the Web is foreshortened, simple, and telegraphic, but it is unlikely to employ the subtlety of language that can inspire collective trust that will endure beyond the protest of the moment. Indeed, "the precipitous decline of the Occupy protests following police raids on the camps may be explained in part by the relatively thin commitments of the large numbers of followers who joined the festival atmosphere from their offices or desktops; many of these people drifted away "when the generative core of physical action was dispersed" (Bennett and Segerberg 2013: Ch. 6, in press).

What was lacking among these secondary participants? I think the answer was the lack of the interpersonal trust that can come only from intense and sustained interaction, such as occurs in the course of a strike, a school occupation, or the experience of working together during a boycott

(Tilly 2005). This may be why so many of the transnationally organized mobilizations that appeared in the first decade of the century did not endure. They diffused quickly, because language like "Go 2EDSA, Wear blck" is easy to understand, to translate, and to communicate to dispersed publics. But without the depth and subtlety that comes from interpersonal interaction, they were thin reeds on which to build a sustained social movement.

The same was true in the Middle East in 2011–12. Navid Hassanpour has shown how the early stages of the Cairo protests were animated by educated activists using the fast gear of social media. But when the Mubarak regime cut off Internet access, the movement in Cairo continued to spread; using the slower and more conventional gear of interpersonal communication in the lower-class neighborhoods of the capital, it denied the regime its technological advantage (Hassanpour in press).

But skepticism about the new digitalized forms of communication would be a dreary way to end a book that has been largely optimistic about the creativity, the diffusion, and the endurance of contentious episodes and contentious language. So let me return to the Occupy movement in a more positive note. As a face-to-face phenomenon, that movement broke up in the face of the cold of winter, the boredom of living in tents day after day, the impending election campaign, and rousting by the police. But to judge by the endurance and diffusion of the language of "the 99 percent" and the sprinklings of Occupy episodes since then, its impact is far from finished. As Bennett and Segerberg conclude from their spirited examination,

> it is possible that its legacy is better understood in terms of the production of enduring discourses and action repertoires that infused popular culture, and continued to spawn small occupations throughout local settings into the future. It is perhaps too early to tell. (Bennett and Segerberg 2013: Ch. 6)

This book has shown that we can understand the linguistic outcomes of contentious episodes only with the passage of time and through an examination of the interaction of new contentious language with different and changing environments. When sailors "struck" the sails of their ships in the port of London, no one would have predicted the eventual development of the strike as an institution of collective bargaining; when Colonel Boycott was "boycotted" by the people of his Irish village in the 1780s, no one guessed that Mexican American farmworkers would one day organize a boycott of grapes in California using essentially the same tool: like the words of Tom Paine's *Common Sense*, words matter most when they inspire people, bring them together, and create networks of trust among emerging collective actors. That is what I hope will be the message of this book.

# Sources

Abbey, Edward. 2000. *The Monkey Wrench Gang*. New York: Perennial Classics.

Abrams, Kathryn. 1998. "The New Jurisprudence of Sexual Harassment." *Cornell Law Review* 83: 1169–230.

Ackerman, Bruce. 1984. "The Storrs Lectures: Discovering the Constitution." *Yale Law Journal* 93: 1044–72.

———. 1998. *We the People: Transformations*. Cambridge, MA: Harvard University Press.

Ackerman, Peter, and Jack DuVall. 2000. *A Force More Powerful*. New York: St. Martin's Press.

Agulhon, Maurice. 1986. "Leçon Inaugurale: Chaire D'histoire contemporaine." Paris: Collège de France.

———. 1982a. *Marianne to Combat: Republican Imagery and Symbolism in France, 1789–1880*. Cambridge: Cambridge University Press.

———. 1982b. *The Republic in the Village: The People of the Var from the French Revolution to the Second Republic*. Cambridge: Cambridge University Press.

Albistur, Maïté, and Daniel Armogathe. 1977. *Histoire du féminisme français du moyen age à nos jours*. Paris: Editions des Femmes.

Alexander, Michelle. 2010. *The New Jim Crow: Mass Incarceration in the Age of Colorblindness*. New York: The New Press.

Alimi, Eitan. 2010. "The Relational Context of Radicalization: The Case of Jewish Settler Contention Before and After the Gaza Pullout." Presented to the *International Studies Association Annual Meeting*. Goteborg, Sweden.

Almog, Oz. 2000. *The Sabra: The Creation of the New Jew*. Berkeley, Los Angeles and London: University of California Press.

Almond, Gabriel A., Scott Flanagan, and Robert J. Mundt, eds. 1973. *Crisis, Choice and Change*. Boston: Little, Brown.

Almond, Gabriel A., and Sidney Verba. 1964. *The Civic Culture: Political Attitudes and Democracy in Five Nations*. Princeton, NJ: Princeton University Press.

Almond, Gabriel A., and Sidney Verba, eds. 1980. *The Civic Culture Revisited.* Boston: Little, Brown.

Alter, Karen, and Jeannette Vargas. 2001. "Explaining Variation in the Use of European Litigation Strategies: EC Law and UK Gender Equality Policy." *Comparative Political Studies* 33: 452–82.

Aminzade, Ronald R., and Doug McAdam. 2001. "Emotions and Contentious Politics." In *Silence and Voice in the Study of Contentious Politics*, edited by Ronald R. Aminzade, Jack Goldstone, Doug McAdam, Elizabeth Perry, William H. Sewell, Jr., Sidney Tarrow, and Charles Tilly. Ch. 2. Cambridge: Cambridge University Press.

Anderson, Benedict. 1991. *Imagined Communities: Reflections on the Origin and Spread of Nationalism.* 2nd ed. London: Verso.

Anderson, Benedict, and Ruth McVey. 1971. "A Preliminary Analysis of the 1 October 1965, Coup in Indonesia." Interim Reports Series, Ithaca, NY. In *Modern Indonesia Project*, edited by Southeast Asia Program. Ithaca, NY: Cornell University.

Andrews, Kenneth. 2004. *Freedom Is a Constant Struggle: The Mississippi Civil Rights Movement and Its Legacy.* Chicago: University of Chicago Press.

———. 2002. "Movement-Countermovement Dynamics and the Emergence of New Institutions: The Case of 'White Flight' Schools in Mississippi." *Social Forces* 80: 911–36.

Andrews, Kenneth T., and Michael Biggs. 2006. "The Dynamics of Protest Diffusion: Movement Organizations, Social Networks, and News Media in the 1960 Sit-Ins." *American Sociological Review* 71: 752–77.

Apter, David E. 1954. *Gold Coast in Transition.* Princeton, NJ: Princeton University Press.

———. 1961. *The Political Kingdom in Uganda: A Study in Bureaucratic Nationalism.* Princeton, NJ: Princeton University Press.

Ariès, Philippe. 1978. "L'histoire des mentalités." In *La Nouvelle histoire*, edited by Jacques le Goff, Roger Chartier, and Jacques Revel, 402–23. Paris: CEPL.

AVFT. 2006. *20 Ans de lutte contre les violences sexuelles et sexistes au travail.* Paris: AVFT.

Avineri, Shlomo, ed. 1971. *Israel and the Palestinians: Reflections on the Clash of Two National Movements.* New York: St. Martin's.

Azaryahu, Maoz, and Arnon Golan. 2001. "(Re)Naming the Landscape: The Formation of the Hebrew Map of Israel, 1949–1960." *Journal of Historical Geography* 27: 178–95.

Baer, Susanne. 2004. "Dignity or Equality? Responses to Workplace Harassment in European, German, and U.S. Law." In *Directions in Sexual Harassment Law*, edited by Catharine MacKinnon and Reva B. Siegel, 582–601. New Haven, CT: Yale University Press.

Bailyn, Bernard. 1992. *The Ideological Origins of the American Revolution.* Cambridge, MA: Harvard University Press, 1992.

Baker, Keith M. 1990. *Inventing the French Revolution: Essays on French Political Culture in the 18th Century.* Cambridge: Cambridge University Press.

Bakhtin, Mikhail M. 1981. *The Dialogic Imagination.* Austin: University of Texas Press.

Balkin, Jack M. 2011. *Constitutional Redemption: Political Faith in an Unjust World*. Cambridge, MA: Harvard University Press.

———. 2004. "Free Speech and Hostile Environments." In *Directions in Sexual Harassment Law*, edited by Catharine MacKinnon and Reva B. Siegel, 437–78. New Haven, CT: Yale University Press.

Bardenstein, Carol B. 1998. "Threads of Memory and Discourses of Rootedness: Of Trees, Oranges and the Prickly-Pear Cactus in Israel/Palestine." *Edebiyât* 8: 1–36.

Barnes, Samuel, and Max Kaase et al. 1979. *Political Action: Mass Participation in Five Western Democracies*. Thousand Oaks, CA: Sage Publications.

Barnes, Samuel, and Giacomo Sani. 1974. "Mediterranean Political Culture and Italian Politics." *British Journal of Political Science* 4: 289–303.

Barreto, Matt, and Christopher Parker. 2013. *The Paranoid Style Revisited: Support for the Tea Party and Contemporary American Politics*. Princeton, NJ: Princeton University Press.

Bartolini, Stefano, and Peter Mair. 2008. *Identity, Competition and Electoral Availability: The Stabilization of European Electorates, 1885–1985*. Cambridge: Cambridge University Press.

Bauer, Raymond R. 1952. *The New Man in Soviet Psychology*. Cambridge, MA: Harvard University Press.

Beckwith, Karen. 1996. "Women against Pit Closures: Women's Standing in a Men's Movement." *Signs* 21: 1034–68.

Beisel, Nicola. 1997. *Imperiled Innocents: Anthony Comstock and Family Reproduction in Victorian America*. Princeton, NJ: Princeton University Press.

Ben-Eliezer, Uri. 1998. *The Making of Israeli Militarism*. Bloomington: Indiana University Press.

Bennett, Lerone Jr. 1962. *Before the Mayflower: A History of the Negro in America*. Chicago: Johnson Publishing Co.

Bennett, W. Lance, and Murray Edelman. 1985. "Toward a New Political Narrative." *Journal of Communication* 35: 156–71.

Bennett, W. Lance, and Alexandra Segerberg. 2013. *The Logic of Connective Action*. Cambridge: Cambridge University Press.

Berezin, Mabel. 1997. *Making the Fascist Self: The Political Culture of Interwar Italy*. Ithaca, NY: Cornell University Press.

Bergmann, Anna. 1992. *Die Anfänge Der Modernen Geburtenkontrolle*. Hamburg: Rasch & Rohring Verlag.

Bernal, Martin. 1987. *Black Athena: The Afroasiatic Roots of Classical Civilization*. London: Free Association Books.

Bernstein, Anita. 1994. "Law, Culture, and Harassment." *University of Pennsylvania Law Review* 142: 1227–1331.

———. 1997. "Treating Sexual Harassment with Respect." *Harvard Law Review* 111: 446–524.

Bernstein, Mary, and Verta Taylor, eds. 2013. *The Marrying Kind: Debating Same-Sex Marriage within the Lesbian and Gay Movement*. Minneapolis: University of Minnesota Press.

Bernstein, Marc S. 2012. "Scofflaws, Prophets, and Other Criminals: Recent Books in English on Israeli Cinema." *Israel Studies Review* 27: 213–25.

Blee, Kathleen M. 2002. *Inside Organized Racism: Women in the Hate Movement*. Berkeley: University of California Press.

Bob, Clifford. 2011. *Globalizing the Right: Conservative Activism and World Politics*. Cambridge: Cambridge University Press.

Bobocel, D. Ramona, Leanne S. Son Hing, Liane M. Davey, David J. Stanley, and Mark P. Zanna. 1998. "Justice-Based Opposition to Social Policies: Is It Genuine?" *Journal of Personality and Social Psychology* 75: 653–69.

Bollinger, Lee C. 1986. *The Tolerant Society: Freedom of Speech and Extremist Speech in America*. Oxford: Oxford University Press.

Brecher, Jeremy. 1972. *Strike!* Boston: South End Press.

Bridges, Amy. 1986. "Becoming American: The Working Classes in the United States before the Civil War." In *Working-Class Formation: Nineteenth Century Patterns in Western Europe and the United States*, edited by Ira Katznelson and Aristide R. Zolberg, 157–96. Princeton, NJ: Princeton University Press.

Briggs, Asa. 1960. "The Language of 'Class' in Early Nineteenth-Century England." In *Essays in Labour History*, edited by Asa Briggs and John Saville, 43–73. London: MacMillan.

Browne, Kingsley R. 2004. "The Silenced Workplace: Employer Censorship under Title VII." In *Directions in Sexual Harassment Law*, edited by Catharine MacKinnon and Reva B. Siegel, 399–416. New Haven, CT: Yale University Press.

Brubaker, Rogers, and Frederick Cooper. 2000. "Beyond Identity." *Theory and Society* 29: 1–47.

Bunce, Valerie. 1999. *Subversive Institutions: The Design and the Destruction of Socialism and the State*. Cambridge: Cambridge University Press.

Burke, Edmund. 1986. *Reflections on the Revolution in France*. London: Penguin.

Burns, Stewart, ed. 1997. *Daybreak of Freedom: The Montgomery Bus Boycott*. Chapel Hill: University of North Carolina Press.

Calhoun, Cheshire. 1999. "Making up Emotional People: The Case of Romantic Love." In *The Passions of Law*, edited by Susan A. Bandes, 217–40. New York: New York University Press.

Calhoun, Craig. 1982. *The Question of Class Struggle: Social Foundations of Popular Radicalism During the Industrial Revolution*. Chicago: University of Chicago Press, 1982.

Calise, Mauro, and Theodore J. Lowi. 2010. *Hyperpolitics: An Interactive Dictionary of Political Science Concepts*. Chicago: University of Chicago Press.

Camus, Albert. 1977. *Les Justes*. Paris: Gallimard.

Caplan, Russell L. 1988. *Constitutional Brinksmanship: Amending the Constitution by National Convention*. Oxford: Oxford University Press.

Caporaso, James A., and Joseph Jupille. 2001. "The Europeanization of Gender Equality Policy and Domestic Structural Change." In *Transforming Europe: Europeanization and Domestic Change*, edited by Maria Green Cowles, James A. Caporaso, and Thomas Risse, 21–43. Ithaca, NY: Cornell University Press.

Carson, Clayborne. 1981. *In Struggle*. Cambridge, MA: Harvard University Press.

Chabot, Sean. 2012. *Transnational Roots of the Civil Rights Movement: African American Explorations of the Gandhian Repertoire*. Lanham, MD: Lexington Books.

Chaliand, Gérard. 2007. *The History of Terrorism: From Antiquity to Al Qaeda.* Berkeley and Los Angeles: University of California Press.

Chase, James S. 1973. *The Emergence of the Presidential Nominating Convention, 1789–1832.* Urbana: University of Illinois Press.

Chauncey, George. 2004. *Why Marriage? The History Shaping Today's Debate.* New York: Basic Books.

Chirot, Dan, and Clark McCauley. 2006. *Why Not Kill Them All? The Logic and Prevention of Mass Political Murder.* Princeton, NJ: Princeton University Press.

Chong, Dennis. 1991. *Collective Action and the Civil Rights Movement.* Chicago: University of Chicago Press.

Cichowski, Rachel A. 2001. "Judicial Rulemaking and the Institutionalization of the European Union Sex Policy." In *The Institutionalization of Europe*, edited by Alec Stone Sweet, Neil Fligstein, and Wayne Sandholtz. Ch. 6. Oxford: Oxford University Press.

Cixious, Helene. 1986. *Entre l'écriture.* Paris: Editions des Femmes.

Clark, Terry Nichols, Seymour Martin Lipset, and Michael Rempel. 1993. "The Declining Political Significance of Social Class." *International Sociology* 8: 293–316.

Collier, David, and Ruth Collier. 1991. *Shaping the Political Arena: Critical Junctures, the Labor Movement, and Regime Dynamics in Latin America.* Princeton, NJ: Princeton University Press.

Crimp, Douglas. 2002. *Melancholia and Moralism: Essays on AIDS and Queer Politics.* Cambridge, MA: MIT Press.

Crouch, Colin, and Alessandro Pizzorno, eds. 1978. *The Resurgence of Class Conflict in Western Europe.* 2 vols. London: McMillan Press.

Dahrendorf, Ralf. 1959. *Class and Class Conflict in Industrial Society.* Stanford, CA: Stanford University Press.

Daly, Mary. 1973. *Beyond God the Father: Toward a Philosophy of Women's Liberation.* Boston: Beacon Press.

Daniel, G. Reginald. 2001. *More Than Black: Multiracial Identity and the New Racial Order.* Philadelphia: Temple University Press.

Darnton, Robert, and Daniel Roche, eds. 1989. *Revolution in Print: The Press in France, 1775–1800.* Berkeley and Los Angeles: University of California Press.

Davis, F. James. 2001. *Who Is Black? One Nation's Definition.* University Park: Pennsylvania State University Press.

de Mari, Eric. 1991. "La Mise hors de la loi sous la révolution française: 19 Mars 1793–9 Thermidor Ann II." Montpellier: University of Montpellier I.

della Porta, Donatella. 2013. *Clandestine Political Violence.* Cambridge: Cambridge University Press.

———, ed. 2007. *The Global Justice Movement: Cross-National and Transnational Perspectives.* Boulder, CO: Paradigm Publishers.

———. 1995. *Social Movements, Political Violence and the State: A Comparative Analysis of Italy and Germany.* Cambridge: Cambridge University Press.

Dorf, Michael C. 2011. "Same-Sex Marriage, Second-Class Citizenship, and Law's Social Meaning." *Virginia Law Review* 97: 1267–1346.

Dorf, Michael C., and Sidney Tarrow. 2013. "Strange Bedfellows: Unlikely Issues: How an Anticipatory Counter-Movement Brought Same-Sex Marriage into the Public Arena." Unpublished paper, Ithaca, NY: Cornell University Law School.

Drucker, Peter. 1993. *Post-Capitalist Society*. New York: Harper Business.

Du Bois, W. E. B. 2005. *The Illustrated Souls of Black Folk*. Boulder, CO: Paradigm Publishers.

Duggan, Lisa. 2002. "The New Homonormativity: The Sexual Politics of Neoliberalism." In *Materializing Democracy: Towards a Revitalized Cultural Politics*, edited by Russ Castronovo and Dana Nelson, 175–94. Durham, NC: Duke University Press.

Edelman, Lauren B., Howard S. Erlanger, and John Lande. 1993. "Internal Dispute Resolution: The Transformation of Civil Rights in the Workplace." *Law and Society Review* 27: 497–534.

Edelman, Lauren B., Christopher Uggen, and Howard S. Erlanger. 1999. "The Endogeneity of Legal Regulation: Grievance Procedures as Rational Myth." *American Journal of Sociology* 105: 406–54.

Edelman, Murray. 1977. *Political Language: Words That Succeed and Policies That Fail*. New York: Academic Press.

———. 1971. *Politics as Symbolic Action: Mass Arousal and Quiescence*. New York: Markham.

———. 1964. *The Symbolic Uses of Politics*. Urbana: University of Illinois Press.

Ehrenreich, Rosa. 1999. "Dignity and Discrimination: Toward a Pluralistic Understanding of Workplace Harassment." *Georgia Law Review* 88: 3–26.

Enyedi, Zsolt. 2005. "The Role of Agency in Cleavage Formation." *European Journal of Political Research* 44: 697–720.

Evans, Geoffrey, and Nan Dirk De Graaf. 2012. "Explaining Cleavage Strength: The Role of Party Positions." In *Political Choice Matters: Explaining the Strength of Class and Religious Cleavages in Cross-National Perspective*, edited by Geoffrey Evans and Nan Dirk De Graaf, 3–26. Oxford: Oxford University Press.

———, eds. 2012. *Political Choice Matters: Explaining the Strength of Class and Religious Cleavages in Cross-National Perspective*. Oxford: Oxford University Press.

Evans, Sara M. 1980. *Personal Politics: The Roots of Women's Liberation in the Civil Rights Movement and the New Left*. New York: Vintage Books.

Faust, Drew Gilpin. 1981. *The Ideology of Slavery: Proslavery Thought in the Antebellum South, 1830–1860*. Baton Rouge: Louisiana State University Press.

Fetner, Tina. 2008. *How the Religious Right Shaped Lesbian and Gay Activism*. Minneapolis: University of Minnesota Press.

Flam, Helena. 2005. "Emotions' Map." In *Emotions and Social Movements*, edited by Helena Flam and Debra King, 19–56. London: Routledge.

Flam, Helena, and Debra King, eds. 2005. *Emotions and Social Movements*. London: Routledge.

Foot, Michael, and Isaac Kramnick, eds. 1987. *The Thomas Paine Reader*. New York: Penguin.

Frank, Jason. 2010. *Constituent Moments: Enacting the People in Postrevolutionary America*. Durham, NC: Duke University Press.

Franklin, Mark, Thomas Mackie, and Henry Valen, eds. 1992. *Electoral Change: Responses to Evolving Social and Attitudinal Structures in Western Countries*. Cambridge: Cambridge University Press.

Freeden, Michael. 1996. *Ideologies and Political Theory: A Conceptual Approach*. Oxford: Oxford University Press.

Friedman, Gabrielle, and James Q. Whitman. 2002–3. "The European Transformation of Harassment Law: Discrimination Versus Dignity." *Columbia Journal of European Law* 9: 241–74.

Friedman, Tom. 1996. "Revolt of the Wannabees." *New York Times*, February 7, p. A15.

Fuentes, Sonia Pressman. 1999. *Eat First: You Don't Know What They'll Give You*. New York: XLibris.

Fukayama, Francis. 1989. "The End of History?" *National Interest* (Summer): 3–18.

Furet, François. 1989. "The Terror." In *Critical Dictionary of the French Revolution*, edited by François Furet and Mona Ozouf, 137–50. Cambridge, MA: Harvard University Press.

Furet, François, and Mona Ozouf, eds. 1989. *Critical Dictionary of the French Revolution*. 4 vols. Cambridge, MA: Harvard University Press.

Gagnon, V. P. Jr. 2004. *The Myth of Ethnic War: Serbia and Croatia in the 1990s*. Ithaca, NY: Cornell University Press.

Galnoor, Itzhak. 1995. *The Partition of Palestine: Decision Crossroads in the Zionist Movement*. Albany: State University of New York Press.

Gamson, William A. 1988. "Political Discourse and Collective Action." In *From Structure to Action: Comparing Social Movement Research across Cultures: International Social Movement Research I*, edited by Bert Klandermans, Hanspeter Kriesi, and Sidney Tarrow, 219–44. Greenwich, CT: JAI Press.

———. 1992a. "The Social Psychology of Collective Action." In *Frontiers in Social Movement Theory*, edited by Aldon Morris and Carol McClurg Mueller, 53–76. New Haven, CT: Yale University Press.

———. 1992b. *Talking Politics*. Cambridge: Cambridge University Press.

Gamson, William A., and Andre Modigliani. 1987. "The Changing Culture of Affirmative Action." In *Research in Social Movements, Culture and Change*, edited by Louis Kriesberg, 137–77. Greenwich, CT: JAI.

Gamson, William, and Catherine Lasch. 1983. "The Political Culture of Welfare Policy." In *Evaluating the Welfare State*, edited by S. E. Spiro and E. Yechtman-Yaar. New York: Academic Press.

Ganz, Marshall. 2009. *Why David Sometimes Wins: Leadership, Organization, and Strategy in the California Farm Worker Movement*. Oxford: Oxford University Press.

Gates, Henry Louis Jr. 1994. *Colored People: A Memoir*. New York: Alfred A. Knopf.

Gates, Henry Louis Jr., and Gene Andrew Jarrett, eds. 2007. *The New Negro: Readings on Race, Representation, and African American Culture, 1892–1938*. Princeton, NJ: Princeton University Press.

Genovese, Eugene D. 1972. *Roll, Jordan, Roll.* New York: Random House.

Gilligan, Carol. 1982. *In a Different Voice: Psychological Theory and Women's Development.* Cambridge, MA: Harvard University Press.

Givan, Rebecca K., Kenneth Roberts, and Sarah A. Soule, eds. 2010. *The Diffusion of Social Movements: Actors, Mechanisms, and Political Effects.* Cambridge: Cambridge University Press.

Glenny, Misha. 1994. *The Fall of Yugoslavia.* New York: Penguin.

Godéchot, Jacques. 1965. *France and the Atlantic Revolution of the Eighteenth Century, 1770–1799.* Glencoe, IL: Free Press.

———. 1968. *Les Institutions de la France sous la révolution et l'empire.* Paris: Presses Universitaires de France.

Goffman, Erving. 1974. *Frame Analysis: An Essay on the Organization of Experience.* New York: Harper Colophon, 1974.

Goldthorpe, John H. 1963. *The Affluent Worker.* Cambridge: Cambridge University Press.

Goodheart, Adam. 2011. *1861: The Civil War Awakening.* New York: Knopf.

Goodwin, Jeff, and James Jasper. 2006. "Emotions and Social Movements." In *Handbook of the Sociology of Emotions*, edited by Jan E. Stets and Jonathan H. Turner, 611–36. New York: Springer.

Goodwin, Jeff, James M. Jasper, and Francesca Polletta, eds. 2001. *Passionate Politics: Emotions and Social Movements.* Chicago: University of Chicago Press.

Gordon, Dexter B. 2003. *Black Identity: Rhetoric, Ideology, and Nineteenth-Century Black Nationalism.* Carbondale: Southern Illinois University Press.

Gordon, Linda. 1977. *Woman's Body, Woman's Right: Birth Control in America.* 3rd ed. New York: Penguin.

Gough, Hugh. 1987. "Genocide and the Bicentenary: The French Revolution and the Revenge of the Vendée." *Historical Journal* 30: 977–88.

———. 2010. *The Terror in the French Revolution.* London: Palgrave Macmillan.

Gould, Deborah. 2009. *Moving Politics: Emotion and Act Up's Fight against AIDS.* Chicago: University of Chicago Press.

Gould, Roger. 1995. *Insurgent Identities: Class, Community, and Protest in Paris from 1848 to the Commune.* Chicago: University of Chicago Press.

Graeber, David. 2011. "Occupy Wall Street's Anarchist Roots: The 'Occupy' Movement Is One of Several in American History to Be Based on Anarchist Principles." http://www.Aljazeera.Com/Indepth/Opinion/2011/11/201111287283590450.8.html.

Gramsci, Antonio. 1971. *Selections from the Prison Notebooks of Antonio Gramsci.* Edited by Quintin Hoare and Geoffrey Nowell-Smith. New York: International Publishers.

Greene, Jack P., and J. R. Pole, eds. 2000. *A Companion to the American Revolution.* Malden, MA: Blackwell.

Grusky, David B., and Jesper B. Sorenson. 1998. "Can Class Analysis Be Salvaged?" *American Journal of Sociology* 103: 1187–234.

Guilhaumou, Jacques. 1989. *La Langue politique et la révolution française.* Paris: Meridiens Klincksieck.

Hardt, Michael, and Toni Negri. 2004. *Multitude: War and Democracy in the Age of Empire*. New York: Penguin.

Hare, Ivan, and James Weinstein, eds. 2009. *Extreme Speech and Democracy*. Oxford: Oxford University Press.

Harris, Cheryl I. 2010. "The Story of Plessy V. Ferguson: The Death and Resurrection of Racial Formalism." In *Constitutional Law Stories*, edited by Michael C. Dorf, 183–230. New York: Foundation Press.

Harris, Middleton, ed. 1974. *The Black Book*. New York: Random House.

Harris, Timothy. 2006. *Revolution: The Great Crisis of the British Monarchy: 1685–1720*. London: Allen Lane.

Harrison, Hubert H. 1920. *When Africa Awakes: The "Inside Story" of the Stirrings and Strivings of the New Negro in the Western World*. New York: Porro Press.

Hassanpour, Navid. In press. "Media Disruption and Revolutionary Unrest: Evidence from Mubarak's Quasi-Experiment." *Political Communication* 30.

Hellman, Judy. 1999. "Real and Virtual Chiapas: Magic Realism and the Left." In *Socialist Register 2000: Necessary and Unnecessary Utopias*, edited by Leo Panich and Colin Leys, 161–86. London: Merlin.

Hellman, Stephen. 1975. "The PCI's Alliance Strategy and the Case of the Middle Classes." In *Communism in Italy and France*, edited by Donald L. M. Blackmer and Sidney Tarrow, 372–419. Princeton, NJ: Princeton University Press.

Hervik, Peter. 2006. "The Predictable Responses to the Danish Cartoons." *Global Media and Communication* 2: 225–30.

Hirigoyen, Marie-France. 2001. *Harcèlement moral: Déméler le vrai du faux*. Paris: Syros.

Hirsch-Hoefler, Sivan. 2008. "Mobilizing Politics: The Mobilization Strategies of the Israeli Settlement Movement." PhD thesis, University of Antwerp Department of Political Science.

Hobsbawm, Eric J. 1984. *Labouring Men: Further Studies in the History of Labour*. London: Weidenfeld and Nocolson.

Hochschild, Jennifer L. 1984. *The New American Dilemma: Liberal Democracy and School Desegregation*. New Haven, CT: Yale University Press.

Hochschild, Jennifer L., Vesla Weaver, and Traci Burch. 2012. *Creating a New Racial Order*. Princeton, NJ: Princeton University Press.

Hoffmann, Stefan, and Katharina Hutter. 2012. "Carrotmob as a New Form of Ethical Consumption." *Journal of Consumer Policy* 35: 215–36.

Hoggart, Richard. 1961. *The Uses of Literacy*. Boston: Beacon Press.

Hollander, Barry A. 2010. "Persistence in the Perception of Barack Obama as a Muslim in the 2008 Presidential Campaign." *Journal of Media and Religion* 9: 55–66.

Holquist, Michael. 1990. *Dialogism: Bakhtin and His World*. London: Routledge.

Hunt, Lynn. 1992. *The Family Romance of the French Revolution*. Berkeley: University of California Press.

———. 2007. *Inventing Human Rights: A History*. New York: W.W. Norton.

———. 1984. *Politics, Culture and Class in the French Revolution*. Berkeley: University of California Press.

Hurst, William. 2009. "Mass Frames and Worker Protest." In *Popular Protest in China*, edited by Kevin J. O'Brien, 71–87. Cambridge, MA: Harvard University Press.

Imig, Doug, and Sidney Tarrow, eds. 2001. *Contentious Europeans: Protest and Politics in an Emerging Polity*. Lanham, MD: Rowman and Littlefield.

Inglehart, Ronald. 1990. *Culture Shift in Advanced Industrial Societies*. Princeton, NJ: Princeton University Press.

———. 1988. "The Renaissance of Political Culture." *American Political Science Review* 82: 1203–30.

———. 1977. *The Silent Revolution: Changing Values and Political Styles among Western Politics*. Princeton, NJ: Princeton University Press.

Janove, Jathan W. 2003. "The Farrager/Ellerth Decision Tree: Lower Courts Put New Growth on Five-Year-Old Branches." *Human Relations* 48: 1047–59.

Jasper, James. 1997. *The Art of Moral Protest: Culture, Biography, and Creativity in Social Movements*. Chicago: University of Chicago Press, 1997.

Jones, Adam. 2010. *Genocide: A Comprehensive Introduction*. London: Routledge.

Kammen, Michael. 1987. *A Machine That Would Go of Itself*. New York: Vintage.

Kanter, Rosabeth Moss. 1972. *Commitment and Community: Communes and Utopia in Sociological Perspective*. Cambridge, MA: Harvard University Press.

Kaplan, Robert D. 1993. *Balkan Ghosts: A Journey through History*. New York: St. Martin's.

Kaplan, Steven L. 1982. "The Famine Plot Persuasion." *Transactions of the American Philosophical Society*, no. 73: Part 3.

Katznelson, Ira. 1981. *City Trenches: Urban Politics and the Patterning of Class in the United States*. New York: Pantheon Books.

———. 1986. "Working-Class Formation: Constructing Cases and Comparisons." In *Working-Class Formation: Nineteenth-Century Patterns in Western Europe and the United States*, edited by Ira Katznelson and Aristide R. Zolberg, 3–44. Princeton, NJ: Princeton University Press.

Kennedy, David M. 1970. *Birth Control in America: The Career of Margaret Sanger*. New Haven, CT: Yale University Press.

Kennedy, Randall. 2002. *Nigger: The Strange Career of a Troublesome Word*. New York: Pantheon Books.

Kertzer, David. 1990. *Comrades and Christians: Religion and Political Struggle in Communist Italy*. Long Grove IL: Waveland Press.

———. 1988. *Ritual, Politics and Power*. New Haven. CT: Yale University Press.

Kestnbaum, Meyer. 2002. "Citizen-Soldiers, National Service and the Mass Army: The Birth of Conscription in Revolutionary Europe and North America." *Armed Forces and Society* 20: 117–44.

Khalidi, Walid. 1992. *All That Remains: The Palestinian Villages Occupied and Depopulated by Israel in the 1948 War*. Washington, D.C.: Institute for Palestine Studies.

Kimmerling, Baruch. 1993. "Patterns of Militarism in Israel." *European Journal of Sociology* 34: 196–223.

Kinder, Donald R., and Lynn M. Sanders. 1996. *Divided by Color: Racial Politics and Democratic Ideals*. Chicago: University of Chicago Press.

King, Desmond S., and Rogers M. Smith. 2011. *Still a House Divided: Race and Politics in Obama's America*. Oxford: Oxford University Press.

King, Martin Luther Jr. 1957. "Facing the Challenge of a New Age." *Phylon Quarterly* 18: 25–34.

Kirchheimer, Otto. 1966. "The Transformation of the European Party Systems." In *Political Parties and Political Development*, edited by Joseph LaPalombara and Myron Weiner. Ch. 6. Princeton, NJ: Princeton University Press.

Kitschelt, Herbert. 1994. *The Transformation of European Social Democracy*. Cambridge: Cambridge University Press.

Klandermans, Bert. 1988. "The Formation and Mobilization of Consensus." In *From Structure to Action: Comparing Social Movement Research across Cultures*, edited by Bert Klandermans, H. Kriesi, and S. Tarrow, 173–96. Greenwich, CT: JAI Press.

Klarman, Michael J. 2012. *From the Closet to the Altar: Courts, Backlash, and the Struggle for Same-Sex Marriage*. Oxford: Oxford University Press.

Koopmans, Ruud. 1996. "Explaining the Rise of Racist and Extreme-Right Violence in Western Europe: Grievances or Opportunities." *European Journal of Political Research* 30: 185–216.

Kriesi, Hanspeter, et al. 1995. *The Politics of New Social Movements in Western Europe*. Minneapolis: University of Minnesota Press.

Krinsky, John. 2008. *Free Labor: Workfare and the Contested Language of Neoliberalism*. Chicago: University of Chicago Press.

Krinsky, John, and Ann Mische. In press. "Formations and Formalisms: Charles Tilly and the Paradox of the Actor." *Annual Review of Sociology* 39: 1–28.

Kubik, Jan. 1994. *The Power of Symbols against the Symbols of Power: The Rise of Solidarity and the Fall of State Socialism in Poland*. University Park: Pennsylvania State University Press.

Lacy, Karyn R. 2007. *Blue-Chip Black: Race, Class, and Status in the New Black Middle Class*. Berkeley and Los Angeles: University of California Press.

Laitin, David. 1986. *Hegemony and Culture: Politics and Religious Change among the Yoruba*. Chicago: Chicago University Press.

———. 1988. "Political Culture and Political Preferences." *American Political Science Review* 82: 589–97.

———. 1977. *Politics, Language and Thought: The Somali Experience*. Chicago: University of Chicago Press.

Landes, Joan B. 1988. *Women and the Public Sphere in the Age of the French Revolution*. Ithaca, NY: Cornell University Press.

LaPalombara, Joseph. 1987. *Democracy, Italian Style*. New Haven, CT: Yale University Press.

LaPalombara, Joseph, and Myron Weiner, eds. 1966. *Political Parties and Political Development*. Princeton, NJ: Princeton University Press.

Le Gal, Sebastien. 2012. "Aux Origines du droit à la sureté." In *Le Droit à la sureté: État des lieux, état du droit*, edited by Ludovic Garrido, 19–42. Paris: Editions Cujas.

————. 2005. "La Suspension du droit en révolution, entre volonté de rupture et permanence d'une tentation: L'article 92 de la constitution de l'an VIII." In *Le Droit en Révolution*, edited by AFHIP. Aix-en-Provence, France: PUAM.

————. 2011. "Les Origines de l'état de siège en France; Ancien régime – révolution." Thesis, University of Lyons Faculty of Law.

Le Magueresse, Catherine. In preparation. "Quand les femmes disent non." Unpublished thesis, University of Paris.

Leader Maynard, Jonathan. 2014. "Rethinking the Role of Ideology in Mass Atrocities," *Terrorism and Political Violence* 25: in press.

Lefkowitz, Mary R., and Guy Maclean Rogers, eds. 1996. *Black Athena Revisited*. Chapel Hill: University of North Carolina Press.

Lepore, Jill. 2011. "Birthright: What's Next for Planned Parenthood." *New Yorker*, November 14, 44–55.

Leunberger, Christine, and Isaak Schnell. 2010. "The Politics of Maps: Constructing National Territories in Israel." *Social Studies of Science* 40: 803–42.

Levy, Yagil. 2007. *Israel's Materialist Militarism*. Lanham, MD: Lexington.

Lewis, Anthony. 2007. *Freedom for the Thought That We Hate*. New York: Basic Books.

Lichbach, Mark, and Helma DeVries. 2007. "Mechanisms of Globalized Protest Movements." In *The Oxford Handbook of Comparative Politics*, edited by Charles Boix and Susan C. Stokes, 461–96. Oxford: Oxford University Press.

Lindkilde, Lasse. 2008. "In the Name of the Prophet? Danish Muslim Mobilization During the Muhammad Caricatures Controversy." *Mobilization* 13: 219–38.

Linebaugh, Peter, and Marcus Rediker. 1990. "The Many-Headed Hydra: Sailors, Slaves, and the Atlantic Working Class in the Eighteenth Century." *Journal of Historical Sociology* 3: 225–52.

Lipset, Seymour Martin, and Stein Rokkan. 1967. *Party Systems and Voter Alignments: Cross-National Perspectives*. Glencoe, IL: Free Press.

Locke, Alain, ed. 1983. *The New Negro*. New York: Atheneum.

Lohmann, Susanne. 1994. "The Dynamics of Information Cascades: The Monday Demonstrations in Leizpzig, East Germany, 1989–1991." *World Politics* 47: 42–101.

Louis, Marie-Victoire. 1994. *Le droit de cuissage*. Paris: Éditions de l'atelier.

Lustick, Ian S. 1999. "Hegemony and the Riddle of Nationalism." In *Ethnic Conflict and International Politics in the Middle East*, edited by Leonard Binder, 332–59. Gainesville: University Press of Florida.

Luxemburg, Rosa. 1968. *Rosa Luxemburg*, Vol. 2. Edited by J. Nettl. Oxford: Oxford University Press.

Lynn, John A. 1983. *The Bayonets of the Republic: Motivation and Tactics in the Army of Revolutionary France, 1791–94*. Urbana: University of Illinois Press.

Lyttelton, Adrian. 2004. *The Seizure of Power: Fascism in Italy, 1919–1929*. London: Routledge.

Machiavelli, Niccolò. 1977. *The Prince*. New York: W.W. Norton.

MacKinnon, Catharine. 2004. "Afterword." In *Directions in Sexual Harassment Law*, edited by Catharine MacKinnon and Reva B. Siegel, 672–704. New Haven, CT: Yale University Press.

———. 1993. *Only Words*. Cambridge, MA: Harvard University Press.

———. 1979. *Sexual Harassment of Working Women: A Case of Sex Discrimination*. New Haven, CT: Yale University Press.

MacKinnon, Catharine, and Reva B. Siegel, eds. 2004. *Directions in Sexual Harassment Law*. New Haven, CT: Yale University Press.

Mansbridge, Jane, and Katherine Flaster. 2007. "The Cultural Politics of Everyday Discourse: The Case of 'Male Chauvinist.'" *Critical Sociology* 33: 627–60.

Margulies, Joseph. 2013. *What Changed When Everything Changed: 9/11 and the Making of National Identity*. New Haven, CT: Yale University Press.

Marlow, Joyce. 1973. *Captain Boycott and the Irish*. New York: Saturday Review Press.

Marshall, Thomas H. 1964. *Class, Citizenship and Social Development*. Garden City, NY: Doubleday.

Martin, Jean-Clément. 1998. *Contre-révolution, révolution et nation en France, 1789–1799*. Paris: Seuil.

———. 2006. *Violence et révolution*. Paris: Editions du Seuil.

Marx, Anthony W. 1998. *Making Race and Nation: A Comparison of South Africa, the United States, and Brazil*. Cambridge: Cambridge University Press.

Marx, Karl, and Friedrich Engels. 2012. *The Communist Manifesto*. Edited by Jeffrey C. Isaac. New Haven, CT: Yale University Press.

Matovski, Aleksandar. 2008. "Macedonia after Bucharest: Avoiding Another European Failure in the Balkans." In *ISS Opinion*. Brussels: European Union Institute for Security Studies.

Mayer, Nonna. 2012. "Comment aborder les métamorphoses du vote ouvrier en Europe." In *Une Droitisation de la classe ouvrière en Europe*, edited by Jean-Michel de Waile and Mathieu Vieira, 27–40. Paris: Economica.

McAdam, Doug. 1988. *Freedom Summer*. New York: Oxford University Press.

———. 1999 [1982]. *Political Process and the Development of Black Insurgency, 1930–1970*. Chicago: University of Chicago Press.

———. 1983. "Tactical Innovation and the Pace of Insurgency." *American Sociological Review* 48: 735–54.

McAdam, Doug, and Hillary Schaffer Boudet. 2012. "Putting Social Movements in Their Place." Cambridge: Cambridge University Press.

McAdam, Doug, and Dieter Rucht. 1993. "The Cross-National Diffusion of Movement Ideas." *The Annals of the American Academy of the Political and Social Sciences* 528: 56–74.

McAdam, Doug, and Sidney Tarrow. 2005. "Scale Shift in Transnational Contention." In *Transnational Protest & Global Activism*, edited by Donatella della Porta and Sidney Tarrow, 121–147. Lanham, MD: Rowman and Littlefield.

McAdam, Doug, Sidney Tarrow, and Charles Tilly. 2001. *Dynamics of Contention*. Cambridge: Cambridge University Press.

McCann, Carole. 1994. *Birth Control Politics in the United States, 1916–1945*. Ithaca, NY: Cornell University Press.

McConahay, John B., and Joseph C. Hough Jr. 1976. "Symbolic Racism." *Journal of Social Issues* 32: 23–45.

Melucci, Alberto. 1988. "Getting Involved: Identity and Mobilization in Social Movements." In *From Structure to Action: Comparing Social Movements across Cultures*, edited by Bert Klandermans, Hanspeter Kriesi, and Sidney Tarrow, 329–48. Greenwich, CT: JAI Press.

Merry, Sally Engle. 2006. "Transnational Human Rights and Local Activism: Mapping the Middle." *American Anthropologist* 108: 38–51.

Meyer, David S. and Suzanne Staggenborg. 1996. "Movements, Countermovements, and the Structure of Political Opportunity." *American Journal of Sociology* 101: 1628–60.

Michelat, Guy, and Michel Simon. 2011. "Inquietudes, dynamiques ideologiques, attitudes politiques: Quoi de neuf?" In *L'état de l'opinion*, edited by Olivier Duhamel and Edouard Lecerf, 137–64. Paris: Editions du Seuil.

Miller, Mary Ashburn. 2011. *A Natural History of Revolution: Violence and Nature in the French Revolutionary Imagination*. Ithaca, NY: Cornell University Press.

Mink, Gwendolyn. 2000. *Hostile Environment: The Political Betrayal of Sexually Harassed Women*. Ithaca, NY: Cornell University Press.

Morris, Aldon. 1984. *The Origins of the Civil Rights Movement: Black Communities Organizing for Change*. New York: Free Press.

Morris, Aldon, and Carol Mueller, eds. 1992. *Frontiers of Social Movement Research*. New Haven, CT: Yale University Press.

Moyn, Samuel. 2010. *The Last Utopia: Human Rights in History*. Cambridge, MA: Harvard University Press.

Mudde, Cas. 2007. *Populist Radical Rightwing Parties in Europe*. Cambridge: Cambridge University Press.

Myrdal, Gunnar. 1944. *An American Dilemma: The Negro Problem and Modern Democracy*. New York: Harper.

Oakes, James. 2012. *Freedom National: The Destruction of Slavery in the United States, 1861–1865*. New York: W.W. Norton.

Offe, Claus. 1985. "New Social Movements: Challenging the Boundaries of Institutional Politics." *Social Research* 52: 817–68.

Ogletree, Charles J. Jr. 2010. *The Presumption of Guilt: The Arrest of Henry Louis Gates Jr. and Race, Class, and Crime in America*. New York: Palgrave Macmillan.

Olesen, Thomas. 2007. "Contentious Cartoons: Elite and Media-Driven Mobilization." *Mobilization* 12: 37–52.

———. 2005. *International Zapatismo: The Construction of Solidarity in the Age of Globalization*. London: ZED Books.

Olson, Mancur. 1965. *The Logic of Collective Action*. Cambridge, MA: Harvard University Press.

Opp, Karl-Dieter. 1989. *The Rationality of Political Protest*. Boulder, CO: Westview Press.

Oppenheimer, David B. 2004. "Employer Liability for Sexual Harassment by Supervisors." In *Directions in Sexual Harassment Law*, edited by Catharine MacKinnon and Reva B. Siegel, 272–89. New Haven, CT: Yale University Press.

Ozouf, Mona. 1988. *Festivals and the French Revolution*. Translated by Alan Sheridan. Cambridge, MA: Harvard University Press.

Paine, Thomas. 1989. *Political Writings*. Edited by Bruce Kuklick. Cambridge: Cambridge University Press.

Palmer, Robert R. 1959. *The Age of the Democratic Revolution: A Political History of Europe and America, 1760–1800*. Princeton, NJ: Princeton University Press.

Palmer, R. R. 1940. "The National Idea in France before the Revolution." *Journal of the History of Ideas* 1: 95–111.

Perrot, Michelle. 1986. "On the Formation of the French Working Class." In *Working-Class Formation: Nineteenth-Century Patterns in Western Europe and the United States*, edited by Ira Katznelson and Aristide R. Zolberg, 71–110. Princeton, NJ: Princeton University Press.

Philippa, M., F. Debrandarere, A. Quak, T. Schoonheim, and N. van der Sijs. 2009. *Etymologisch Soordenboek Van Het Nederlands*. Amsterdam: Amsterdam University Press.

Pickerill, Jenny, and John Krinsky, eds. 2012. Special Issue: "Occupy!" *Social Movement Studies* 11: 279–409.

Pickles, John. 1991. "Texts, Hermeneutics and Propaganda Maps." In *Writing Worlds: Discourse, Text and Metaphor in the Representation of Landscape*, edited by T. J. Barnes and J. S. Duncan, 193–230. London: Routledge.

Pizzorno, Alessandro. 1964. "The Individualistic Mobilization of Europe." *Daedalus* 93: 199–224.

Plongeron, Bernard. 1973. *Théologie et politique au siècle des lumières: 1770–1820*. Paris: Droz.

Plows, Andrea, Derek Wall, and Brian Doherty. 2004. "Covert Repertoires: Ecotage in the UK." *Social Movement Studies* 3: 199–219.

Pocock, John. 1975. *The Machiavellian Moment: Florentine Political Theory and the Atlantic Republican Tradition*. Princeton, NJ: Princeton University Press.

Polanyi, Karl. 2001. *The Great Transformation: The Political and Economic Origins of Our Time*. Boston: Beacon Press.

Polenberg, Richard. 1999. *Fighting Faiths: The Abrams Case, the Supreme Court, and Free Speech*. Ithaca, NY: Cornell University Press.

Polletta, Francesca. 2006. *It Was Like a Fever: Story-Telling in Protest and Politics*. Chicago: University of Chicago Press.

Portes, Alejandro. 2000. "The Resilient Importance of Class: A Nominalist Analysis." *Political Power and Social Theory* 14: 249–84.

Przeworski, Adam, and John Sprague. 1986. *Paper Stones: A History of Electoral Socialism*. Chicago: University of Chicago Press.

Putnam, Robert D. 1971. *The Beliefs of Politicians*. New Haven, CT: Yale University Press.

Pye, Lucien, and Sidney Verba, ed. 1965. *Political Culture and Political Development*. Princeton, NJ: Princeton University Press.

Rana, Aziz. 2010. *The Two Faces of American Freedom*. Cambridge, MA: Harvard University Press.

Rancière, Jacques. 1981. *La Nuit des proletaires*. Paris: Fayard.

Ravaillon, Martin. 2011. "The Two Poverty Enlightenments: Historical Insights from Digitalized Books Spanning Three Centuries." Washington, DC: World Bank Development Research Group.

Rials, Stephane, ed. 1982. *Textes constitutionnels français*. Paris: PUF.

Riley, Denise. 1988. *"Am I That Name?" Feminism and the Category of "Women" in History*. Minneapolis: University of Minnesota Press.

Roberts, Dorothy. 1998. *Killing the Black Body*. New York: Vintage.

Rodgers, Daniel T. 2011. *Age of Fracture*. Cambridge, MA: Harvard University Press.

———. 1987. *Contested Truths: Keywords in American Politics since Independence*. New York: Basic Books.

Roggeband, Conny. 2010. "Transnational Networks and Institutions: How Diffusion Shaped the Politicization of Sexual Harassment in Europe." In *The Diffusion of Social Movements: Actors, Mechanisms, and Political Effects*, edited by Rebecca Kolins Givan, Kenneth M. Roberts, and Sarah A. Soule, 19–33. Cambridge: Cambridge University Press.

Rojas, Fabio. 2007. *From Black Power to Black Studies: How a Radical Social Movement Became an Academic Discipline*. Baltimore: Johns Hopkins University Press.

Roth, Benita. 2004. *Separate Roads to Feminism: Black, Chicana, and White Feminist Movements in America's Second Wave*. Cambridge: Cambridge University Press.

Roth, Silke. 2005. "Sisterhood and Exclusionary Solidarity in a Labor Women's Organization." In *Emotions and Social Movements*, edited by Helena Flam and Debra King, 189–206. London: Routledge.

Rousseau, Jean-Jacques. 1972. *The Government of Poland*. Translated by Willmoore Kendall. Indianapolis: Bobbs-Merrill.

———. 1978. *On the Social Contract with the Geneva Manuscript and Political Economy*. Translated by J. R. Masters. New York: St. Martin's.

Roy, William G. 2010. *Reds, Whites, and Blues: Social Movements, Folk Music, and Race in the United States*. Princeton, NJ: Princeton University Press.

Rupp, Leila J., and Verta Taylor. 1987. *Survival in the Doldrums: The American Women's Rights Movement, 1945 to the 1960s*. Oxford: Oxford University Press.

Saguy, Abigail C. 2000. "Employment Discrimination or Sexual Violence: Defining Sexual Harassment in American and French Law." *Law and Society Review* 34: 1091–128.

———. 2004. "French and American Lawyers Define Sexual Harassment." In *Directions in Sexual Harassment Law*, edited by Catharine MacKinnon and Reva B. Siegel, 602–17. New Haven, CT: Yale University Press.

Sanger, Margaret. 1921. *What Every Girl Should Know*. New York: Maisel.

Sapir, Edward. 1934. "Symbolism." In *Encyclopedia of the Social Sciences*, edited by Edward R. A. Seligman and Alvin Johnson, 492–95. New York: MacMillan.

Saussure, Ferdinand de. 1983. *Course in General Linguistics*. Oxford: Oxford University Press.

Schama, Simon. 1977. *Patriots and Liberators: Revolution in the Netherlands, 1780–1813.* New York: Knopf.

Schauer, Frederick. 2004. "The Speech-ing of Sexual Harassment." In *Directions in Sexual Harassment Law,* edited by Catharine MacKinnon and Reva B. Siegel, 347–64. New Haven, CT: Yale University Press, 2004.

Scheff, Thomas J. 1994. *Bloody Revenge.* Boulder, CO: Westview.

Scheppele, Kim Lane. 2000. "The Constitutional Basis of Hungarian Conservatism." *East European Constitutional Review* 9: 51–62.

Schiffrin, Steven H. 1994. "Racist Speech, Outsider Jurisprudence, and the Meaning of America." *Cornell Law Review* 80: 43–103.

Scott, James C. 1990. *Domination and the Arts of Resistance: Hidden Transcripts.* New Haven, CT: Yale University Press, 1990.

———. 1976. *The Moral Economy of the Peasant: Rebellion and Subsistence in Southeast Asia.* New Haven, CT: Yale University Press.

———. 1985. *Weapons of the Weak: Everyday Forms of Resistance.* New Haven, CT: Yale University Press, 1985.

Sears, David O., and P. J. Henry. 2005. "Over Thirty Years Later: A Contemporary Look at Symbolic Racism." *Advances in Experimental Social Psychology* 37: 95–150.

Selbin, Eric. 1993. *Modern Latin American Revolutions.* Boulder, CO: Westview Press.

Semelin, Jacques. 2007. *Purify and Destroy: The Political Uses of Massacre and Genocide.* New York: Columbia University Press.

Sewell, William H., Jr. 1990. "Collective Violence and Collective Loyalties in France: Why the French Revolution Made a Difference." *Politics and Society* 18: 527–52.

———. 1996. "Historical Events as Transformations of Structures: Inventing Revolution at the Bastille." *Theory and Society* 25: 841–81.

———. 1986. "Artisans, Factory Workers, and the Formation of the French Working Class, 1789–1848." In *Working-Class Formation: Nineteenth-Century Patterns in Western Europe and the United States,* edited by Ira Katznelson and Aristide R. Zolberg, 45–70. Princeton, NJ: Princeton University Press.

———. 1980. *Work and Revolution in France: The Language of Labor from the Old Regime to 1848.* Cambridge: Cambridge University Press.

Shapira, Anita. 1992. *Land and Power: The Zionist Resort to Force, 1881–1948.* Oxford: Oxford University Press.

———. 2005. *L'imaginaire d'Israel: Histoire d'une culture politique.* Paris: Calmann-Levy.

Sheffer, Gabriel, Oren Barak, and Amiram Oren, eds. 2008. *An Army That Has a State? New Approaches to Civil-Security Relations.* Jerusalem: Carmel.

Shefter, Martin. 1977. "Party and Patronage: Germany, England and Italy." *Politics and Society* 7: 403–51.

———. 1986. "Trade Unions and Political Machines: The Organization and Disorganization of the American Working Class in the Late Nineteenth Century." In *Working-Class Formation: Nineteenth-Century Patterns in Western Europe and the United States*, edited by Ira Katznelson and Aristide R. Zolberg, 197–278. Princeton, NJ: Princeton University Press.

Shelef, Nadav G. 2010. *Evolving Nationalism: Homeland, Identity, and Religion in Israel, 1925–2005.* Ithaca, NY: Cornell University Press.

Siegel, Reva B. 2004. "Introduction: A Short History of Sexual Harassment." In *Directions in Sexual Harassment Law*, edited by Catharine A. MacKinnon and Reva B. Siegel, 1–42. New Haven, CT: Yale University Press.

Skocpol, Theda, and Vanessa Williamson. 2011. *The Tea Party and the Remaking of Republican Conservatism.* Oxford: Oxford University Press.

Skretny, John. 2002. *The Minority Rights Revolution.* Cambridge, MA: Harvard University Press.

Smith, Arthur L. 1969. *Rhetoric of Black Revolution.* Boston: Allyn and Bacon.

Smith, Michelle. 2010. "Beyond the Watch and Guard of Statistics: Race, Art and the Political Theory of Alan Locke." Unpublished paper, Ithaca, NY: Cornell University Department of Government.

Smith, Rogers M. 1997. *Civic Ideals: Conflicting Visions of Citizenship in U.S. History.* New Haven, CT: Yale University Press.

———. 2010. "Understanding the Symbiosis of American Rights and American Racism." In *America's Liberal Tradition Reconsidered: The Contested Legacy of Louis Hartz*, edited by Mark Huilliung, 55–89. Lawrence: University of Kansas Press.

Snow, David A. 2004. "Framing Processes, Ideology, and Discursive Fields." In *Blackwell Companion to Social Movements*, edited by David A. Snow, Sarah A. Soule, and Hanspeter Kriesi, 380–412. Oxford: Blackwell's.

Snow, David A., and Robert Benford. 2000. "Mobilization Forum: Clarifying the Relationship between Framing and Ideology." *Mobilization* 5: 55–60.

———. 1988. "Ideology, Frame Resonance, and Participant Mobilization." In *From Structure to Action: Social Movement Participation across Cultures*, edited by Bert Klandermans, Hanspeter Kriesi, and Sidney Tarrow, 197–217. Greenwich, CT: JAI Press.

———. 1992. "Master Frames and Cycles of Protest." In *Frontiers in Social Movement Theory*, edited by Aldon Morris and Carol McClurg Mueller, 133–55. New Haven, CT: Yale University Press.

Snow, David A., E. Burke Rochford, Jr., Steven K. Worden, and Robert D. Benford. 1986. "Frame Alignment Processes, Micromobilization and Movement Participation." *American Sociological Review* 51: 464–81.

Snow, David A., Sarah A. Soule, and Hanspeter Kriesi, eds. 2004. *The Blackwell Companion to Social Movements.* Oxford: Blackwell.

Somers, Margaret. 1994. "The Narrative Constitution of Identity: A Relational and Network Approach." *Theory and Society* 23: 605–49.

———. 1992. "Narrativity, Narrative Identity, and Social Action: Rethinking English Working-Class Formation." *Social Science History* 16: 591–630.

Soule, Sarah A. 1992. "Populism and Black Lynching in Georgia, 1890–1900." *Social Forces* 71: 431–49.

Soysal, Yasmin. 1994. *Limits of Citizenship: Migrants and Postnational Membership in Europe.* Chicago: University of Chicago Press.

Spriano, Paolo. 1975. *The Occupation of the Factories: Italy, 1920*. London: Pluto.

Sprinzak, Ehud. 1981. "Gush Emunim: The Tip of the Iceberg." *Jerusalem Quarterly* 21: 28–47.

———. 1991. *The Ascendance of Israel's Radical Right*. Oxford: Oxford University Press.

Stedman Jones, Gareth. 1983. *Languages of Class: Studies in English Working Class History*. Cambridge: Cambridge University Press.

Steinberg, Marc W. 1999a. *Fighting Words: Working-Class Formation, Collective Action, and Discourse in Early Nineteenth-Century England*. Ithaca, NY: Cornell University Press.

———. 1995. "The Roar of the Crowd: Repertoires of Discourse and Collective Action among the Spitalfields Silk Weavers in Nineteenth-Century London." In *Repertoires and Cycles of Collective Action*, edited by Mark Traugott, 57–87. Durham, NC: Duke University Press.

———. 1999b. "The Talk and Backtalk of Collective Action: A Dialogic Analysis of Repertoires of Discourse." *American Journal of Sociology* 105: 736–80.

Sternberg, Robert J. 2003. "A Duplex Theory of Hate: Development and Application to Terrorism, Massacres, and Genocide." *Review of General Psychology* 7: 299–328.

Sternhell, Zeev. 1998. *The Founding Myths of Israel: Nationalism, Socialism, and the Making of the Jewish State*. Princeton, NJ: Princeton University Press.

Stout, Christopher T. 2012. "Do Voters Prefer Post-Racial Black Candidates? An Analysis of Racialization and Electoral Support." Paper presented at the Midwest Political Science Association Annual Meeting, Chicago.

Strang, David, and John Meyer. 1993. "Institutional Conditions for Diffusion." *Theory and Society* 22: 487–511.

Strum, Philippa. 1999. *When the Nazis Came to Skokie: Freedom for Speech We Hate*. Lawrence: University of Kansas Press.

Stuckey, Sterling, ed. 1972. *Ideological Origins of Black Nationalism*. Boston: Beacon.

Summers Effler, Erika. 2010. *Laughing Saints and Righteous Heroes: Emotional Rhythms in Social Movement Groups*. Chicago: University of Chicago Press.

Swain, Carol. 1998. "Affirmative Action: A Search for Consensus." Presented to the National Science Foundation Conference on Racial Trends in the United States, Washington D.C.

Swarts, Heidi. 2008. *Organizing Urban America: Secular and Faith Based Progressive Movements*. Minneapolis: University of Minnesota Press.

Swidler, Ann. 1995. "Cultural Power and Social Movements." In *Social Movements and Culture*, edited by Hank Johnson and Bert Klandermans, 25–40. Minneapolis: University of Minnesota Press.

Tarrow, Sidney. 1977. *Between Center and Periphery: Grassroots Politicians in Italy and France*. New Haven, CT: Yale University Press.

———. 1992a. "Costumes of Revolt: The Symbolic Politics of Social Movements." *Sisyphus Social Studies* 8: 53–71.

———. 1995. "Cycles of Collective Action: Between Moments of Madness and the Repertoire of Contention." In *Repertoires and Cycles of Collective Action*, edited by Mark Traugott, 281–307. Durham, NC: Duke University Press.

———. 1989. *Democracy and Disorder: Protest and Politics in Italy, 1965–1974*. Oxford: Oxford University Press.

———. 2010. "Dynamics of Diffusion." In *The Diffusion of Social Movements: Actors, Mechanisms and Political Effects*, edited by Rebecca K. Givan, Kenneth Roberts, and Sarah A. Soule, 204–19. Cambridge: Cambridge University Press.

———. 1992b. "Mentalities, Political Cultures and Collective Action Frames: Constructing Meanings through Action." In *Frontiers in Social Movement Theory*, edited by Aldon Morris and Carol McClurg Mueller, 174–202. New Haven, CT: Yale University Press.

———. 2005. *The New Transnational Activism*. Cambridge: Cambridge University Press.

———. 1967. *Peasant Communism in Southern Italy*. New Haven, CT: Yale University Press.

———. 2011. *Power in Movement*. Revised and updated ed. Cambridge: Cambridge University Press, Third Revised Edition.

———. 2012. *Strangers at the Gates: Movements and States in Contentious Politics*. Cambridge: Cambridge University Press.

Tartakowsky, Danielle. 2005. *La Part du rêve: Histoire du 1er Mai en France*. Paris: Hachette Littératures.

———. 1997. *Les Manifestations de rue en France, 1918–1968*. Paris: Publications de la Sorbonne.

Taylor, Verta. 2009. "Culture, Identity, and Emotions: Studying Social Movements as If People Really Matter." *Mobilization* 15: 113–34.

———. 1995. "Watching for Vibes: Bringing Emotions into the Study of Feminist Organizations." In *Feminist Organizations: Harvest of the New Women's Movement*, edited by Myra Marx Ferree and Patricia Yancey Martin, 223–33. Philadelphia: Temple University Press.

Taylor, Verta, Katrina Kimport, Nella Van Dyke, and Ellen Ann Anderson. 2009. "Culture and Mobilization: Tactical Repertoires, Same-Sex Marriage, and Their Impact on Gay Activism." *American Sociological Review* 74: 865–90.

Taylor, Verta, and Leila Rupp. 2002. "Loving Internationalism: The Emotion Culture of Transnational Women's Organizations, 1888–1945." *Mobilization* 7: 141–58.

te Brake, Wayne P. 1985. "Popular Politics and the Dutch Patriot Revolution." *Theory and Society* 14: 199–222.

Thompson, E. P. 2009. *Customs in Common*. London: Merlin.

———. 1966. *The Making of the English Working Class*. New York: Vintage Books.

Tilly, Charles. 1986. *The Contentious French*. Cambridge, MA: Harvard University Press.

———. 2008. *Contentious Performances*. Cambridge: Cambridge University Press.

————. 1995a. "Contentious Repertoires in Great Britain, 1758–1834." In *Repertoires and Cycles of Collective Action*, edited by Mark W. Traugott, 15–42. Durham, NC: Duke University Press.

————. 1978. *From Mobilization to Revolution*. Reading, MA: Addison-Wesley.

————. 2005a. *Identities, Boundaries and Social Ties*. Boulder, CO: Paradigm Publishers.

————. 2003. *The Politics of Collective Violence*. Cambridge: Cambridge University Press.

————. 1995b. *Popular Contention in Great Britain, 1758–1834*. Cambridge, MA: Harvard University Press.

————. 2006a. *Regimes and Repertoires*. Cambridge: Cambridge University Press.

————. 1983. "Speaking Your Mind without Elections, Surveys, or Social Movements." *Public Opinion Quarterly* 47: 461–78.

————. 2002. *Stories, Identities and Political Change*. Lanham, MD: Rowman and Littlefield.

————. 2005b. *Trust and Rule*. Cambridge: Cambridge University Press.

————. 1964. *The Vendée*. Cambridge, MA: Harvard University Press.

————. 2006b. *Why?* Princeton, NJ: Princeton University Press.

Tilly, Charles, and Sidney Tarrow. 2007. *Contentious Politics*. Boulder, CO: Paradigm Publishers.

Tilly, Charles, and Chris Tilly. 1998. *Work under Capitalism*. Boulder, CO: Westview Press.

Tilly, Charles, and Lesley Wood. 2009. *Social Movements, 1768–2008*. 2nd ed. Boulder, CO: Paradigm Press.

Tocqueville, Alexis de. 1955. *The Old Regime and the French Revolution*. Garden City, NY: Doubleday, 1955.

————. 1992. *Recollections: The French Revolution of 1848*. New Brunswick, NJ: Transaction Books.

Touraine, Alain. 1971. *The May Movement: Revolt and Reform*. New York: Random House.

Tournier, Maurice. 1992. "La Loi dans la langue, loi de langue à travers une chronique de la grève des origines à 1848." *Langage et société* 60: 17–48.

Traugott, Mark. 2010. *The Insurgent Barricade*. Berkeley and Los Angeles: University of California Press.

Trejo, Guillermo. 2012. *Popular Movements in Autocracies: Religion, Repression, and Indigenous Collective Action in Mexico*. Cambridge: Cambridge University Press.

Trigilia, Carlo. 2011. "Social Class." In *International Encyclopedia of Political Science*, edited by Bernard Badie, Dirk Berg-Schlosser, and Leonardo Morlino, 270–75. London: Sage Publications.

Tronti, Mario, Giorgio Napoletano, Aris Accornero, and Massimo Cacciari, eds. 1978. *Operaismo e centralità operaia*. Rome: Editori Riuniti.

Turner, Lowell, Harry Katz, and Richard W. Hurd. 2001. *Rekindling the Movement: Labor's Quest for Relevance in the 21st Century*. Ithaca, NY: Cornell University Press.

Vasi, Ion Bogdan, and Chan Suk Suh. 2013. "Predicting the Spread of Protests with Internet and Social Media Activity." Unpublished paper. New York and Ithaca, NY: Columbia University and Cornell University.

Verhoeven, Claudia. 2008. "The Making of Russian Revolutionary Terrorism." In *Enemies of Humanity: The Nineteenth-Century War on Terrorism*, edited by Isaac Land, 99–116. New York: Palgrave Macmillan.

———. 2009. *The Odd Man Karakazov: Imperial Russia, Modernity, and the Birth of Terrorism*. Ithaca, NY: Cornell University Press.

Vovelle, Michel. 2004. *Les Mots de la révolution*. Toulouse, France: Presses Universitaires du Mirail.

Wada, Takeshi. 2009. "Demonstrating Repertoires of Contention." Paper presented at the American Sociological Association Annual Conference, San Francisco.

———. 2012. "Modularity and Transferability of Repertoires of Contention." *Social Problems* 59: 544–71.

Walgrave, Stefaan, and Dieter Rucht. 2011. *Protest Politics: Antiwar Mobilization in Advanced Industrial Democracies*. Minneapolis: University of Minnesota Press.

Walker, David. 1965. *David Walker's Appeal, in Four Articles*. New York: Hill and Wang.

Ward, Harry W. 1995. *The American Revolution: Nationhood Achieved, 1763–1788*. New York: St. Martin's.

Warner, Michael. 2000. *The Trouble with Normal: Sex, Politics and the Ethics of Queer Life*. Cambridge, MA: Harvard University Press.

Washington, Booker T., Fannie Barrier Williams, and Norman Barton Wood. 1969. *A New Negro for a New Century*. New York: Arno Press and the New York Times.

Weitz, Eric D. 2003. *A Century of Genocide: Utopias of Race and Nation*. Princeton, NJ: Princeton University Press.

Wildavsky, Aaron. 1987. "Choosing Preferences by Constructing Institutions: A Cultural Theory of Preference Formation." *American Political Science Review* 81: 3–22.

Williams, Heather. 2003. "Of Labor Tragedy and Legal Farce: The Han Young Factory Struggle in Tijuana, Mexico." *Social Science History* 27: 525–50.

Williams, Kim M. 2006. *Mark One or More: Civil Rights in Multiracial America*. Ann Arbor: University of Michigan Press.

Williamson, Joel. 1980. *New People: Miscegenation and Mulattoes in the United States*. New York: Free Press.

Wilson, William Julius. 1999. *The Bridge over the Racial Divide: Rising Inequality and Coalition Politics*. Berkeley, Los Angeles, and London: University of California Press.

———. 1978. *The Declining Significance of Race*. Chicago: University of Chicago Press.

———. 1987. *The Truly Disadvantaged: The Inner City, the Underclass, and Public Policy*. Chicago: University of Chicago Press.

Woloch, Isser. 1994. *The New Regime: Transformations of the French Civic Order, 1789–1820s*. New York: W.W. Norton and Co.

Womack, John. 1971. *Zapata and the Mexican Revolution*. New York: Knopf.

Wood, Gordon S. 2002. *The American Revolution: A History*. New York: Modern Library.

———. 1991. *The Radicalism of the American Revolution*. New York: Vintage 1991.

Woodward, C. Vann. 1971. *Origins of the New South, 1877–1913*. Baton Rouge: Louisiana State University Press, 1971.

Woycke, James. 1988. *Birth Control in Germany, 1871–1933*. London: Routledge.

Zippel, Kathrin. 2006. *The Politics of Sexual Harassment: A Comparative Study of United States, the European Union, and Germany*. Cambridge: Cambridge University Press.

Zolberg, Aristide. 1972. "Moments of Madness." *Politics and Society* 2: 183–207.

# Index

Cambridge Studies in Contentious Politics *(continued from page iii)*